Re-visioning Television

Re-visioning Television

Policy, strategy and models for the sustainable development of community television in South Africa

Adrian Hadland, Mike Aldridge & Joshua Ogada

OHIO UNIVERSITY LIBRARY ATHENS OHIO

Compiled by the Society, Culture and Identity Research Programme of the Human Sciences Research Council

Published by HSRC Press
Private Bag X9182, Cape Town, 8000, South Africa
www.hsrcpress.ac.za

© 2006 Human Sciences Research Council

First published 2006

All rights reserved. No part of this book may be reprinted or reproduced or utilised in any form or by any electronic, mechanical, or other means, including photocopying and recording, or in any information storage or retrieval system, without permission in writing from the publishers.

ISBN 0-7969-2160-1

Copy editing by Laurie Rose-Innes
Cover design by Jenny Frost and Jacob Erasmus
Cover photograph by Christine Nachmann. Mural by The Lines of Attitude Team: www.falko1.co.za, www.faith47.com, www.mode2.org, www.dreph.com and Phiks.
Print management by Compress

Distributed in Africa by Blue Weaver
PO Box 30370, Tokai, Cape Town, 7966, South Africa
Tel: +27 (0) 21 701 4477
Fax: +27 (0) 21 701 7302
email: orders@blueweaver.co.za
www.oneworldbooks.com

Distributed in Europe and the United Kingdom by Eurospan Distribution Services (EDS)
3 Henrietta Street, Covent Garden, London, WC2E 8LU, United Kingdom
Tel: +44 (0) 20 7240 0856
Fax: +44 (0) 20 7379 0609
email: orders@edspubs.co.uk
www.eurospangroup.com/bookstore

Distributed in North America by Independent Publishers Group (IPG)
Order Department, 814 North Franklin Street, Chicago, IL 60610, USA
Call toll-free: (800) 888 4741
All other enquiries: +1 (312) 337 0747
Fax: +1 (312) 337 5985
email: frontdesk@ipgbook.com
www.ipgbook.com

CONTENTS

List of tables and figures   vi
Acknowledgements   viii
Preface   ix
Executive summary   xi
Acronyms and abbreviations   xiii

CHAPTER 1   INTRODUCTION TO COMMUNITY TELEVISION   1

CHAPTER 2   REGULATORY OVERVIEW   15

CHAPTER 3   LESSONS FROM COMMUNITY RADIO   37

CHAPTER 4   CTV IN SOUTH AFRICA TODAY   43

CHAPTER 5   PARTNERSHIPS   67

CHAPTER 6   SIGNAL DISTRIBUTION   97

CHAPTER 7   PRODUCTION   103

CHAPTER 8   PROGRAMMING   125

CHAPTER 9   AUDIENCE RESEARCH   141

CHAPTER 10   RURAL CTV   145

CHAPTER 11   FUTURE TECHNICAL DIRECTIONS FOR CTV   153

CHAPTER 12   BUSINESS MODELS   165

CHAPTER 13   CONCLUSION   185

CHAPTER 14   CASE STUDY: CTV CAPE TOWN BUSINESS MODEL   187

APPENDIX A   LOCAL CTV SCOPING REPORT: TECHNICAL PARAMETERS – UNIVERSITY OF CAPE TOWN   203

APPENDIX B   LOCAL CTV SCOPING REPORT: TECHNICAL PARAMETERS – UNIVERSITY OF THE WESTERN CAPE   206

GLOSSARY   209

REFERENCES   213

TABLES AND FIGURES

Tables

Table 8.1	Weekly CTV programming	133
Table 8.2	Daily programming, Monday to Friday	136
Table 14.1	AMPS audience ratings (000s), April 2004	193
Table 14.2	Cape Town income demographics	193

Figures

Figure 7.1	Prosumer to professional camera price range	110
Figure 7.2	Low to medium camera price range	111
Figure 7.3	Manual broadcast workflow	115
Figure 7.4	Automated digital workflow solution	116
Figure 8.1	Weekly programming hours	134
Figure 8.2	Daily programming, Monday to Friday	135
Figure 11.1	Video sharing network	156
Figure 11.2	The PanAmSat (PAS) 7 footprint	157
Figure 12.1	Total TV viewing	171
Figure 12.2	Total TV households (TVHHs)	171
Figure 12.3	Audience share, all adults (South Africa)	172
Figure 12.4	Audience share, all adults (Western Cape)	173
Figure 12.5	Audience share, all adults (Gauteng)	173
Figure 12.6	Audience share, all adults (KwaZulu-Natal)	174
Figure 12.7	African audience share	175
Figure 12.8	White audience share	175
Figure 12.9	Coloured audience share	175
Figure 12.10	Indian audience share	176
Figure 12.11	English audience (home language)	176
Figure 12.12	Afrikaans audience (home language)	177
Figure 12.13	IsiXhosa audience (home language)	177
Figure 12.14	South Sotho audience (home language)	177
Figure 12.15	IsiZulu audience (home language)	178
Figure 12.16	Audience by age group, 16–24 years	178
Figure 12.17	Audience by age group, 25–34 years	179
Figure 12.18	Audience by age group, 35–49 years	179
Figure 12.19	Universal LSM 3, TVA	180
Figure 12.20	Universal LSM 3, TVHH	180
Figure 12.21	Universal LSM 6, TVA	180
Figure 12.22	Universal LSM 6, TVHH	181

Figure 12.23   Universal LSM 8, TVA   181
Figure 12.24   Universal LSM 8, TVHH   181
Figure 12.25   Universal LSM 10, TVA   182
Figure 12.26   Universal LSM 10, TVHH   182
Figure 14.1   Cape Town income demographics   194
Figure 14.2   Coverage for CT CTV   200

ACKNOWLEDGEMENTS

The authors of this report would like to thank the following individuals and organisations for their invaluable help and support:

Karen Thorne, Khululekile Banzi, Andrei Naidoo, Jean Witten of the HSRC, the Cape Town Community Television Collective (CT CTVC), Greater Durban Television (GDTV), the Media Development and Diversity Agency (MDDA) and the Media Institute of Southern Africa – South Africa (MISA-SA).

PREFACE

This report on the policy, strategy and models for the sustainable development of community television (CTV) in South Africa is the result of a deeply participative research process led by the Society, Culture and Identity (SCI) Research Programme of the Human Sciences Research Council (HSRC). The HSRC is a statutory organisation that conducts research aimed at supporting the country's drive to a better, more equitable and brighter future. Media and its role and impact on society remain a key research interest of the SCI team, which has already produced some important work on the subject (see, for instance, Hadland & Thorne [2004: 9]).

Conceptualised by HSRC Chief Research Specialist Adrian Hadland with the assistance of CTV activist and Arts and Media Access Centre Director Karen Thorne, the project was intended to provide support to South Africa's nascent local television sector. Underpinning this interest is the assumption that improved access to more diverse media is good for democracy, development and empowerment. Funded initially with the HSRC's parliamentary grant, the Media Development and Diversity Agency (MDDA) has again joined hands to support an HSRC media research project. Further assistance has been forthcoming from the Media Institute of Southern Africa (MISA).

The work contained in this report has been informed by a process of participation and collaboration that has involved many key members and organisations within the CTV community. Two of the principal authors, Mike Aldridge and Joshua Ogada, as well as the assistant and intern Khululekhile Banzi, boast many years of work in and around community media and have a special interest in CTV. The project also relied heavily on the Cape Town Community Television Co-operative and its steering committee, the body that is driving the CTV process in the Cape and which represents a wide range of stakeholders. A regional workshop and a series of sectoral workshops were held during the course of this research project, which helped root the work in the real needs and priorities of people involved in, or wishing to become involved in, CTV.

In addition, another formal collaborative partner in this research has been Greater Durban Television (GDTV), one of the pathfinders of CTV in South Africa. GDTV's willingness to share its experiences and knowledge and to support the drive to a broad-access national television network for the people has been important. Readers will find these elements along with the Cape Town Collective's inputs reflected in particular in the case study section of this report. Their collective wisdom, however, is inherent in this research from one end of the report to the other.

Once a draft report had been completed, a national workshop was held at the HSRC's Pretoria office in late October 2005. Here, stakeholders and interested parties from across the country assembled to debate the principles, values, models and recommendations contained in this report. MISA played a key role in ensuring the success of the workshop, which had as its keynote speaker the former CEO of the MDDA, Libby Lloyd. Feedback and inputs from the workshop are incorporated into this report to make it a truly inclusive and participative work reflecting the experiences, needs and beliefs of many people who have worked hard for years to bring CTV to South Africa.

The authors would like to thank the stakeholders, activists and interested parties who have participated in this research project in one way or another, from filling out questionnaires and taking part in workshops to debating the issues that the report contains. We have sought to reflect as many of the opposing and divergent views as possible. We hope, in the end, to have combined many strands of experience, research and opinion and to have knitted them together to provide a solid platform from which CTV in South Africa can go onward and upward. We also acknowledge the work, often unseen or unreported, that has been done over the last decade by people who care about CTV to keep the hope alive. We stand, at last, on the very brink of success.

Adrian Hadland, Mike Aldridge and Joshua Ogada
Cape Town
January 2006

EXECUTIVE SUMMARY

This report deals with the policy, strategy and models for the sustainable development of community television (CTV) in South Africa. It is the result of a deeply participative research process led by the Society, Culture and Identity (SCI) Research Programme of the Human Sciences Research Council (HSRC), and was conceptualised to provide support to South Africa's nascent local television sector.

Funded initially with the HSRC's parliamentary grant, the Media Development and Diversity Agency has again joined hands to support an HSRC media research project. Further assistance has been forthcoming from the Media Institute of Southern Africa.

This report is divided into 14 chapters. Chapter One is an introduction to the issues, debates and concerns of CTV and its development in South Africa. The chapter also reviews various examples of CTV internationally and draws out some useful pointers and models. Compiled by Joshua Ogada and Mike Aldridge.

Chapter Two presents a detailed look at the laws, regulations and policies that have a direct bearing on CTV. The chapter highlights the Independent Communications Authority of South Africa's position paper, considers the implications of the Convergence Bill and refers to various legal and regulatory parameters within which CTV organisations will need to operate. Compiled by Mike Aldridge.

Chapter Three looks at lessons to be learned from the history of the community radio sector in South Africa. It argues that CTV should partner with community radio stations as part of its strategy for sustainability. Compiled by Joshua Ogada.

Chapter Four considers the current state of CTV in South Africa. It examines the history of the CTV initiative and presents case studies of five local CTV outfits: Soweto TV, Cue TV, Bush TV, Greater Durban TV and the Cape Town Community Television Collective. Compiled by Mike Aldridge, with contributions by Khululekile Banzi.

Chapter Five looks at partnerships. It lists possible funding partners and content partners, and considers institutions and organisations that could provide important strategic and training collaboration opportunities for CTV. Compiled by Mike Aldridge.

Chapter Six deals with the more technical area of signal distribution. It describes the operations and parameters of Sentech and Orbicom and grapples with the various challenges CTV faces when it comes to distribution. Compiled by Mike Aldridge.

Chapter Seven focuses on the complex issue of production. Topics discussed include broadcast tape formats, outside broadcasts and field production, as well as the office equipment that a CTV organisation can expect to need. Compiled by Mike Aldridge.

Chapter Eight hones in on the important area of programming. Issues raised include the role and management of programming committees, as well as programme acquisition and syndication. The chapter also lists potential programming partners and sources. Compiled by Mike Aldridge.

Chapter Nine looks into the vital area of audience research. It establishes a theoretical framework and provides a template on which future research into audience perceptions of CTV can be based. Compiled by Joshua Ogada and Andrei Naidoo.

Chapter Ten deals with the challenges facing the development of CTV in South Africa's rural areas. It considers a definition of what constitutes a rural area and proposes various options for supporting rural CTV. Compiled by Mike Aldridge and Joshua Ogada.

Chapter Eleven considers future technical directions for CTV. It examines the possibilities of using Internet TV, netcasting, video content delivery over data networks and cellular communications, as well as still-developing technologies allowing for interactive television and the issues raised by digital broadcasting. Compiled by Mike Aldridge.

Chapter Twelve examines business models for CTV. It discusses issues of sustainability, advertising, demographics, content and audience analysis. Compiled by Mike Aldridge and Andrei Naidoo.

Chapter Thirteen is the concluding chapter. It highlights some of the recommendations contained within the report, including the authors' preference for the 'consortium model' favoured by Australian CTV. Other recommended options include the establishment of media access centres and the creation of a development fund for broadcasting. The chapter, and the report, conclude that the technology, the people, the will, the models and the experience exist to make sustainable CTV in South Africa a reality.

Finally, in Chapter Fourteen, a case study of CTV in Cape Town is presented, wherein a proposed business model, along with potential partnerships for facilities and transmission, is discussed. Compiled by Joshua Ogada and Mike Aldridge.

ACRONYMS AND ABBREVIATIONS

ABET	adult basic education and training
ACB	Association of Christian Broadcasters
ADSL	Asymmetric Digital Subscriber Line
AFDA	South African School of Motion Picture Medium and Live Performance
AMAC	Arts and Media Access Centre
AMPS	All Media Products Survey
ATSC	Advanced Television Systems Committee
AVEA	Audio-Visual Entrepreneurs of Africa
AV	audio-visual
CBO	community-based organisation
CCD	charge-coupled device
CDH	Community Digital Hub
CMOS	complementary metal oxide semiconductor
CTN	Community Television Network
CTV	community television
CT CTV	Cape Town community television
CT CTVC	Cape Town Community Television Collective
CVET	Community Video Education Trust
DAC	Department of Arts and Culture
dB	decibel
DoC	Department of Communications
DTT	digital terrestrial transmission
DV	digital video
ENG	electronic news gathering
FRU	Film Resource Unit
GB	gigabyte
GCIS	Government Communication and Information System
GDTV	Greater Durban Television
HD	high definition
HH	household
HSDPA	High-speed downlink packet access
HSRC	Human Sciences Research Council
IBA	Independent Broadcasting Authority
ICASA	Independent Communications Authority of South Africa
ICT	information and communications technology
IDASA	Institute for Democracy in South Africa
IDP	integrated development plan
IP	Internet protocol
IPDC	International Programme for the Development of Communication
ISDN	integrated services digital network

IWT	Independent World Television
kW	kilowatt
LAN	local-area network
LSM	Living Standards Measure
MAPP	Media, Advertising, Publishing, Printing and Packaging
MB	megabyte
MBps	megabytes per second
MDDA	Media Development and Diversity Agency
MHz	megahertz
MISA	Media Institute of Southern Africa
MPCC	Multi-purpose Community Centre
MPEG	Moving Picture Experts Group
NAB	National Association of Broadcasters
NCRF	National Community Radio Forum
NEMISA	National Electronic Media Institute of South Africa
NFVF	National Film and Video Foundation
NGO	non-governmental organisation
NTSC	National Television System Committee
OB	outside broadcast
OSS	open-source software
PAL	phase alternating line
PATV	public access television
RAM	random-access memory
RAMS	Radio Audience Measurement Survey
SAARF	South African Advertising Research Foundation
SABC	South African Broadcasting Corporation
SACOD	Southern Africa Communications for Development
SAMRO	South African Music Rights Organisation
SD	standard definition
SETA	Sector Education and Training Authority
SMME	small, medium and micro enterprise
SMPTE	Society of Motion Picture and Television Engineers
TVA	television audience
UHF	ultra-high frequency
UMTS	Universal Mobile Telecommunications Service
USA	Universal Service Agency
VHF	very high frequency
VTR	videotape recorder
WAN	wide-area networks

CHAPTER 1

Introduction to community television

Introduction

The idea of media begins with the reproduction of the human voice through a medium. This most basic form of human communication has evolved through the mediums of print, radio and television into the modern information era, where through-flows of data converge into the meta-medium of computer networks. Just as the voice enables us to communicate our thoughts with one another through the medium of air, so the technologies we have developed as a species enable us to reflect on the nature of our world in a wider collective manner. The media are conduits for information in society, but they also reflect the power relationships that shape the dominant voices conveyed by these mechanisms.

Perhaps South Africans have become more sophisticated consumers of media following the success of the national liberation struggle that displaced the previously dominant ideology of apartheid and concomitant state repression. The conflict of ideologies between the antagonists in this struggle was fought through disparate media ranging from the mainstream to alternative press and *samizdat* liberation media. The fact that a different meta-narrative is being transmitted through the media today has shaken people's perceptions of a single, monolithic ideology that remains unchanged and unchallenged over time, which in turn enables them to question the worldview presented through the media.

Ten years after the new dispensation took effect, different priorities dominate the airwaves in South Africa. The state's ability to control or manipulate the media is limited, although it does have a dominant relationship with the public broadcaster, the South African Broadcasting Corporation (SABC). The interests of capital are also served by the SABC, which for sustainability relies heavily on commercial income to add to its government and public allotments. The commercial broadcasters are supported by advertising and subscription revenue, with the free-to-air eTV and subscription channels such as M-Net, DSTV and Vivid falling into this category. The government also makes use of community media in both radio and print to convey its messages and information to the people.

The dominant discourses within this media landscape remain those of government and commerce, although it must be said that today's broadcasters do make valiant efforts to represent the views and preferences of the populace. Nevertheless, in terms of economic and political affiliations, the SABC strives to retain an uneasy balance between the demands of government support, public interest and advertiser returns. The commercial channels turn their collective interest to garnering audiences that they sell on to advertisers, maintaining a nominal notion of serving the public interest by producing popular material in tried-and-tested genres.

The democratic struggle has left its imprint on the minds of South Africans, and today's socio-political environment favours the growth of democratic mechanisms, which include equitable media representation and public control. Through passing enabling media legislation and setting up the Independent Communications Authority of South Africa (ICASA) as the broadcast media regulator, the government has delivered on its promise of creating three tiers of broadcasting. Still, gaps remain in this media landscape, with community television (CTV) being an obvious missing piece in the jigsaw puzzle.

The media and development objectives identified by the government to carry through its struggle-born democratic impulse include the creation of mechanisms to redress the imbalances in media representation that marked the apartheid past. These include restructuring and transforming the SABC, the establishment of the National Electronic Media Institute of South Africa (NEMISA), setting up the Media Development and Diversity Agency (MDDA), and funding the programme for universal telephonic communications through the Universal Service Agency (USA).

In this fertile climate, media enterprises have proliferated, and new radio, television and netcasting media have opened their respective windows on the world for South Africa's people. Community radio stations have sprung up across the nation to challenge the dominance of public and commercial channels, while television channels too have multiplied; but the media explosion is still happening, with technology opening up new frontiers for media forms and numbers. Digital broadcasting will usher in more television channels, while broadband networks and Internet protocol (IP) connections are offering new ways of reaching audiences. Reception and transmission devices are also evolving and proliferating, with cellphones and hand-held devices enabling mobile data downloads and diverse levels of interactive communication.

South Africans live out their lives within this media and information environment based on the historical situation that has placed them within the socio-economic and political matrix of the 'new' South Africa. The structure of the past has left its imprint on the demographic profile of the population, which when viewed in terms of economic, social and political factors reveals wide disparities that yet reflect the racial inequities of the apartheid and colonial years.

Whether for good or ill, the forced marriage between black and white that marked the official end of the liberation struggle has continued the reign of capitalism as the dominant economic paradigm. The ensuing profile of the wealth continuum between rich and poor remains pyramidal in shape, with a great majority of poor people and relatively few well-off or affluent people. The demographics of this pyramid are skewed in favour of the previous beneficiaries of apartheid, the so-called white races that fitted into the 'right' side of the racial divide.

This demographic profile is slowly changing as a new South African society evolves, but the media, like other sectors of society, have a role to play in its readjustment to the current objectives of racial parity within the overall economic framework. There are inherent limitations in the ability of the media to affect the broader socio-economic and political environment, but there is nevertheless an important role for the media to play in the evolution of this broader historical context.

The extent to which community media can play a part in participatory democracy and development is still open to question, particularly in the absence of CTV, in a context where 'the emergence and deepening of a new democratic era in South Africa with its emphasis on transparency, accountability, accessibility, empowerment and equity is essential to the core principles and basic objectives of the small media sector' (Hadland & Thorne 2004: 19).

The essential motivation for community media is to enable a form of communication through media that is substantially different to that presented in other media forms. This is a vision of media that have different masters to their mainstream cousins, and that reflect the issues, interests and concerns of people at the local level in a way that national media do not. For one thing, they are meant to operate in a way that is not dominated by the interests of commerce, and so must be structured on a non-profit basis. Secondly, they are accountable to the interests of groupings of people at the small scale. Thirdly, they are designed to continue the democratic project that is still in the process of transforming our society.

To achieve this vision, ICASA has examined examples of CTV in action in other countries and has established a set of basic principles to govern the sector in South Africa. These measures are designed to free CTV of domination by political and commercial interests. On the other hand, ICASA sees the sustainability of CTV in terms of a partnership between stakeholders that include government and commerce, where these organs of society provide funding for CTV in return for it conveying their messages to their target audiences. This may be an uncomfortable and difficult relationship to maintain where the demands of commerce may compete with the democratic objectives of the broadcaster.

Moreover, CTV broadcasters find themselves in an environment where they face significant competition for viewers from free-to-air and public service channels, particularly if the SABC receives the necessary government funding to implement its proposed regional, indigenous language channels. CTV channels will have to provide programming that is significantly different to what is available on these other channels and, at the same time, attract viewers away from these competitors.

While it may be desirable for CTV to reach small-scale niche audiences, the financial dynamics of the media depend on maximising audience reach through attracting large numbers of viewers within the target groups that funders and advertisers wish to reach. In providing an enabling environment for CTV, the government has striven to create a platform for sustainability in terms of a diversity of funding sources, but it remains to be seen whether CTV broadcasters are capable of straddling the divides of commerce and participatory democratic and development objectives to both establish themselves and sustain their long-term existence.

Furthermore, there are particular challenges with regard to digital broadcasting and convergence that will demand courageous initiatives and creative solutions from CTV. This occurs within an environment where there remain huge gaps between First- and Third-World economies within the country and their attendant populations of information rich and information poor. As the experience of community radio has shown, CTV will demand strong management capacity to breach these barriers and to provide a socially useful, sustainable sector in the long term.

The mere fact that South Africa has created a legislative-enabling environment for CTV is a significant step for the fledgling democracy, for there are many states in the world where the very idea of free media and/or community media is anathema to repressive governments. However, to actually develop a functional, sustainable CTV sector will be very challenging, particularly since there is no legislated means of financial sustainability, for instance through a national fund that derives revenue from commercial or public service broadcasters, or through legislated government support. There are various international examples where CTV has failed, so we cannot think that just because we are able to establish CTV broadcasts that stations will survive or prosper in the long term. There are many profound challenges that face CTV on the road ahead and the sector will have to leverage every resource, human and otherwise, that it can in order to meet them.

A review of existing CTV models

CTV has been described as a logical next step to community-led development. Its ability to engage with activities at local level, many already using video and arts for advocacy, raising awareness, training and indeed for creative pleasure, sets it apart as a powerful tool with immense potential. The current underutilisation of media facilities in the community, as is identified in this research, and the huge need to disseminate information and to reach within and between communities, provide a basic rationale for CTV.

Set in the context of the impending conversion of television transmission facilities from analogue to digital technologies, and against a background of the current debate on digital convergence, it is clear that CTV can play a special role in ensuring that the visual media enhance people's creativity, interactivity and means of expression, and not merely their consumption. Developments in the media also add to the rationale for a CTV channel. The experiences of community radio in South Africa and of CTV where it exists in strength in numerous countries around the world demonstrate their capacity to enhance diversity and to bring media closer to people, especially by engaging communities in the process of programme production and management of the stations themselves.

What we seek to achieve with this overview is to synthesise the CTV discourse in South Africa in one coherent document. The discourse has been characterised by successive peaks that have coincided with policy development as well as an underlying need for the development of CTV. This discourse has benefited from the experiences of other countries where community or public access television exists. The fact that the South African policy environment for CTV is still in its nascent form means that we are able to benefit from experiences in other countries in the course of developing our own model of CTV.

The National Community Radio Forum (NCRF) states that while we have to learn from international best practice, these models must be adapted to suit our own national priorities and conditions. It further states that CTV should thus have a clear mandate to:
- strengthen civil society by giving a powerful voice to citizens and encouraging debate and dialogue in order to find solutions to common concerns – in so doing, CTV will have a powerful role to play in promoting social cohesion and integration;
- promote participatory governance by providing a platform for the government to communicate directly to citizens and for citizens to communicate their needs to the government and hold elected officials accountable for community needs;
- give expression to a diversity of languages and community cultural activities such as local theatre, music and dance groups;
- give real meaning to freedom of expression by creating opportunities for citizens to exercise their right to communicate through public access time slots; and
- provide education and information that aims to improve the quality of people's lives. (Moalosi & Thorne 2003)

In the South African context, CTV is expected to play an important role in job creation and skills development as an entry-level training ground for a new generation of media producers and broadcasters. The financial realities require CTV to operate as a lean and mean, cost-efficient organisation with a small, highly skilled staff contingent. While the CTV station would be a small operation, there is the possibility of relying on a decentralised network of community producers. In this way, CTV provides more opportunities for 'community' producers, whether individuals or non-governmental organisations (NGOs). In this respect, CTV is different from a community radio station where staff produce the majority of programming. The decentralised network option would then reduce the numbers of permanent in-house staff.

Volunteers participating through structured internships or work-based skills development programmes will offset the running costs, while at the same time producing a new crop of skilled and experienced learners for placement in an industry under pressure to conform to employment equity targets.

It will be important for CTV operators to forge partnerships with outside training service providers. CTV can also provide the space for experimentation and innovation through the airing of student productions. This would give learners the opportunity to get practical work experience; and CTV could enhance the income potential of organisations providing training and media access to aspirant film makers. Although the proposed audience for CTV channels may not elicit much interest from commercial advertisers, if targeted at lower Living Standards Measure (LSM) levels, there are organisations and foundations in the areas of development and social upliftment that might support CTV and its feeder bodies.

CTV has existed for varying periods of time around the world for some time now. Whereas this makes South Africa a bit of a late-starter in the field, it provides us with a banquet of experiences to learn from in the establishment of our own initiatives.

The Independent Broadcasting Authority Act of 1993 (IBA Act) set in place a definition of community broadcast media as a service that is owned and controlled by the community it serves. Another useful definition of community or public access television is: 'a system that provides television production equipment, training and airtime on a local cable channel, so members of the public can produce their own shows and televise them to a mass audience' (Olson 2000: 1). From this definition it is clear that the mandate of CTV extends beyond simply broadcasting content to the public. Although this definition pertains to the North American model of public access television (PATV), which is supported by statutory income from cable television channels, it nevertheless indicates the principle of public participation in the production process and the concomitant de-professionalisation of the medium.

The distinction between commercial and community media lies in the position of the audience vis-à-vis the medium. Community media place the audience at the centre of the production process as opposed to merely being at the receiving end. This broad principle characterises community media anywhere in the world. CTV as we refer to it here is variously known elsewhere as PATV, open channels, and community access television, to name but a few.

Whereas the broad principles may remain largely the same, the nature and form that CTV takes internationally depends on several factors that determine its character.

The national or regional media environment plays a major role in determining the form of community media. Commercial, state-owned or public media existing in a particular environment, and how the public interacts with them, will affect the existence of community media and their role. For instance, communities may feel marginalised in the coverage offered by the dominant media, which would then motivate the need for an alternative or oppositional voice. In other instances, the relative positions of commercial and community media may be of a more complementary nature. In the US, the privately owned media are required by law to support PATV in order to fulfil the requirement that they serve the public interest. This means that PATV complements privately owned commercial television by providing community-specific information and allowing vital access for communities to the media.

The levels of media saturation and penetration in a given environment also determine the form that CTV takes. In countries such as Australia, for instance, great geographical distances between centres of human settlement have an isolating effect that motivates the existence of CTV, because local issues can be so specific that it is impossible for national television to address them adequately. This is also the basis for rural television such as Mayan TV in Central America, which serves a population that is geographically as well as culturally untouched by the mainstream media (Mayan TV 2005).

Further, one can look at the levels of technological advancement in different environments and how this dictates the need or lack thereof for CTV. For instance, in some settings the prevalence of the Internet has allowed citizens to access information beyond that which is provided by mainstream television. Cellphone technology has penetrated the developing world in a big way, thanks mostly to the inadequate coverage of landlines and the lack of necessary infrastructure, especially in rural areas.

There has been a sharp increase in Internet accessibility. Governments are increasingly providing access through public libraries, community centres and other institutions. In the private sector, cyber cafés are springing up everywhere and allowing citizens access to the Net. These developments demonstrate that the demand for information in rural areas is no less urgent than in urban settings. This also illustrates the demand for information that can potentially be met by CTV. At the same time, it underlines the need to explore technical options available for CTV, given that the relative lack of infrastructure has not hindered development in other forms of media. Moreover, there is greater opportunity for multimedia approaches to CTV. The advent of digital and satellite broadcasting has opened up a whole new perspective, offering both opportunities and challenges for community media.

The level of socio-economic development is another important determining factor for CTV. Although this broadly covers the above-mentioned factors, one could look specifically at the rural/urban population distribution in a given environment with all its attendant ramifications as a key element in the role that CTV plays. It is commonly the case that urban populations benefit from higher levels of media saturation than their rural counterparts as a function of infrastructural development and other factors. This has the effect of sidelining the issues that are important to rural populations because of their limited access.

The media needs of a population also determine the nature of CTV. In developing countries such as South Africa there is still a huge need to disseminate development information. The public broadcaster can only fulfil this role to a certain extent. Commercial and privately owned media do not deem this task to be commercially viable and, therefore, largely neglect it. Community media can play a critical role in fulfilling this need. In markets characterised by high levels of media concentration there tends to be a dearth of locally relevant information on existing commercial channels. In the US, for instance, small television stations serving local communities have been progressively acquired by large conglomerates, which operate on economies of scale by providing content that is as generic and as widely relevant as possible. Researching locally specific information becomes too costly and falls by the wayside.

There are cases, however, where CTV is simply a forum that fulfils the information needs of civil society – this is when it truly serves as alternative media. It is important though to bear in mind the preferences of audiences. Whereas the ideological rationale for CTV may prioritise locally relevant and socially uplifting information, this may not be what the audience wants. A broad-based consultative process coupled with comprehensive audience research can yield information about audience needs and preferences that, in turn, should inform programming format.

An analysis of different models of CTV provides us with a framework upon which to build a model that would best suit the South African environment. The perceived successes and failures of different models around the world, combined with a snapshot of the local environments in which they operate, will help to define the requirements of the South African environment and what model of CTV will best serve our needs. Here are some of the experiences and models presented by other countries in the realm of CTV and which are relevant to South Africa's need to create its own form.

Australia

Australia has a wealth of experience with CTV. Boasting about ten stations spread across the country, the CTV sector has entrenched itself firmly in the Australian media landscape. Australian CTV is built on the 'consortium model', which brings together different players, including media NGOs and community groups, in a partnership that has yielded success. Partnerships and stakeholders are an integral part of any CTV initiative. The nature of these partnerships can take different forms, which ultimately define the character of the initiative. The governance structure includes representatives from the local community, the government and non-profit organisations.

In the South African environment, this kind of structure would be useful, given the necessity to include as many constituencies as possible. The nature of government involvement in the partnership is also noteworthy. The financial involvement of the government is limited to special project funding, with no direct contributions to the stations. Community radio in South Africa has long been cautious about government involvement through funding. The sector has always been wary that with financial support comes the risk of undue influence. It would be logical to assume that CTV would have the same concerns. Furthermore, ICASA regulation does not allow for government representation. However, community radio has had a measure of success when partnering with local or national government on special projects. This makes for partnerships that are finite in nature while ensuring the autonomy of the media institution, and does not necessitate the inclusion of the government in management structures.

In the South African context, this type of relationship could involve tying in with the Sector Education and Training Authorities (SETAs) through which the government can contribute to the sector. CTV in Australia funds itself largely through sponsorships and membership fees. They do not raise any money from commercial sponsorship. Whereas this has worked well for them, it may not be as applicable in a South African context. In a socio-economic environment like Australia's, it is much more feasible to raise sufficient money from sponsorships to run a television station. They also rely on grants and revenue from sales of merchandise and airtime. South Africa does not have that luxury, due to lower average levels of income.

More specifically, the proposed audience profile for Cape Town CTV, for example, comprises much lower LSMs than in Australia. The aims of CTV and the means to achieve them depend on its target audience. As will be discussed later, there is more of a need here to consider some level of commercial advertising to bring in additional revenue that may not be available from audience or community support.

In Australia, signal distribution is via UHF and, in some cases, via neighbourhood cable. Programme production is one of the areas in which the consortium model has worked well for Australia. Included among the partners are media NGOs with significant production capacity. There are also independent producers who contribute significantly in terms of content.

An oft-mentioned exemplar of Australian CTV is C31 Melbourne. Boasting an audience of approximately three million, it caters for a constituency very close in size to what, say, a Cape Town initiative would serve. Although the population of Melbourne is greater than this, C31 seeks to serve a small and loyal audience and meet its needs as well as it can (C31 Melbourne 2005). In the local context, CTV would probably take this approach and find its niche within the broader media landscape, as opposed to competing with public and commercial stations. This is especially pertinent when one considers that CTV has been seen as another hand in the finite pot of advertising budgets available to media in an already highly competitive environment.

C31 broadcasts in 20 languages, allowing it to cater to the needs of the local language groups as well as immigrant communities, of which there is a significant population. Their programming is a mix of entertainment, education and information, with priority given to that which is relevant to the constituent community. C31's audience comprises groups that tend to be underrepresented in mainstream media: immigrant Somali and Eritrean communities, special interest groups such as the deaf community, the gay community as well as students and youth are all actively catered for by the station (C31 Melbourne 2005).

US and Canada: PATV

In North America, PATV arose out of the needs of communities to have their voices heard. In Canada, public access first made use of film as part of the government's 'war on poverty', whereby it became possible to put a face to the problems confronting ordinary citizens by documenting their lives (Olson 2000). At the same time, it allowed the government to showcase what services were available to the public to help them improve their lives. Right from the outset, the ethos of public access was radically different; when the initial attempts at documenting citizens' lives were not well received, the subjects were allowed to preview the footage and participate in the editing. This privilege, however, did not extend to politicians or public officials. It was clear that public access was destined to take the side of ordinary citizens and prioritise their voices.

Throughout the 1960s in Canada, the system developed with the public becoming more involved in the process, and selecting the topics to be covered. Meanwhile in the US, the first community-owned service was set up in 1968, operating a closed-circuit channel under the name Cable TV Incorporated (Olson 2000). In the 1960s and 1970s, counter-culture video collectives were taking root in the US, and developing an ideology that centred on getting information to the masses. One of the founders of this movement, Michael Shamberg, labelled the movement 'Guerrilla Television', and its aim was to 'break down the barriers imposed by broadcast television' by, among other things, 'allowing the people to speak for themselves' (Shamberg 1971: 8).

From this auspicious beginning, PATV in the US grew steadily over the ensuing years into the entity it is today, comprising over 1 800 stations across the country. The early 1970s saw the introduction of legislative benchmarks that served to entrench the presence and role of PATV in the US. In 1972, the Federal Communications Commission issued a report requiring operators in the 100 largest markets to provide three access channels for local government, education and public access, or at least one if the demand for three was deemed insufficient. The ruling was extended in 1976 to include cable systems that had a client base of 3 500 or more. Although there were challenges to this along the way, the strong presence of PATV today is a testament to the strength of the values and convictions underpinning it, as well as the continuing need for it.

PATV also draws strength from its partnerships and stakeholders, primarily local government, the public and educational institutions. All of these provide content, training and resources, as well as constituting audiences. Included among educational institutions are Media Access Centres, which serve as hubs for training, production and general access for the public.

Municipal concession fees, fees from cable operators, donations and sponsorships mean that PATV is generally well resourced in the US; and the support for PATV is firmly legislated, meaning sustainability is assured. Of course, levels of funding vary according to the market in which the service operates as well as the nature of its partners.

Although it is unlikely that the policy-making bodies in South Africa will deem it necessary at any time soon to legislate financial and/or material support for CTV, the formation of partnerships with local government and potential partner institutions can guarantee the success and sustainability of CTV. Of particular interest is the Media Access Centre model, which would formalise the relationships between stakeholders and centralise the much-needed resources and skills. One such centre has been proposed for the community of Asheville in North Carolina. It envisions a centre that can bring together community-based information and media arts activities. The focus would be to provide a forum for community dialogue and media education and training, and the centre would subsidise access to members of the community and to media organisations.

This Community Access Centre approach offers a common organisational framework and allows for concerted funds-mobilisation efforts as well as financial planning. Run by civic leaders, such a centre can also function as a forum for community meetings that can be both open to the public and televised. In South Africa, there is potential that such a centre could be housed in a Multi-purpose Community Centre (MPCC), and training could be provided through accredited institutions and SETAs. This model can provide access to the community through participation, it can build capacity through the training offered and it can even provide a cultural hub for the community.

Europe: open channels

In Europe, the term 'open channel' denotes a frequency allocated to free-to-air public access radio and television broadcasting. Like PATV in the US, open channel television is a public service legislated and supported by the government as well as commercial media through a percentage of licence fees. In 1997, six European countries (Germany, France, Britain, Poland, Norway and Sweden) got together and signed the Berlin Declaration on Open Channels for Europe. This declaration formalised the existence of open channels in Europe. The principles of the declaration are based on citizens' inalienable right to communicate and take into account the threats to this right. The Declaration combats discrimination of all kinds and decries the limited access to media available to the ordinary citizen. It notes the trend toward liberalisation and conglomeration in the European broadcast industry and considers these factors to be key threats to the rights of citizens to communicate.

Although community or public access television had existed in Europe prior to the open channel definition, the aim of the Berlin Declaration was to bring together different organisations in order to constitute a representative body that could lobby at the level of the European Union. It would also serve as a forum for exchange and sharing of expertise and resources to the benefit of all.

Offener Kanal Radio and TV of Germany is a typical example of the European open channel system. Its existence was established through legislation, just like PATV in the US, and the government contributes 15 per cent of the television licence fees it collects. The federal government teams together with local government structures in the regions, NGOs and individuals to constitute the governance structure of the various stations.

Another example is Denmark's Non-Commercial Television, which is also supported by the government through a licence fee but is subsidised by the commercial television sector. Again the ties with community radio are strong. This relationship allows for sharing of content, facilities and expertise across formats, as well as allowing for the pooling of resources for development.

South Africa, as a whole, has a well-established community radio sector from which CTV could benefit greatly. Issues of sustainability, policy and regulation and audiences have all been dealt with at length in the community radio sector, and this knowledge would be of substantial aid to CTV.

Dublin has also begun the process of setting up CTV, whose focus is on affording public access to transmission, training and production. The educational element is strong in the Dublin approach, which plans to provide educational access from basic literacy all the way to an advanced level. This is a counter-hegemonic approach that challenges the norms and values of commercial television that seeks to homogenise audiences to the detriment of local specificities and points of view (Dublin Community Television 2005).

Dublin CTV aims to play a central role in civic life by televising council debates and proceedings to enhance government transparency. Governance of Dublin CTV will be based on a coalition of citizens' groups, local government and educational institutions.

South Korea

In RTV, South Korea offers an example of CTV in the context of a technologically advanced environment, characterised by satellite broadcasting and high levels of media saturation (RTV South Korea 2005).

RTV is run by the Citizens' Broadcast Foundation, a civil society organisation mandated with this specific purpose. The station is funded by the Digital Satellite Broadcasting Company (the platform company of Korea's digital satellite broadcasting capability) and from public funds, such as the Development Fund for Broadcasting, distributed by the Korean Broadcasting Commission. RTV also accepts contributions from individual citizens, firms and foundations and generates revenue from its own production and other activities.

RTV provides facilities and training through a Citizens' Network Centre. All programming is of local origination, and the station broadcasts for 15 hours on weekdays and 16 hours over weekends. RTV is sustainable as a result of the specifically earmarked funds allocated through the Foundation. Its strength also derives from operating in a technologically advanced environment affording digital satellite distribution.

In South Africa, the SABC may be a likely partner in a development fund for broadcasting, depending on the levels of support it is able to give. The Citizens' Network Centre is also a viable option worth adopting. Existing media training institutions could be earmarked to fill this role. The Citizens' Network Centre must facilitate public access, allowing for entry-level training, for instance, as opposed to benefiting only those who are already in the industry. In the case of South Africa, where the issue of access is paramount and there is a dearth of trained and qualified personnel, this is a key concern.

Fiji

CTV Fiji was established in 1997 and has an audience of 95 000. It broadcasts in three languages via VHF, and the main focus of programming is education and information. The governance structures of CTV Fiji consist of representatives drawn from the community (Nandi CTV Fiji 2005).

Funding for the station remains a weak point, with heavy reliance on grants from international agencies and in-house initiatives such as quiz shows, which provide some revenue through advertising and sponsorships. CTV Fiji underscores the possibility of operating within a linguistically diverse environment. Whereas this may be perceived to be expensive in terms of programming and staff training needs, Fiji has shown that there are substantial payoffs in terms of audience size and loyalty.

Dependence on external funding, however, calls into question the levels of accountability to the local community. Although this can be achieved, it is preferable to rely on local funding.

Certain kinds of innovative programming such as quiz shows can bring in much-needed revenue by attracting sponsorship and advertising, especially given the relatively low levels of investment needed to produce these formats. The use of cellphone interactivity also provides a potential source of revenue; the technology exists to set up systems with service providers where viewers call in or SMS and a share of the rates goes to the station.

New Zealand

Triangle TV in New Zealand offers a good example of how CTV operates in that country. The channel was established in August 1998 and broadcasts via UHF on a government-owned channel. Triangle TV's main focus is access, public service and ethnic television programming. The station does not own any production facilities, relying on facilities owned by independent producers or housed at other media institutions (Triangle TV 2005).

South African CTV could follow the Triangle TV example, given the option to broadcast for fixed periods on SABC-owned frequencies, at least until such time that it is sufficiently sustainable. Although the lack of production facilities may be seen as a weakness, it has great strength in terms of lower running costs. If production facilities are available in the market and through partners and stakeholders at competitive rates to the extent that this can be outsourced, then it substantially reduces the costs of running CTV. However, this would require a network of independent producers who are sufficiently well established to attract sponsorship or even have independent access to production facilities, in addition to being dedicated to CTV. The latter caveat is important in so far as independent producers sourcing sponsorship and advertising is concerned; the principles and values of CTV need to be adhered to and understood in order to avoid potential conflicts of principle. For instance, if the CTV initiative champions social upliftment in a constituency where alcohol abuse is a problem, would it allow a programme sponsored by a beer company?

South Africa

The nature and structure of partnerships and stakeholders should be as inclusive as possible but, at the same time, strategically thought out. These could potentially include the community, city/local and regional government, educational institutions, local business, civic organisations and NGOs. The issues to take into consideration here are revenue streams, sources of programming and the smooth operation of the station.

Signal distribution remains an open debate in terms of when the switch-over process from analogue to digital transmission takes place, along with the issue of frequency availability. The time frame of the migration is as yet undetermined. There would need to be a clear idea of when a given initiative could be up and running technically and financially and what infrastructural options would be available at the time.

Full community access and training could be achieved by borrowing from the Media Access Centre model. As discussed above, the use of MPCCs remains a viable option, depending on how well the management structure of these units enables CTV.

In terms of structure, one option is a combination of public access, educational and government programming, while allowing for commercial income generation through the sale of advertising and airtime. This model is based on the PEG structure of US and Canadian public access broadcasting, where Public access, Education and Government programming underpins the channel. In the South African context, Aldridge (1996) has suggested that a commercial component be added to form a C-PEG structure. Commercially viable and cheap formats such as game and quiz shows need to be investigated. In the initial stages, the focus may need to be on formats that require less production time and fewer human resources and skills, together with lower equipment levels than would be found at national broadcasters.

Producers should be encouraged to act independently in securing sponsorship and advertising for their content. As noted above, producers would need to work within the governing principles and values of the station. It remains to be seen how viable a C-PEG model would be in a South African context. Its potential lies in the flexibility of combinations in the mix. Aldridge (1997) points out the concern that exists in harmonising the interests of the station and those of commercial sponsors and advertisers. Ross (in Aldridge 1996) indicates that there are a few cases where commercial considerations have not interfered with stations' commitments to their constituent groups.

Public access can be enhanced further through the purchase or licensing of programmes from independent producers, media departments at training institutions (local universities, for example) as well as bodies such as the Film Resource Unit (FRU) and the National

Film and Video Foundation (NFVF). Paid programming could also be provided by local organisations (civic, religious and other stakeholders).

Educational institutions and media-related NGOs will not only be able to provide training, but will also be a potentially rich source of quality programming for the station. The government, both local and national, through bodies such as the Government Communication and Information System (GCIS) and the Department of Communications (DoC) must be engaged to form partnerships that encompass issues of programming, policy support and possibly funding, as is the case with CTV initiatives in other parts of the world.

Conclusion

There is a great deal to be learned from models of CTV around the world. The external environments offer similarities that South Africa can learn from as well as differences that must be considered. However, the internal characteristics of the various initiatives offer an important insight to us: the basic principles that underpin the need for CTV are similar – ensuring the right of ordinary citizens to communicate, by providing the means to do so.

CHAPTER 2

Regulatory overview

Constitutional framework

Community television (CTV) operations must be carried out in the primary context of legislation passed by the government of the Republic of South Africa. Broadcasting policy is developed and controlled principally by the country's broadcast regulator, the Independent Communications Authority of South Africa (ICASA), which has replaced the Independent Broadcasting Authority (IBA). Underpinning this environment is the historical legacy of the democratic struggle against apartheid. One aspect of this was civil society's struggle to gain representation on the airwaves in a way that is not mediated by state-managed public service broadcasting, on the one hand, or the imperatives of commerce, on the other.

One consequence of the liberation struggle is the country's Constitution, under which framework all other policy-making occurs. The Constitution contains several provisions that have a bearing on CTV. The Founding Provisions express the values on which the notions of state and nation are constituted, including human dignity, the achievement of equality, the advancement of human rights and freedoms, non-racialism and non-sexism, in addition to universal adult suffrage and attendant measures to ensure the current Republic's democratic functioning.

It is these values that have created an enabling environment for the emergence of community media, an eventuality that was made possible by the Independent Broadcasting Authority Act of 1993 (IBA Act), which mandated three tiers of broadcasting – community, public and private/commercial. The IBA's successor, ICASA, has set value parameters for CTV that include public access, local origination, community participation and non-profitable functioning. The essential idea is that 'viewers get involved in the production and management of communication systems and in the ownership and control of the means of communication' (ICASA 2004).

Since the community covered by local CTV channels will include wide metropolitan areas, many communities of interest must be involved in this manner. This is a very democratic model of functioning, but in order for it to be effective it should take place within a framework that respects the rights of all, which is the kind of structure that the Constitution provides for the country as a whole.

In a similar manner, the constitutional provisions that recognise the rights of citizens as being equal in terms of privileges and benefits, as well as duties and responsibilities, have a direct bearing on the manner in which the CTV sector conducts itself. This is because the notion of CTV is founded on a humanistic proposition that values those mechanisms that promote people's involvement in public life and in the governance of the nation through open debate and freedom of expression.

These democratic values have been born of the struggle for freedom by the people of South Africa, who recognised the media, particularly the South African Broadcasting Corporation (SABC), as a prime mechanism for controlling public consciousness. The mass democratic movement used media to good effect in its battle against apartheid, and the media activists of yesteryear have become the media producers and owners of today. It is against this background that the long march to CTV takes place, as South Africa breasts the information tides of the 21st century.

Rights to access

The transformation that has taken place over the last few decades has often been painful, but it has resulted in a national culture that supports the attainment of equal and unassailable human rights. The role of community media in this context is captured by John van Zyl (2002) who declares that the restoration of human rights and of learning to countries whose people have been damaged by conflict can be achieved through developing democratic, interactive communications mediums.

In this scenario, access to information can be seen as a fundamental human right that plays a role in ensuring other rights with respect to areas such as the environment, health, gender equality and education. Fundamental rights are ubiquitous and indivisible, residing equally in each person unless diminished by some socially determined means such as a prison term.

In Van Zyl's view, the mass media are a necessary mechanism to 'enlighten public opinion and help ordinary people understand their rights'. This notion can be traced back to the 1970s, the dawn of the information society and its computer networks, when the issue of the 'right to communicate' rose to the fore. This two-way, interactive communication aims to enable all citizens to participate in public affairs, or to engage in what Habermas (in Louw 1991) refers to as the public sphere. In this environment, even marginalised or otherwise disempowered people – previously the subjects of development rather than actors therein – have the right to contribute to debates about their well-being and their future.

For CTV, the implications of democratic communications extend further than the boundaries of disadvantaged communities, because access to media – in the sense of it being a civil right – must extend to all citizens. It is therefore dangerous to privilege any one section of the population, even marginalised communities, as having the sole prerogative to air their views, screen their preferred programming or otherwise access the airwaves without a guarantee that all might do the same.

The tradition that South Africa belongs to all who live in it extends back to the *Freedom Charter* of 1956, and is enshrined in the Preamble to the country's Constitution:

> We, the people of South Africa,
> Recognise the injustices of our past;
> Honour those who suffered for justice and freedom in our land;
> Respect those who have worked to build and develop our country; and
> Believe that South Africa belongs to all who live in it, united in our diversity.

The definition of rights is further elucidated in the Bill of Rights. Section 7(1) of the Constitution provides that the 'Bill of Rights is a cornerstone of democracy in South Africa', and 'enshrines the rights of all people in our country and affirms the democratic values of human dignity, equality and freedom', values that also underpin CTV internationally. For example, the Australian regulations for CTV are very similar to those being applied in South Africa and, in addition to their non-profit and community participation provisos, allow for written policies and procedures 'that apply to all station activities, which promote tolerance and respect of social and cultural difference and attempt to break down prejudice on the basis of ethnicity, race, chosen language, gender, sexual preference, religion, age, physical or mental ability, occupation, cultural belief or political affiliation' (CBAA 2003).

The notion of equality is expanded in Section 9(2) of the Constitution, in terms of which the state reserves its ability to balance or redress inequality by taking legislative or other means 'to protect or advance persons, or categories of persons, disadvantaged by unfair discrimination'. This provision has to be seen in conjunction with Section 9(3) and (4), which prohibits unfair discrimination on grounds such as race, gender, sex, pregnancy, marital status, ethnic or social origin, colour, sexual orientation, age, disability, religion, conscience, belief, culture, language and birth.

Other rights are also listed, including the right to life, to freedom and security of the person and freedom of religion, belief and opinion. Bearing on this is the right to freedom of expression, in Section 16, which includes 'freedom of the press and other media; freedom to receive or impart information or ideas; freedom of artistic creativity; and academic freedom and freedom of scientific research'. These rights are limited in the sense that they do not extend to 'propaganda for war; incitement of imminent violence; or advocacy of hatred that is based on race, ethnicity, gender or religion, and that constitutes incitement to cause harm'.

It is interesting to note that one of the rights often cited with regard to CTV (access to information) is dealt with on a rather sketchy basis in the Bill of Rights, and does not seem to pertain to media in general. Instead, Section 32 refers to the right to access information held by the state and to any information held by a third party that may be required for the exercise or protection of rights held by others.

Indeed, there is no specific provision in South Africa's Constitution or broadcasting-related legislation that sets out public rights with regard to access to the airwaves. In its *Triple Inquiry Report* into broadcasting, the IBA echoed the constitutional provision for public access to government information via broadcasting, which duty the IBA ascribes to 'the domain of the public broadcaster' (IBA 1995).

ICASA position paper on community television

In November 2004, ICASA set the stage for the creation of permanent CTV stations in South Africa through its *Community television broadcasting services: Position paper*. This document sets out various submissions on CTV that ICASA received from interested parties, as well as establishing ICASA's policy on CTV with regard to issues ranging from frequency allocations to viability, licence applications, principles and obligations in terms of language, news, actuality and children's programming, local content and independent production.

The position paper represents the most comprehensive consideration that ICASA has given to CTV following the inception of policy in this regard by its predecessor, the IBA. The IBA Act made provision for CTV services as the third tier of broadcasting in South Africa, and the IBA consequently granted a few temporary event broadcasting licences under the rubric of this legislation. ICASA has made passing reference to CTV in other policy documents pertaining to the television sector; but in the absence of a particular regulatory policy, CTV stations could not be licensed on a permanent basis.

ICASA's position paper firstly considers CTV in relation to the Authority's mandate to ensure the provision of 'a diverse range of sound and television broadcasting services on a national, regional and local level, which, when viewed collectively, cater for all language and cultural groups and provide entertainment, education and information' (ICASA 2004: 4). CTV is but one aspect of the total broadcast media landscape, although, along with its commercial and public service counterparts, it must be responsive to public needs. Additionally, in terms of Section 2 of the IBA Act, CTV must promote 'identity, culture and character' at its geographic level of operations and provide 'regular news services; actuality programmes on matters of public interest; programmes on political issues of public interest; and programmes on matters of international, national, regional and local significance'.

Primarily, these considerations mean that CTV fits into the context of being a player, separate and distinct from the other players, in the arena of national television services. At the same time, it has an obligation to reflect and build cultural identities at the local level and be responsive to public needs. It must also provide a range of programming in the genres identified by ICASA, within the parameters specific to CTV that the Authority has defined.

An onus has been placed on ICASA to license CTV stations in terms of the Broadcasting Act of 1999, which is now contained in the new Convergence Bill before Parliament. As part of this process, ICASA conducted an inquiry into local television that it published as a discussion paper in 2003, and it commissioned a feasibility study on the viability of commercial local television. Both of these initiatives drew a number of written and oral submissions that commented on local and community television in terms of the overall television market in South Africa. Particular concerns raised by stakeholders related to the maintenance of stability within the broadcasting industry, as well as ensuring fair competition between broadcasting licensees. Submissions were received from signal distributors Sentech and Orbicom as well as the National Association of Broadcasters (NAB), focusing on frequency availability and allocation, while M-Net additionally commented on the issue of advertising regulation.

Despite the intentions of the enabling legislation to establish a viable CTV sector in South Africa, there remains some doubt as to the extent to which ICASA has fully understood the implications of its policies for the type of CTV broadcasting it has envisaged. The problem is that the regulator has seen community broadcast media in much the same light as public service broadcasters, requiring them to produce content such as news, drama and educational programming, which is expensive even for public service and commercial stations. As Van Zyl (2006) points out in his discussion on community radio, the issue of financial sustainability has been given little attention: 'In effect, the regulator was making the community radio sector a parallel public broadcaster without the benefit of licence fees, government support (e.g. in the form of tax relief, or lower telephone charges) and actual state subsidies'.

The same is true for the CTV sector, where the regulator has high expectations of the type of content stations are expected to provide, but at the same time has made no provision for statutory financial support. While commercial free-to-air television services such as eTV can utilise the tried-and-tested formulas of delivering mass audiences to advertisers by providing mostly cheap, foreign-produced entertainment programming, the same is not true for the CTV sector. On the contrary, this sector has to produce a very high percentage of local content, while still relying on the services of volunteers and support from 'the community', which, in the South African context, is made up largely of the lower Living Standards Measure (LSM) levels. These problems are dealt with extensively in Chapter 12 of this report (Business models), but the lack of statutory financial support for the CTV sector remains a problem that should be addressed by further lobbying for such assistance in the future.

It is essential to point out here that the term 'community' is very politically loaded in South Africa. As Bosch (2003) points out, in the apartheid years the state used it to refer to white areas while, on the other hand, black activists conscripted the term as a euphemism for the townships. It is this latter signification that has come to define the term in the minds of most South Africans today and this, together with the developmental needs of the bulk of the country's population, constrains consideration of CTV both in public forums and in the ideological thrust of many CTV initiatives. This puts CTV in a precarious position in the racially charged atmosphere of South African society; white people are often seen as intruders in the realm of media that should be owned and managed solely by the 'previously disadvantaged' population sectors and there is a strong sentiment that such media should serve only the lower-income groups. Thus, there are contradictions between the nature of communities of interest, the extent of CTV's mandate to service all those within a geographic area and the potential for sourcing funding or revenue that aims at particular economic strata (higher LSMs for commercial purposes or low-income groups for donor funding).

Frequency availability

The issue of frequency availability is fundamental to the viability of local CTV broadcasting. There is currently a scarcity of available frequencies for local transmissions for the following reasons:

- most of the available spectrum is either used by existing commercial and public broadcasters or earmarked for the expansion of their analogue broadcasting reach;
- the need to prevent interference between broadcast channels necessitates that barrier frequencies be left vacant between broadcast frequencies;
- the proposed migration from analogue to digital terrestrial transmission (DTT) requires spare frequencies to be made available during the migration process;
- the proposed regional public service television channels will require broadcast frequencies; and
- the possible migration of current VHF television channels 11 and 13 to the spare UHF assignments in view of accommodating digital audio broadcasting.

Submissions suggested the need for frequency allocations within a national frequency allocation plan, giving particular regard to the issue of planning for the analogue-to-digital migration. Respondents were worried that the allocation of additional analogue television frequencies would adversely affect the migration process, as well as limit the expansion of existing analogue broadcast services.

CTV finds itself emerging onto the South African broadcast landscape at a difficult time, when two proposed regional television channels are demanding airspace and when the frequency-hungry migration from analogue to digital transmission is imminent. Nevertheless, ICASA has made space available for CTV on the frequency spectrum by reallocating spare analogue frequencies for CTV use in Durban, Johannesburg and Port Elizabeth, as well as in a scattering of rural areas. In Cape Town, the Authority has allowed CTV to 'squat' on a frequency earmarked for the analogue-to-digital migration, with the caveat that a CTV licence in Cape Town will be valid for no longer than 12 months.

Even with these frequency allocations, there may be significant gaps in coverage in the metropolitan areas because 'gap-filler' frequencies will not be available where the terrain obstructs the single frequency signal.

ICASA acknowledges that analogue frequency will be freed up after the migration to DTT, which would then be available for CTV use. While it may be assumed that CTV broadcasts in Durban, Johannesburg and Port Elizabeth would continue unhindered by the migration process because it would not affect their allocated channels, the same cannot be said for Cape Town. The Mother City's CTV channel is confronted by the prospect of a limited time period in which to establish itself through analogue broadcasting. Once the migration process begins, the channel would have to shut down broadcast operations for the migration period (the duration of which, according to the IBA's *Triple Inquiry Report*, might be some 10–20 years), or find windows on other broadcast channels such as the SABC's, or surf the DTT wave and gear up to begin digital broadcasting as soon as the migration process is initiated.

While there are frequencies available for CTV in a few rural towns, the small size of their populations mitigates against dedicated CTV services in these areas. DTT may well be a better solution for rural television services, particularly if there is a national CTV service that provides programming for these areas. Another option to consider for rural towns is low-power broadcasting that falls outside the scope of ICASA's regulatory ambit.

Conflation with local TV

One major headache for CTV in South Africa is that it is conflated with local television; that is, it is seen as serving a large area such as a metropolitan city region rather than a small zone such as a city suburb. ICASA's investigation into local television showed that commercial local TV was unlikely to be sustainable in the long term, because it would be competing for advertising revenue with the existing national broadcasters. Moreover, it would have to compete for audiences against the proposed regional channels; and the Authority's latest move with regard to the regional channels has been to allow them to run advertising, whereas previously they were to be funded solely by government grants and sponsorships.

For these reasons, ICASA decided against licensing local commercial TV broadcasting and it also declined to license local public TV because of the proposed regional channels. This left the field open for licensing local community television in line with the IBA Act; as the ICASA position paper on CTV states: 'As only one of the three tiers of broadcasting is being introduced at local level, there is no need to distinguish between different types of local television and it will be referred to henceforth as community television' (ICASA 2004: 14).

The problem here is that the notion of community media generally refers to small-scale media (Lundby 1995; Hadland & Thorne 2004) and, while local television may be on a small scale relative to national or regional media, a metropolitan area, for example, covers numerous communities and hundreds of thousands, if not millions, of people. This poses an essential paradox for CTV because, at this scale, it is difficult to define the station's ownership and target audience by a single identifiable community.

ICASA's stance regarding the granting of CTV licences within this ambit is to privilege geographic region rather than interest group in defining the community to be served. The reason for this is the scarcity of broadcast frequencies, which prohibits multi-channel broadcasting on the small scale, at least above the unregulated 200 GHz frequency. The implications of this definition of geographic community are clarified by ICASA counsellor Pfanani Lishivha, who responded to a query concerning the status of a metropolitan area as an identifiable geographic community:

> Geographic community means the entire community served and covered by the channel. If the channel serves and covers the entire metro such a metro becomes the geographic community. Special interest groups are also members of a geographic community. The board of the station will need to be made of reps from various community organisations within the coverage area.
> (Lishivha 2005a)

Limitations on CTV

Another stricture that ICASA sets out is the prohibition on political ownership, control or influence over CTV. ICASA will not license any organisation that has party political affiliations to run a CTV channel, and the regulator considers features of control such as ownership, funding, board membership, management, programming and consistent public identification with a particular political entity in determining levels of political influence. This provision implicitly excludes government bodies from involvement in the ownership and management of CTV stations, as well as excluding such bodies from dominating the stations through provision of a major portion of funding and/or revenue.

In the licence application process, ICASA must first determine the economic nature of the organisation applying for a licence. This must be of a non-profit nature and purpose-built to serve the interests of the community it represents. The applicant must demonstrate that it has the support of the particular community concerned, either through direct representation or through the medium of persons 'associated with promoting the interests of such community' (ICASA 2004: 15). However, such representatives may not be merely passive functionaries of the organisation and must also be shown to participate in the selection and provision of programmes during the course of the broadcast.

These provisos relate to the basic definition of a CTV station – that it is fully controlled by a non-profit entity and is carried on for non-profit purposes and that it serves a particular community. In terms of governance, the CTV station must be managed and controlled by a board that is democratically elected from members of the community in the licensed geographic area.

Principles of CTV

ICASA has specified certain principles that underlie CTV. The first of these is public access, a notion that is supposed to obviate the divide between broadcast professionals, on the one hand, and the public at large, on the other. In ICASA's terms, this means that 'the viewer becomes the broadcaster' (ICASA 2004: 16) and the role of CTV is to act as a 'responsible civic custodian' in ensuring that anyone who chooses to appear on television does so in a responsible manner.

This definition of access is unclear with regard to how persons engage with television, for the notion of simply appearing on television (i.e. appearing in front of the camera) is different to the process of producing programming, which requires training to be effective. The word 'appear' is vague and does not specify the level of representation that an individual might enjoy. It could mean simply that a person is part of an audience at a show, or that they have a very brief opportunity to state their opinion. In addition, the Authority uses the words 'anyone who chooses to appear on television' (ICASA 2004: 16), which implies that everyone has a right to appear, provided that they do so in a way that is acceptable to the CTV station's management.

The principles that follow this point on access amplify the nature of viewer participation, in terms, firstly, of a requirement for local origination of programming and, secondly, for community participation in 'the production and management of communication systems and in the ownership and control of the means of communication' (ICASA 2004: 16). This means that there must be mechanisms in place for members of the geographic community served by the station to participate in its activities at all these various levels, in addition to their right of access through simply appearing on television.

This suggests that there is an onus on the station to engage in training activities that will empower citizens to participate in a meaningful and effective way. There is, however, no directive to engage in training activities *per se*, so these might be outsourced to a separate entity, for example, tertiary education institutions.

Programming committees

A further stipulation for community involvement is through the selection and provision of programmes, which must take place through the medium of programming councils or committees that are representative of different sectors within the community served by the station. These committees must both select programmes to be shown in terms of ICASA's content regulations and provide programmes, presumably through programme acquisition.

No criteria are given for programme selection other than the content quotas set out in the ICASA position paper, so policy and methodology in this regard are left up to the programming committee. However, the committee would have to take into account citizens' right of access, in other words the right of persons from the community to appear in programmes. Whether such programmes are to be studio-based or pre-recorded is not prescribed, so presumably both instances would apply.

This raises the question of how the committee will determine what programmes get shown and when. For example, can an individual from the geographic community demand that a programme that he or she has made must appear on the CTV channel because they have a right to such access? ICASA's position is that 'viewers' have a right to appear on television, but the manner in which they do so is not spelt out. Would the programming committee then have the power to reject a programme based on quality or other programming considerations, if the person is afforded some other way of appearing on the channel or if they themselves do not actually appear in the programme and it merely represents their point of view?

Noting that the position paper merely sets out principles of community broadcasting and guidelines on how to ensure that a community broadcasting service fulfils its purpose in serving the community, Lishivha (2005b) points out that determining access to programming or appearing on television will be the function of the CTV channel's programming committee. This body must develop criteria to govern its functioning and the nature and scope of community programming. In terms of ICASA policy:

> ...the chief responsibility of management is not to ensure that anyone who chooses to appear on TV may do so freely, but to require that those who

do appear do so responsibly. It is up to the community, through the board, programming committee, and management to determine the acceptable quality of the production that can be broadcast, times of such broadcast, etc. The right to access is not an absolute right. (Lishivha 2005b)

Nevertheless, the definition of what constitutes 'doing so responsibly' is open to contention and this, together with questions of 'acceptable quality', may be a site of struggle in the future.

Financial sustainability

The final principle of CTV as enunciated by ICASA is the requirement of non-profit status. The CTV broadcaster must be a non-profit entity and be run for non-profit purposes, although this does not mean that its activities cannot generate income. The regulation specifies that surplus income generated by the station must be reinvested in the particular community that it serves. While this might take forms such as 'giving financial study assistance to needy members of the community, establishing and/or funding community projects' (ICASA 2004: 17), the actual form of such reinvestment is left up to the broadcaster.

CTV funding may be derived from a broad base of advertising, grants, donations and sponsorships. In terms of the 1998 White Paper on Broadcasting Policy, there is a specific onus on the government's Media Development and Diversity Agency to fund CTV in accordance with its mandate to promote development and diversity in the South African media, with particular regard to gaining government assistance to train broadcast trainers.

Funding may also be obtained from advertising revenue and in this regard the Authority decrees that CTV stations may carry an average of ten minutes of advertisements per hour measured annually, with a maximum of 12 minutes allowed in any hour. It is significant to note that M-Net's submission to ICASA's local television inquiry on advertising limits requested that public regional and local TV stations be limited to a maximum of six minutes in the hour for advertising; the fact that ICASA has allowed CTV stations double this amount suggests that it sees CTV stations obtaining a significant portion of their revenue from advertising and that this will not detract significantly from the overall amount of 'adspend' available to television stations on a national basis (i.e. it will not have a significant effect on the advertising revenues of the existing broadcast players).

The station's financial sustainability will depend on its ability to attract funds from these disparate sources, which in turn will depend on its ability to deliver relevant programming to attract viewers among its various target audiences within the geographic region it serves. Programming is also a basis for legitimacy in terms of broadcasting regulations in that it must 'reflect the needs of the people in the community which must include amongst others cultural, religious, language and geographic needs' (ICASA 2004: 18).

The above stricture is elaborated through distinct responsibilities that the broadcaster is obliged to fulfil with regard to producing programming that meets the needs of viewers in terms of particular criteria set by regulations (the ICASA position paper cites the Broadcasting Act, the IBA Act, which will be superceded by the Convergence Act, and the Constitution).

Programming

Firstly, the broadcaster must provide a service that is both distinct from other broadcasters and which deals 'specifically with community issues which are not normally dealt with by the broadcasting service covering the same area' (ICASA 2004: 18). This is somewhat ambiguous in terms of CTV because there are no other local television broadcasters, but we can assume that the context for CTV broadcasters will be the coverage of local events and issues by the existing national and proposed regional channels.

The broadcasting service must provide programming that informs, and also offers educational material and entertainment. No criteria are given for judging these aspects, but the broadcaster will have to show a range of programming that fits into one or more of these categories.

The station is also obliged to focus on 'grassroots community issues'. These issues must fall under areas such as development, health care, basic information and general education, environmental affairs, local and international content and the reflection of local culture. These categories are not exclusive and the broadcaster will be expected to cover other areas of interest or information that may be relevant to the community. It is clear that the station must reflect a multiplicity of issues rather than being based on a single area of interest, for example education.

It is significant that the term 'international' is included here because it locates the local community within the context of an international information environment. There is then a need to reflect international issues in programming, which content can then also be sourced from other countries.

The station will be expected to 'promote the development of a sense of common purpose with democracy' (ICASA 2004: 18). This is another ambiguous point. It could mean that the station must endeavour to represent the interests of disparate groups within society in order to give people a sense of striving towards a common purpose in ensuring a democratic society. On the other hand, it could mean that principles of democratic action should be promoted, for example voting in elections or discussing political issues. In other words, this would promote the democratic process in a socio-political sense and so unite people behind the project of working at democracy in society. Still, whatever interpretation is given to this proviso it is clear that the station must afford its constituency a sense of democratic action and unity of purpose in striving towards this ideal.

Within this same injunction to promote a sense of democracy is embedded a developmental goal in improving quality of life. This is a rather awkward conjunction that enjoins the station to provide programming that supports developmental goals as well as enhancing the democratic project. The question of just who are to be the beneficiaries of these provisos is also left out, so we do not know who should feel the sense of common purpose with regard to democracy or whose quality of life is to be improved – whether it is participants in the station's activities or its audience, where the two sectors do not coincide. In other words, it is unclear whether these statements refer to those engaged in production activities or to viewers, and this can be a critical point in examining the nature of an organisation applying for a CTV licence.

Nevertheless, an onus is placed on the station to broadcast programming that 'supports and promotes sustainable development, participatory democracy and human rights as well as the educational objectives, information needs, language, culture and entertainment interests of participating groups such as women, youth, civic and sport interest groups' (ICASA 2004: 18).

It is interesting that the locus of programming requirements is shifted here from 'viewers' to 'participating groups'. This sets the station to serving primarily the interests of those groups that participate in the station's activities in terms of the particular aspects of programming content listed, rather than those of the public at large.

Language is another aspect of programming that must be taken into consideration. Here ICASA merely stipulates that CTV must broadcast in the languages used in the relevant communities, and no language quotas are required.

Programme types

ICASA also specifies certain types of programming that a CTV station must carry. The first of these is news and here the Authority will specify the duration of daily news bulletins in the licensee's licence conditions, without any prior indication of such duration being given. However, there is a clear onus on the station to provide news bulletins in addition to actuality and children's programmes.

Actuality programmes must offer a range that includes genres such as documentaries, docu-dramas, informal knowledge-building and regular current affairs features. Again the Authority will set out the number of hours per week of such programming in the licensee's licence conditions.

Children's programming is another required area. Here programmes must be produced that entertain, inform and educate children and which reflect their culture, language and life experiences. It must also affirm their sense of self, community and place. The Authority enjoins the station to broadcast children's programming 'at times when children form part of a larger audience', which presumably means when children are available to watch TV (i.e. when they are not at school).

The position paper lists three values that safeguard the welfare of children and juveniles in the media environment. The first of these is 'respect for the child's personality and development needs', which implies 'the affordable and convenient provision of media materials that will foster creativity and imagination, broaden horizons, stimulate curiosity and critical awareness and encourage social, cultural and civic competence' (ICASA 2004: 20).

The medium of CTV is in itself a means of delivering 'affordable and convenient' material, while it will be up to the station to ensure that the other criteria are met in its children's programmes.

Secondly, children's programmes must set limits on advertiser's ability 'to reach and influence children'. Thirdly, they must avoid exposing children to 'harmful materials and overly adult fare before they are ready for it'. Here again the station will have to use its discretion in judging the content of children's programmes to meet these criteria.

South African content

More specific criteria are set for South African content in programming. Firstly, South African content is defined in terms of who produces it – persons, companies or organisations (i.e. juristic persons) who are citizens permanently resident in the Republic.

Where groups of people are involved in production (as companies or organisations), the majority of key personnel must be citizens; and a prescribed percentage of production costs must be incurred in the country.

ICASA's thinking with respect to programming is guided by its South African Television Content Regulations of 2006, which incentivise the production of South African programme genres. These include drama, African language drama, children's drama, children's informal knowledge-building programmes, arts programming and a diversity of commissioning from provinces outside the main production areas of Gauteng and the Western Cape (ICASA 2006).

The Authority scores programmes according to an incentive point system. In addition to the above genres, ICASA scores African language programming with high incentive points, specifically for CTV. These African language genres include documentaries, children's programming and arts programming.

Most importantly for CTV, the Authority prescribes a quota of 55 per cent South African programming content from start-up. ICASA sees South African content as 'both a social necessity and an economic opportunity for South Africa', and in this context the content quota has been set to aid 'the promotion and development of the South African television production industry' (ICASA 2006: 22).

It is important that community broadcasters understand that this requirement of South African content is meant to stimulate the local television production industry. While no specific criteria for ensuring this are set out, emphasis is placed on the production of drama as a means of creating jobs in the industry. This proviso in Section 8 of the Content Regulations should be read in conjunction with Section 9, which deals with independent television production (i.e. by non-juristic persons who are independent producers). Here the Authority sets a quota for independent production, which is not produced by the broadcaster, at 40 per cent of overall content. This quota is set with the intention of increasing 'the opportunities for local producers to contribute to the diversity of South African programming' (ICASA 2006: 23).

This creates a dilemma for CTV practitioners, some of whom believe that CTV should have no direct relationship with the professional production industry because:
- they believe CTV should stimulate production initiatives in the non-profit (NGO) sector;
- CTV broadcasters in some other countries specifically exclude professional productions;
- they fear that professional producers with skills and resources could come to dominate CTV broadcasts; and
- the ethos of professional production is often based on commercial considerations that they believe have no place in community media.

In addition to the above factors, CTV would have to be financially successful on a fairly large scale in order to finance such productions, especially local drama. It may be that community arts groups or other amateur or student groups could be called upon to produce low-budget drama, but professional productions are expensive. For example, SABC budgets go up to R13 500 per minute for a drama, or R324 000 per 24-minute programme; the public broadcaster budgets documentary production at up to R4 500 per minute, or R216 000 per 48-minute programme. These costs are normal for the professional production sector but may be difficult for a CTV broadcaster to match.

While a CTV broadcaster may pass on such costs to developmental funders, the station would have to justify this expense in terms of the effectiveness of the programme to reach the target audience on a large enough scale and to have sufficient impact on that target sector to justify the expense.

It may be that ICASA is overly optimistic in expecting the CTV sector to deliver on this respect, in view of the latter's animosity towards the professional production sector and the frailty of its financial base. On the other hand, Thorne (2005) has suggested that emerging black producers, who may be positioned to leverage low-cost production techniques in order to produce content, should be favoured by CTV stations as sources of independent production.

Despite these contentious areas, ICASA's position paper sets the stage for the emergence of permanent CTV broadcasters in South Africa. At this stage in media history, however, the very notion of broadcasting itself is shifting as digital technologies open up new channels for content distribution and interactive communication. For this reason, the South African government is considering legislation that attempts to set the regulatory boundaries of broadcasting and other communications mechanisms in the information age, within the ambit of the Convergence Bill.

Implications of the Convergence Bill

In terms of its Preamble, the Convergence Bill aims to 'promote convergence in the broadcasting, broadcasting signal distribution and telecommunications sectors and to provide the legal framework for convergence of these sectors'. This legislation has significant implications for CTV, recognising as it does the interconnectedness of modern broadcasting and netcasting mediums.

One of the major effects of the Bill for CTV is that it repeals parts of the Broadcasting Act of 1999, which covers regulations governing the radio frequency spectrum and broadcasting services, including community broadcasting.

Interestingly, the term 'broadcasting service' does not refer to netcasting technologies, which are specifically excluded from the definition. There is also a distinction made between 'communications services' and 'content services'; it seems that communications here are defined as two-way transactions between sender and receiver, although broadcast frequencies are included among the means of transmitting this interactive information.

While this distinction may have been clear in the past, differentiating between, say, telecommunications and television, the boundaries between these mediums are somewhat less distinct today than the Bill allows. Television has traditionally been a one-way transmission medium, but new distribution technologies are changing it into a two-way communications medium. For example, BSkyB's interactive television in Britain enables viewers to interact with broadcast content via their set-top box (digital decoder) remote control, albeit that the viewer-to-station leg of the transaction takes place over telephone lines rather than the airwaves (Doherty 2004).

The legislation also does not take into account the interactive nature of Internet protocol (IP) communications, whereby video can be delivered to IP devices and the receiver can select content, record it, regulate its flow and interact with attendant information.

In October 2004, Lord Currie, the chairman of the British broadcasting regulator Ofcom, gave a speech in which he said:

> The rapid growth of first multi-channel, then digital, then PVRs and soon higher-speed broadband are simply the pre-tremors of the real volcanic eruption that technology is about to unleash. At the risk of being over-dramatic I would say that most traditional television broadcasters are today standing about the equivalent of one mile from Mount St Helen. When it blows, frankly, that is too close and then it will be too late to run. (Currie 2004)

Definitions of community broadcasting

Definitions of and regulations for community broadcasting are now covered by the Convergence Bill, which takes its parameters directly from the Broadcasting Act that it supersedes. The term 'community' continues to pertain to 'a geographically founded community or any group of persons or sector of the public having a specific, ascertainable common interest'.

Community broadcasting is defined in Section 1 of the Bill as a broadcasting service that:
- is fully controlled by a non-profit entity and is carried on for non-profit purposes;
- serves a particular community;
- encourages members of the community served by it, or persons associated with or promoting the interests of such a community, to participate in the selection and provision of programmes to be broadcast in the course of such broadcasting service; and
- may be funded by donations, grants, sponsorships or advertising or membership fees, or by any combination of the aforementioned.

The aim of the legislation with regard to broadcasting, set out in Section 2, remains clearly democratic. Its intent is to provide a diversity of broadcast services that serve the broadest public interest in providing a range of programming. So broadcasters must 'cater for all language and cultural groups and provide entertainment, education and information', in the form of news and actuality programmes that cover matters of public interest from politics to regional issues.

The need for diversity is clearly spelt out as the Bill specifies the requirement to cover the needs of 'language, cultural and religious groups', as well as education, regions and local communities.

For community broadcasters, the effect of this democratic imperative is to entrench them firmly as pillars of the public sphere, to provide a public space or forum where a diversity of voices is heard. This thrust towards democratic representation is reinforced by tasking the government with the responsibility of ensuring that broadcasting services are owned by a diverse range of communities, and that broadcasting services are controlled by South Africans.

The Bill aims to 'promote an environment of open, fair and non-discriminatory access to communication networks', although this is balanced by the imperative to 'promote the empowerment of historically disadvantaged persons' (Section 2).

Signal distribution and convergence

It is important to note that content providers must be given access to signal distribution services. This implies that, at least once a body has been licensed to convey content to the public or sections thereof, it is the government's duty to ensure that communications service licensees provide the necessary network space for this purpose.

The government undertakes to provide signal receivers with the means to access distributed signals. It is significant for content providers that ICASA must 'encourage the development of multi-channel distribution systems into the broadcasting framework' (Section 2), another marker to the effects of convergence on the broadcasting landscape and one that should promote the integration of broadcast and netcast technologies.

The premise underlying the Convergence Bill, and indeed its central thrust, is 'to promote and facilitate the convergence of broadcasting and signal distribution' (Section 2), as well as promoting universal access to communications services and encouraging innovation and investment in the communications sector.

The legislation leaves final control of licences to ICASA, and empowers the Authority to 'promote a diversity of views and opinions', as well as promoting ownership and control of communications services by 'previously disadvantaged' groups, together with encouraging competition in the communications sector.

Frequency issues are of particular concern to CTV broadcasters, especially in Cape Town where no spare frequencies are available for CTV broadcasts. Section 30 of the Bill acknowledges that, in carrying out its functions, the Authority 'controls, plans, administers and manages the use and licensing' of broadcast frequencies.

In managing the frequency spectrum, ICASA must comply with the requirements of the International Telecommunication Union and ensure that the spectrum is utilised efficiently and effectively to reduce 'harmful interference'. This could mean that content providers share the spectrum in order to harmonise the use of broadcast frequencies, although the details of this are not spelled out and so are open to interpretation in the future.

It is also significant to note that ICASA is enjoined to give 'high priority' to applications for digital communications using the radio frequency spectrum. This ties in with plans to migrate analogue broadcasting services to digital distribution mechanisms, in the context of a modified frequency plan. The rationale for this is most likely that digital broadcasting makes more effective use of the available spectrum because more digital channels can be squeezed into a particular frequency band than is the case with analogue broadcasting.

This aspect of the legislation might be leveraged by CTV in the future, although it poses the problem of reception, for end-users will have to have digital devices to decode digital transmissions. While this sets before us the hurdle of how digital transmissions are to be received, it is not impossible to imagine a future scenario where local broadcasts leverage either set-top boxes or a combination of high-band and low-band broadcasting technologies, where data streams are broadcast to a wide area via digital terrestrial or satellite distribution and re-packaged for low-band, local area broadcast. This low-band system is a localised neighbourhood television service based on small VHF/UHF transmitters or a 2.4 GHz system (Rushton 2004).

An important point for CTV stations is the requirement to record all programmes and archive them for a period of 30 days after transmission, in addition to keeping scripts or transcripts of the programmes. This means keeping all broadcast material on tape or storing it in digital form. While it may be easy to store programmes that are originated on tape (i.e. pre-packaged material), live-on-air programmes must also be recorded, placing concomitant demands on station infrastructure for making these recordings, storing them and archiving them. Such material must be made available to ICASA's Complaints and Compliance Committee on demand.

Broadcasting standards

ICASA is enjoined by Section 60 of the Bill to draw up a Code of Conduct for broadcasting services to which all broadcasting services licensees must adhere, unless they belong to a body that has drawn up its own set of rules to which its members are compelled to adhere by set disciplinary mechanisms. This body and procedure must be duly acknowledged by ICASA as being an acceptable alternative. Since there is as yet no specific body to which CTV stations can belong (which would probably be along the lines of the National Community Radio Forum), such broadcasters will have to adhere to the conditions of the Code of Conduct (see below).

There are other legislated standards (specified in Section 52(1) and (2) of the Bill) to which CTV broadcasters must adhere. One is the Code of Advertising Practice that governs the nature of broadcast advertisements. Complaints against broadcasters in terms of this code are dealt with by ICASA's Complaints and Compliance Committee.

Party political messages are also subject to restraint. For one thing, party propaganda can only be broadcast during specified election periods and ICASA must determine the timing and scheduling restrictions to be applied. Such advertisements must adhere to standards of legality and technical quality, and may be broadcast no later than 48 hours prior to the commencement of the polling period. CTV broadcasters will still have a choice as to whether or not to broadcast party political messages, and will have to determine their policy on this issue for election periods. If the station chooses to broadcast such advertisements, it must provide equal opportunities to all political parties and may not discriminate against any of them.

Access to the airwaves is an important consideration for CTV broadcasters. It is interesting to note that Section 58 of the Bill requires communications service providers to prioritise 'the carriage of South African broadcasting channels, including local programming'. These signal distributors must also provide universal access for all South Africans to broadcast services as well as a diversity of broadcast service types and content. They must deliver public services, including educational, commercial and community services; and they must 'be open and interoperable, harmonised with the Southern African region, and be able to meet international distribution standards'.

Code of Conduct for Broadcasters

The revised Code of Conduct for Broadcasters (ICASA 2003a) replaces Section 56 (Schedule 1) of the IBA Act. The Code of Conduct (hereafter 'the Code') is underpinned by two elements, the first of which pertains to ensuring adequate viewer and listener information. The Authority believes that 'within reason', audiences should be able to choose what programmes they wish to see or hear as well as what material they wish to avoid. Secondly, broadcasters must be sensitive about their programme scheduling in that they must avoid programming that falls into time slots where it may be detrimental to particular categories of viewers, especially children.

In essence, the Code seeks to protect freedom of expression as a fundamental right, as it is enshrined in the South African Constitution. The Code's Preamble states: 'Freedom of expression ... is one of the basic pre-requisites for this country's progress and the development in liberty of every person. Freedom of expression is a condition indispensable to the attainment of all other freedoms.'

Constitutional provisions

Provisions protecting this right are included in Section 16 of the Constitution, which provides for various freedoms (see above). In addition, Section 36 of the Constitution sets certain limitations on rights; thus, the right to free expression must be weighed against other rights, including equality, dignity, privacy, political campaigning, fair trial, economic activity, workplace democracy, property and, in particular, the rights of children and women.

Not only must all broadcast licensees ensure that their broadcasts comply with the Code, but they must also have adequate procedures in place to fulfil this requirement. In this regard, they must ensure that all relevant employees and programme-makers, including independent producers, understand the Code's contents and significance. To do this, they require procedures 'for ensuring that programme-makers can seek guidance on the Code within the licensee's organisation at a senior level' (Paragraph 9).

The Authority notes that in drawing up the Code it has taken into account 'the objectives of the [IBA] Act and the urgent need in South Africa for the fundamental values which underlie our legal system to accommodate to the norms and principles which are embraced by our Constitution' (Paragraph 13).

Content categories

Conditions pertain to aspects of content such as violence, protection of women and children, language, the depiction of sexual activities and viewer information. In the first category, violence, broadcasters are enjoined not to broadcast material that contains gratuitous violence or which sanctions, promotes or glamorises violence. Needless to say, this is an extremely vague and wide-ranging prohibition that is undoubtedly frequently broken or ignored by broadcasters.

In particular, violence against women is prohibited by Paragraph 15, in that material may not be broadcast 'which, judged within context, sanctions, promotes or glamorises any aspect of violence against women'. Women may not be depicted as victims of violence 'unless the violence is integral to the story being told', and material must not 'perpetuate the link between women in a sexual context and women as victims of violence'. This prohibition is arguably easier to enforce because it is more in line with social mores and is easier to identify than cases falling within the general provisions for depicting violent behaviour.

Violence against specific groups is also prohibited where it 'sanctions, promotes or glamorises violence based on race, national or ethnic origin, colour, religion, gender, sexual orientation, age, or mental or physical disability' (Paragraph 16).

All of the above provisions do not apply to the subject of violence where it is examined as a topic of discussion in the context of a bona fide scientific, documentary, dramatic, artistic or religious programme.

Children's rights

Paragraph 18 of the Code protects the rights and status of children as viewers by enjoining broadcasters not to broadcast material that is unsuitable for children at times when large numbers of children may be expected to be watching. The depiction of violence in programming aimed at children is problematised in various ways. Where 'real-life characters' are involved, violence of a physical, verbal or emotional nature may only be portrayed when it is 'essential to the development of a character and plot'. In animated programming for children, the depiction of 'non-realistic violence' is permissible as long as violence is not the central theme and where it does not 'invite dangerous imitation'.

Programming for children must deal sensitively with themes that could 'threaten their sense of security', and examples here include the portrayal of domestic conflict, death, crime or the use of drugs. Similar precautions must be taken where content may entice children to imitate potentially dangerous acts, 'such as the use of plastic bags as toys, use of matches, the use of dangerous household products as playthings, or other dangerous physical acts'.

Realistic scenes of violence must also be avoided where children might gain the impression that violence 'is the preferred or only method to resolve conflict between individuals' or where violent scenes could 'minimise or gloss over the effect of violent acts'. Realistic depictions of violence must instead 'portray, in human terms, the consequences of that violence to its victims and its perpetrators'. In addition, children's programming should not contain 'frightening or otherwise excessive special effects not required by the story line'.

The Code identifies and regulates a 'watershed period' between 21h00 and 05h00 (Paragraphs 19–25). This is a kind of 'safety zone' where it is presumed that children (under 16 years of age) are not watching. Before this time period, no programming may be broadcast that 'contains scenes of violence, sexually explicit conduct and/or offensive language intended for adult audiences'. In addition, because older children may still form part of the audience during the watershed period, broadcasters must still provide 'advisories' (i.e. a means of flagging programmes containing violence, sexual conduct and/or offensive language so that parents can prevent their children from viewing them). Nevertheless, the Authority accepts that some programming falling outside of this watershed period may still not be suitable for 'very young children', and here broadcasters must provide 'sufficient information, in terms of regular scheduling patterns or on-air advice, to assist parents to make appropriate viewing choices'.

Broadcasters must also be sensitive to time slots within the watershed period, with more risqué programming occupying later time slots. Similarly, material restricted for adults should not start within the watershed period and then run beyond it.

Offensive conduct

With regard to offensive language, 'profanity, blasphemy and other religiously insensitive material' may not be used in children's programmes (Paragraph 26). Children are also protected from 'excessively and grossly offensive language' in programmes, whether during or outside of the watershed period; and where it does find use, it should, 'where practicable, be approved in advance by the licensee's most senior programme executive or the designated alternate' (Paragraph 27).

The depiction of sexual conduct is likewise restricted (Paragraphs 28–31). No scenes may be broadcast that depict a person under the age of 18 years 'participating in, engaging in or assisting another person to engage in sexual conduct or a lewd display of nudity'. Furthermore, no scenes may be broadcast that depict 'explicit violent sexual conduct; bestiality; or explicit sexual conduct which degrades a person in the sense that it advocates a particular form of hatred based on gender and which constitutes incitement to cause harm'. With the exception of scenes depicting sexual conduct by people under 18, the other provisions prohibiting depictions of sexual activities are suspended in the case of bona fide scientific, documentary or dramatic material.

In addition to the above: 'Scenes depicting sexual conduct, as defined in the Films and Publication Act 65 of 1996, should be broadcast only during the watershed period. Exceptions to this may be allowed in programmes with a serious educational purpose or where the representation is non-explicit and should be approved in advance by the most senior programme executive or a delegated alternate.'

In terms of Paragraphs 32 and 33, broadcasters must also assist audiences in choosing programmes to watch by providing information about them. This information can include age-restriction guidelines and indications of where programmes contain scenes of violence, sexual conduct and/or offensive language. These advisories may use classifications by the Film and Publications Board as a guideline. No programme that has been refused a Film and Publications Board classification certification may be broadcast.

News programmes

Particular responsibilities are spelt out in Paragraph 34 with respect to news programming. Broadcasters must 'report news truthfully, accurately and fairly'. News must be 'presented in the correct context and in a fair manner, without intentional or negligent departure from the facts, whether by distortion, exaggeration or misrepresentation; material omissions; or summarisation'. News reports are subject to the provision that only 'that which may reasonably be true, having due regard to the source of the news, may be presented as fact, and such fact shall be broadcast fairly with due regard to context and importance. Where a report is not based on fact or is founded on opinion, supposition, rumours or allegations, it shall be presented in such manner as to indicate clearly that such is the case.'

Reports must be verified where there is any reason to doubt their correctness and where such verification is practicable. Where verification is not practicable, that fact must be mentioned in the report. If it subsequently appears that a broadcast report was incorrect in any significant way, the broadcaster must rectify the situation by stating the fact as soon as possible and by announcing it in such as way that it will be noticed by its audience.

The identity of rape victims and other victims of sexual violence is protected and may only be broadcast with the prior consent of the victim concerned. Viewers must be advised in advance when news reports depict scenes of 'extraordinary violence, or graphic reporting on delicate subject-matter such as sexual assault or court action related to sexual crimes'. This is particularly important 'during afternoon or early evening newscasts and updates when children would probably be in the audience'.

Broadcasters must use their discretion when it comes to using 'explicit or graphic language' to describe 'destruction, accidents or sexual violence which could disturb children and sensitive audiences'. Comment on and criticism of any actions or events of public importance is permitted, provided that such comment is 'an honest expression of opinion' and that it is clearly presented as such, based on facts 'truly stated or fairly indicated and referred to' (Paragraph 35).

Where programmes deal with controversial issues of public importance, the broadcaster must make reasonable efforts to present opposing points of view fairly. This must be done either within the programme or in a subsequent programme that forms part of the same series, and this must be done 'within a reasonable period of time of the original broadcast and within substantially the same time slot'. A right of reply is granted to anyone whose views are criticised in such programmes (Paragraph 36).

Specific provisions and restrictions regarding political and election reporting are contained within the provisions of Sections 58–61 of the Broadcasting Act.

The 'private lives and private concerns' of individuals must be given due regard in news and comment programmes. Here the Authority urges that these personal concerns be afforded 'exceptional care and consideration', bearing in mind that 'a legitimate public interest' can override the right to privacy (Paragraph 38).

Lastly, there is an injunction against paying criminals or those who engage in 'notorious behaviour' for information about their nefarious doings, unless there are 'compelling societal interests' that require such information (Paragraph 39).

Legal parameters of implementation

Non-profit entity

In order to obtain a CTV broadcasting licence a legal entity must be formed that can be licensed, raise funds and enter into contracts with suppliers and staff. Because a CTV broadcaster must be a non-profit entity, there are three registration options open under South African law. These are a trust, a Section 21 company or a voluntary association.

The Trust Property Control Act of 1988, which regulates trusts in South Africa, describes a trust as a relationship whereby the trustee has ownership of the trust property, but only in so far as such control is exercised for the benefit of the trust beneficiary. In terms of the Act, a trust is defined as 'any legal arrangement in terms of which a functionary controls and administers property on behalf of another or in pursuance of an impersonal object'.

In effect, this means that if the members of a CTV initiative register as a trust, ownership of the CTV station will reside with trustees who will administer the entity on behalf of its members. A trust could also function in terms of pursuing an 'impersonal object' by pursuing the objectives of CTV broadcasting – for instance, those outlined in the discussion document on CTV produced by the Cape Town CTV Collective (Thorne 2005).

Registration of a Section 21 company is regulated by the Companies Act of 1973, specifically Sections 19(1)(b), 19(3) and 21. Section 21 sets out the requirements and guidelines for the registration of a company as an 'association not for gain', which is what the proposed licensee will be. A Section 21 company has the advantage of being the most widely recognised form of non-profit entity. One possible disadvantage is that as a registered company it has to comply with certain legislation, especially the Access to Information Act, which means it has to keep records of all its activities. This is a slightly onerous administrative duty but, on the other hand, would make the organisation fully accountable to its stakeholders.

Registration as a voluntary association is regulated by Common Law and does not involve the complexities associated with registration under the Companies Act. A voluntary association may be established by its founding members adopting a constitution whereby they commit themselves collectively to the pursuit of a common endeavour. The advantage of registering as a voluntary association is that it eliminates the necessity of producing audited reports, registering resolutions, and so on.

Registering as one of the above-mentioned options does not in any way prejudice CTV from taking advantage of government initiatives to help in finding ways of getting benefits like tax incentives and funding opportunities.

Such registration would enable the CTV broadcaster to apply for registration as a non-profit organisation (NPO) in terms of Section 13(5) of the Non-profit Organisations Act of 1997. It also allows the organisation to register for tax exemption as a public benefit organisation in terms of the Income Tax Act of 1962. Registration as an NPO is done by submitting certain documents to the NPO Directorate: an application form that is available from the Department of Social Development, and two copies of the organisation's founding documents.

The benefits of registering as an NPO with the Department of Social Development are: assistance from the department in obtaining benefits such as tax incentives and funding opportunities, and improving the organisation's credibility because it will be accountable to a public office.

Applying for tax exemption in terms of Section 10(1)(cN) of the Income Tax Act as a public benefit organisation is done by forwarding the following information to the Tax Exemption Unit: a detailed list of the organisation's programme of action, a list of present and future sources of income, and an explanation of how the organisation's assets will be distributed on dissolution.

The organisation will be able to access particular incentives as a non-profit entity and be eligible for public funding, regardless of whether it is registered as a voluntary association or as a Section 21 company. However, the advantage of registration as a Section 21 company is that this is a more formal structure than a voluntary association. It establishes the organisation as an entity on its own, separate from its conveners, which is then solely responsible for any debts incurred or any litigation that may arise. As a separate entity it would also have greater credibility in terms of fund-raising from donors and government.

Copyright

Issues of copyright have a major impact on television broadcasting. Typically, major broadcasters commission and pay for programme production and retain copyright to the resulting material. Where ready-made material is acquired from third-party sources, the broadcaster may be licensed to broadcast the programme either on a once-off basis or for a set number of repeats.

Where programmes are owned by producers, copyright may be granted to a broadcaster for local redistribution but this would exclude international distribution. This means that many programmes that could be sourced from CTV stations in other countries are restricted to being broadcast in that country in terms of the copyright agreement between the station and the producer. South African CTV stations would then have to negotiate copyright and payment costs with individual producers.

An innovative solution has been proposed by C31 Melbourne, an Australian CTV channel, which intends to develop a distribution and acquisition website to help local Melbourne producers get access to international community broadcasters. Once producers have secured the appropriate clearances for their products, C31 will be able to launch the website to non-community stations in Australia and then internationally to CTV stations. The website would enable buyers to see what programmes are available and then negotiate a sale with the relevant programme producer (El-Khoury 2005).

This suggests that South African CTV stations would face similar hurdles in trying to sell programmes to other broadcasters, whether nationally or internationally.

Music rights

The rights to broadcast music represent similar problems for broadcasters. Music reproduction rights in South Africa are managed by the South African Music Rights Organisation (SAMRO), which extracts revenue from broadcasters based on the number of times that music tracks created by signed artists are played. This means that broadcasters must keep track of every piece of music that is used as broadcast content, whether it be as a complete music video, live music programme or soundtrack.

SAMRO does not always demand income from non-profit community stations. SAMRO dues are usually pegged at around 1 per cent of a station's income, but the organisation has not enforced this requirement with temporary event broadcasts.

Where CTV channels do earn income from their operations, they fall into a particular SAMRO tariff category called DDS/DDSR – Radio and Television Diffusion Services. This tariff applies to diffusion services as defined in the Copyright Act of 1978. The term 'diffusion service' means 'any telecommunication service of transmissions consisting of sound, images, signs or signals, which take place over wires or other paths provided by material substance and intended for reception by specific members of the public' (SAMRO 2005).

SAMRO licences for CTV channels can be obtained from the Broadcasters and Online Transmissions Department, which also issues licences to other television, radio and Internet radio channels.

CHAPTER 3

Lessons from community radio

Community radio in South Africa

When community radio emerged and began to establish itself in South Africa in the mid- to-late 1990s, it took up a position that challenged the state-owned and commercial media that had existed until then. For a long time, community radio has been the most visible form of community media because of its reach and relative ease of installation, operation and maintenance. Whereas community newspapers may have existed at the same time, low literacy levels have limited their spread, a constraint to which radio is not subject.

Community radio offered an infrastructure that allowed people to participate in media activities, wherein the content was relevant to their media needs and aspirations. By allowing non-professionals to participate actively for the first time in a hands-on manner in the production of community media, community radio fulfilled an important empowerment need. Therefore, community participation was understood as meaningful action on the part of local citizens in a medium otherwise dominated by commercial and corporate interests.

Community radio was seen to represent a radical shift in the country's media industry (Bosch 2003). Today, there are over a hundred community radio stations operating in South Africa, licensed by the Independent Communications Authority of South Africa (ICASA) as either geographic or 'community of interest' stations. It is unfortunate that there have been no comprehensive studies detailing the successes and failures of the community radio sector since 1994 beyond the purely speculative and anecdotal. Furthermore, in the post-1994 period there has been a change in the relationship between the government and the mainstream media that continues to evolve. Undoubtedly, this has had an impact on the community radio sector, as it relates to both its mainstream counterpart as well as to the government.

Evidence shows that levels of success experienced by these stations vary widely, rarely achieving the same levels as commercial radio, but it is clear that community radio has managed to entrench itself securely in the media environment. Indeed, the nature of the service that community radio renders has allowed it to become a useful agent in social change.

Dooms (2002) estimated that there were over 1.6 million community radio listeners across the country in 1991. South African Advertising Research Foundation (SAARF) Radio Audience Measurement Survey (RAMS) figures for June to August 2004 indicate a total community radio listenership of approximately 4.1 million.

Community radio is participatory media, owned and controlled by its community and dedicating itself to addressing the human right to information and communication. It has succeeded in creating and promoting a culture of information through its particular form of media education and literacy.

By promoting the cause of its constituency, community radio has been able to promote the social and, in some cases, economic emancipation and upliftment of its audiences. The participatory and interactive nature of community radio also elevates the self-worth of its audiences. This sets community radio above other forms of broadcasting – by being able to cater to the spiritual and psycho-social needs of the people, it provides a useful forum for debate, discussion and participation in the growth and progress of society. Community radio also plays a vital role in the preservation and promotion of group identity. It is able to resist the homogenising tendencies of broad-interest commercial media by focusing on and reflecting the local environment.

It is vital, therefore, to understand the role that community radio has played in fostering the growth of democracy in South Africa, and consequently how community television (CTV) can develop in a way that furthers this goal, by providing new forms of participation and access to citizens.

Knowledge of communities

Existing community radio stations have established community structures to which they are accountable. ICASA guidelines spell out the conditions that must be met by community broadcasters, forming the basis of licensing for community radio stations. With regard to community participation and ownership, Section 1 of the Independent Broadcasting Authority Act of 1999 (IBA Act) defines a community broadcasting service as one that 'serves a particular community; encourages members of the community served by it or persons associated with or promoting interests of such community to participate in the selection and provision of programmes to be broadcast in the course of such broadcasting service'. Community radio stations applying for licences have to demonstrate this process of consultation and inclusion of the community. In the years since the first broadcast licences were issued to community radio, these stations have succeeded to varying degrees in entrenching themselves in their communities.

Schramm (1964) observes that local media are important for social and economic development because they are familiar with the needs of local areas and allow local people access to the media. Although there is a dearth of research that is specific to community media audiences and how well community media have fared in fulfilling their role, some initiatives have been undertaken to assist these stations in gaining a more accurate profile of their constituent communities. In collaboration with the Department of Communications (DoC), IDASA has developed a template for community mapping that allows the radio stations to conduct in-depth research in their communities. Clearly, much more attention is needed for developing research models that are better suited to community media and their audiences. At the core of this is the realisation that conventional audience research for commercial media focuses mainly on audiences as markets, with a strong emphasis on advertising potential – an approach that is not very useful to community media whose focus is more on relating to audiences, identifying their unmet needs along social, political and economic continuums and engaging with them in a concerted effort to find solutions.

Experience with grassroots mobilisation

Arguably, community radio is positioned closer to grassroots communities than any other media form. Being community-owned and community-run, it draws its mandate from the people and exists to meet their needs and give them a voice. The extent to which this is the case may vary from one station to the next, depending on the interaction and participation mechanisms in places. More often than not, the interaction between grassroots communities and their media is based on issues that they aim to address mutually. This perforce implies consultation and mobilisation around needs and issues.

CTV can benefit from the community radio/stakeholder relationship in a number of ways. By partnering with community radio, it can offer communities value by providing an additional forum for community issues to be discussed and addressed. The benefit is mutual in the sense that once CTV is seen to be engaged deeply with community issues, it is legitimised in the eyes of the community. The extent to which it becomes institutionalised in the community depends on the perceived benefits accruing to its audience. If CTV is seen to be trying to 'reinvent the wheel' by serving a purpose that is already being served by community radio then its legitimacy may be called into question.

CTV needs to develop a unique selling point that justifies its existence while at the same time complementing the media that already exist. Television can offer a visual window for communities by 'putting a face to the voices of the community', so to speak. Any process of mobilisation has two sides to it – those whose issue needs to be addressed and those who need to know about this issue and possibly address it. This is where CTV has the potential to go beyond the reach of community radio, based on the assumption that television as a medium, whether commercial or community, has a higher likelihood of attracting an audience of decision-makers.

It is, however, important to learn from the perceived shortcomings of community radio. Hadland & Thorne (2004), for instance, state that community radio has failed to engage with communities in a real sense beyond annual meetings and talk shows, and that there is a need to engage more with local non-governmental organisations (NGOs) and community-based organisations (CBOs). They also point out that in the search for quality programming there is a danger of neglecting the importance of participatory processes that allow members of the community access. CTV can learn from this by setting structures in place that will ensure horizontal linkages with grassroots organisations and represent community interests, as well as vertical linkages with service providers such as local government. Community radio has relied on horizontal linkages to ensure its growth, not in terms of audience size or revenue, but in importance and value to the community. It is a safe assumption that the same approach can work for CTV.

Policy and regulatory experience

Community radio has been operating under policy guidelines and regulations that are elaborated for community broadcast services in general and will perforce apply to CTV as well. The National Community Radio Forum (NCRF) has an interest in the development of CTV and has stated its willingness to extend membership to include such initiatives. There has been considerable interest in CTV from a regulatory perspective. The CTV community has made its presence felt through submissions and other forms of engagement with ICASA; consequently, ICASA issued a position paper in November 2004 that set out the broad parameters for CTV. A number of CTV activists were involved in the process. Subsequently, there have been workshops in Gauteng and Cape Town, where issues of policy and regulation were discussed.

In October of 2004 a workshop convened by the University of the Witwatersrand brought together CTV activists from all over the country. During this workshop, a national advocacy group was established, whose task it has been to monitor policy developments in so far as they affect CTV and to seek support from stakeholders and partners where necessary. This group could benefit from increased interaction with organisations like the NCRF and the National Association of Broadcasters. To date, the CTV sector has relied on the efforts of dedicated individuals. The NCRF has been able to build a national organisation on a membership base of functioning community radio stations, while the

CTV sector has not yet reached this stage of development. Communications policy is also influenced by external factors and pressures. On the international scene, bodies such as the World Association of Community Radio have provided the opportunity for groups from all over the world to share experiences and combine efforts to change policy in favour of community media. Meetings convened by such bodies are attended by policy-makers and regulators and provide good opportunities for lobbying and advocacy.

Experiences with sustainability

Financially, community radio stations continue to face considerable challenges. By virtue of the fact that they generally serve under-represented and low-income audiences, they tend not to be attractive to big-budget advertisers. Most of these stations also have mandates that effectively restrict the kind of advertising and sponsorship that they can accept. This is because the principles and values upon which they operate tend to focus on strong social values that eschew messages that are not seen to edify the target community. An oft-quoted example is lucrative advertising for alcohol companies. While some stations have achieved a degree of success at tapping into local business for advertising and sponsorship, this is the exception rather than the rule. Furthermore, this rarely yields sufficient financial benefits to secure the bottom line.

Internal constraints include a lack of skills in vital areas such as marketing, planning, budgeting and fund-raising. Acquiring personnel equipped with these skills entails being able to pay and keep them. It is ironic that community radio has served as a fertile training ground for people acquiring these skills through internships and accredited learnerships. Unfortunately, these individuals tend to move on and find work in the more lucrative commercial and mainstream media, which are able to remunerate them at a level commensurate with the skills they have acquired. While training is an important function for community radio, its success in this regard leaves it constantly wanting in the self-same skills. Some stations have managed to break the vicious cycle by formalising training and attracting financial support from institutions. With these funds, they are able to keep skilled staff, who work for the station and serve as trainers as well.

The community radio sector has learned that diversity and innovation are the keys to sustainability. One example of this is the sector's success in targeting issue areas that tend to be well funded and that are relevant to their audiences. Organisations dealing with issues such as HIV/AIDS have discovered the potential that community radio has to reach and communicate effectively with grassroots communities, which tend to be most affected. Stations that have invested in training are able to not only provide a medium for campaigns but also offer assistance in designing the campaigns, because of the intimate knowledge they have of their communities.

Thus, CTV has the benefit of hindsight thanks to the radio sector. This is not to say that these same challenges will not continue to exist; rather, they will be easier to confront, and television will be able to build on the experiences of radio. There will also be ample room for cross-media partnerships to overcome these challenges.

Aside from the aforementioned challenges, there have been notable successes, such as the partnerships with local, provincial and national governments entailing the broadcasting of live feeds of important events like speeches, special occasions and meetings. These have gone a long way towards making community radio an indispensable information source while increasing its audience share, as well as providing a steady stream of much-needed revenue. Another example of this is the NCRF's South African Community Radio Initiative, which has facilitated the exchange of programmes between radio stations, so ensuring revenue from the programmes they produce on various informational and educational topics in addition to carrying national satellite feeds.

Partnership opportunities and cross-media platforms

The Convergence Bill currently under consideration is the manifestation of trends in the media sector towards confluence of media through information and communications technology (ICT). Community radio has been exploring the distribution of content across platforms. Bush Radio, for instance, began webcasting in August of 2005, targeting a broader constituency that may not be physically within its broadcast radius but which has an interest in its content. Community radio has also formed partnerships with community newspapers that allow them to share content and reach audiences more effectively. It is no surprise, therefore, that community radio has shown a keen interest in being a key partner in CTV.

Community radio stations already have skills in areas such as programming and production for radio. Whereas television is a very different medium requiring a separate set of skills, there are aspects of radio programming and production that are applicable and transferable. Involving community radio in CTV initiatives harnesses these skills while, at the same time, possibly pre-empting and mitigating potential competition between the two media forms or, worse still, the domination of new CTV initiatives to the extent that CTV becomes a subsidiary of community radio.

Another area of possible partnerships is the initiatives aimed at skills development at a local level; these centre on collaborating with local and national NGOs to tackle issues of social justice and democracy building. By offering these organisations an additional platform, CTV can set itself up to benefit from programme-based sponsorship and funding.

Community radio has taken tentative steps into ICT, making increasing use of, and introducing communities to, the Internet. CTV is well positioned to advance this course, especially because it is a visual medium.

Community radio offers valuable experience in the area of human resources management and capacity building. In order to maintain quality and to function effectively in the face of financial constraints, the sector has come to rely on networks of individuals who are able to volunteer their skills to serve the community by contributing their time and training abilities to the stations. This has enabled the sector to function without the massive financial implications of hiring and maintaining a skilled workforce. It is important to note that the technical requirements for television are greater, implying that there is likely to be a smaller pool of skilled volunteers on which CTV will be able to draw. This will put additional pressure on the area of training and capacity building, in order to increase the number of volunteers available for initiatives.

Institutional linkages: the NCRF

The NCRF was formed in 1993 to 'lobby for the diversification of the airwaves in South Africa, and to foster a dynamic broadcasting environment in the country through the establishment of radio stations' (Hadland & Thorne 2004).

In 2001 the NCRF engaged in an organisational development process aimed at strengthening the ability of its members to function more effectively and sustainability.

One of the issues identified was a lack of collective networking and communication structures at the provincial level. Hence, the NCRF mooted the idea of setting up a hub structure in each province, the mission of which would be to promote improved networking, collaboration and support between community radio stations at a provincial level and to facilitate the development of human resources capacity and financial sustainability – two areas where community radio has not performed to its potential.

In terms of sustainability, the hub structure seeks to improve performance by ensuring that transparent governance structures are developed that are representative of local demographics. It also envisions a concerted drive towards developing effective marketing and branding. The hub structure further seeks to help stations streamline internal administrative and organisational processes. Stations will be able to benefit from research and assistance in the process of licence renewal. As representatives of previously disadvantaged communities, community radio stations will play a bigger role in the process of economic redistribution. The NCRF has expressed willingness to include local TV operators in its membership, whatever form that will take (Hadland & Thorne 2004). At the level of regional hubs, consultations are already taking place to determine what synergies can be created to assist with the establishment of CTV.

Conclusion

In the South African context, it is clear that CTV has the benefit of building on what has been achieved by community radio since 1994. Although radio continues to face the challenge of financial sustainability, it is clear that it has succeeded in entrenching itself by providing a service whose value is recognised by its audiences as well as its partners.

Community radio will continue to occupy a secure place within the media landscape of the country. Whether it will move beyond merely existing and actually start to thrive is debatable. There are those who argue that by virtue of its important function it deserves to be publicly subsidised, but that is a policy hurdle yet to be confronted. The same challenges, and more, await CTV. Possibly the greatest of these challenges is justifying the role that CTV will play, either complementary or supplementary to community radio. Suffice it to say that CTV can push the position of community media further away from perceptions of simplicity and towards the sophistication and abundant possibilities of mainstream media while maintaining community ownership, control and access. The real future for CTV lies in partnering with community radio and learning from its successes and failures.

CHAPTER 4

CTV in South Africa today

The presence of community television (CTV) initiatives in South Africa in the early years of the 21st century is the result of many years' work in policy development, advocacy, lobbying and various temporary event television broadcasts under the enabling CTV legislation. At the time of writing in late 2005, there are emerging CTV initiatives in three of South Africa's cities: Durban, Cape Town and Johannesburg.

Durban and Cape Town have the longest tradition of CTV broadcasts dating back to the mid-1990s when this form of broadcasting was first allowed. Temporary event broadcasts have also been undertaken in Grahamstown but there is at present no initiative in that town to establish a permanent CTV station.

It is surprising that while Gauteng is South Africa's most populous region with the strongest economy of all the provinces, there is no assertive initiative to establish a permanent CTV station in the region. Some attempts have been made to this end, but perhaps the fact that the national television industry is largely based in the province diverts attention away from non-profit CTV broadcasting towards the more lucrative and professionally appealing industry sector. Nevertheless, given the new enabling legislation, it is a matter of time before people get it together to form a CTV body that is capable of taking on the challenge and the rewards of providing a television broadcasting service to communities in this populous and affluent region. Looking at the history and present state of CTV in South Africa is informative in considering how CTV initiatives can go forward to establish themselves as sustainable entities serving the public good in the context of an emerging economy.

History

The emergence of CTV as a mechanism for public participation in broadcasting goes back to the struggle against apartheid, where people fought for recognition of the rights of black South Africans and for their inclusion in the life of the South African state.

The genesis of community broadcasting in South Africa may be placed at the 1991 Jabulani Freedom of the Airwaves conference that took place in the Netherlands. Some 60 delegates representing a wide range of NGOs and civic structures concerned with broadcasting gathered to discuss the future of broadcasting in South Africa. The resolutions that emerged from this conference revolved around the issue of opening broadcasting to include all sections of South African society.

It was also declared that broadcasting should have a public duty to help overcome the divisions and imbalances in South African society caused by apartheid. To do this, it should encourage the development of a society and culture in South Africa that all citizens could identify with, and it should express the full diversity of language and culture in the country (Van Zyl 2002).

Besides these overarching cultural imperatives, the conference opted for future modalities of broadcasting that would involve democratic participation in the production of media in order to reflect the issues and concerns of collective groupings of people with a distinct self-identity – in other words, the concept of community. Here the audience is not seen as mere passive consumers, but as active citizens contributing their views to the expression of group concerns, aspirations and information needs.

This conclusion to the process of evaluating broadcasting by civil society provided a clear basic mandate for future discussions on the role that radio and television can play in South African society. These media can play a role in developing civil participation in the public sphere to influence government thinking, as well as to express cultures, beliefs and value systems and to serve certain communication needs.

The IBA Act

Other initiatives subsequently arose to press for broadening representation in the South African broadcasting environment. These included the ANC Media Charter, the Windhoek Declaration on Promoting an Independent and Pluralistic African Press of 1991 and the Campaign for Independent Broadcasting in 1992 (Armstrong 2004). However, the basis for community broadcasting was established in 1993, when the South African government passed the Independent Broadcasting Authority Act (IBA Act), which mandated the creation of an independent broadcast regulator and called for three tiers of broadcasting: community, public and private/commercial.

These initiatives culminated in the formation of the Independent Broadcasting Authority (IBA) in 1994, with the aim of regulating South Africa's airwaves in order to cater for the information, education and entertainment needs of all South Africans. One of the IBA's first acts was to compile its *Triple Inquiry Report* (1995) on broadcasting, wherein the Authority considered the nature and extent of radio and television broadcasting services in the spheres of public, private and community broadcasting.

The report noted a particular need for broadcasting 'to provide opportunities for historically disadvantaged people to participate at every level – ownership, management, on air, and support positions'. It also noted the importance of 'a special type of educational programming appropriate to our needs' and of communication taking place 'in the languages people understand and prefer' (IBA 1995: 5).

One of the mechanisms to achieve these objectives was to establish community broadcasting services on radio and television. The Authority initiated two measures in this regard; firstly, licensing a number of community radio stations and, secondly, allowing for temporary CTV broadcasting licences of up to one year's duration.

Consequently, in 1995, the Authority granted temporary broadcast licences to two CTV initiatives, these being World Cup Rugby TV in Cape Town and Greater Durban Television (GDTV) in Durban. Following these early initiatives, the Cue TV project of the Department of Journalism at Rhodes University, Grahamstown, was granted special event broadcasting licences (in 1998 and 1999) in order to cover events at the annual Grahamstown Festival; and in 1998, the Cape Community Broadcast Channel was on air for 15 days on an SABC breakaway channel (Armstrong 2004).

GDTV went back on air in 2004 with a temporary one-month licence after a long interval of inactivity, and broadcast on two subsequent occasions over the 2004–2005 period on a similar basis. GDTV has formalised its operations since its first experimental broadcast from the University of Natal campus in 1995, having registered as a Section 21 (non-profit) company.

Community of interest broadcasting

We must differentiate between local, public access CTV, on the one hand, and community of interest TV, on the other. This report is concerned solely with the development of the former mode, by virtue of the fact that it is this form of CTV that has been introduced in South Africa by government legislation and ICASA policy, resulting from the years of struggle for national liberation and media freedom. Community of interest broadcasting is a different modality that may take place on either a local or a national basis.

Currently, community of interest broadcasting is followed in two ways in South Africa. It occurs primarily in the form of community of interest programming or channels on national subscriber networks, where commercial production houses produce programming for interest-groups such as Afrikaans speakers or the Portuguese and Indian ethnic groups. Christian religious broadcasting also falls into this category. Professional Christian television broadcasters buy airtime on national subscriber channels and on SABC and eTV. According to the Association of Christian Broadcasters (ACB) there are currently seven Christian television broadcasters that provide such content on these national channels (Rosenthal 2005). These professional broadcast operations fit into the category of independent media, despite the desire of such sectors to encroach on the CTV terrain. Hadland and Thorne (2004: 10) regard independent media as being substantially different to community media; they define the former category as 'privately-owned, commercial media which is free of control by corporate or government interests'.

The incongruity of the aforementioned aspiration is evident in a second form of community of interest broadcasting that currently exists in South Africa. This has resulted from an anomaly in the CTV environment where South Africa's only existing long-term CTV licence is held by a private, foreign-owned Christian broadcaster, Trinity Broadcasting Network (TBN). This company acquired its broadcast licence from the apartheid government, which saw no challenge to its hegemony in the conservative Christian values espoused by TBN. The rights to this licence, which enable TBN to broadcast via analogue terrestrial transmission on a frequency in the Eastern Cape, were subsequently protected by post-apartheid broadcasting legislation that allowed TBN to continue its operations under a so-called 'grandfather' clause (IBA 1995).

TBN and its ilk do not fit into the space allocated for community broadcasters; firstly, because it is a privately owned company that relies on high-quality, professional production methods to draw mass audiences. Most of the channel's content is produced in other countries (principally the US). Secondly, the company, along with the other professional Christian television broadcasters in South Africa, is inimical to the idea of democratic community involvement in its activities (Rosenthal 2005), as well as pursuing a narrow ideological line of conservative, evangelical 'born-again' Christianity that eschews consideration of any other religious perspective, Christian or otherwise. This is directly counter to the ethos of CTV, which seeks to provide 'a voice for the voiceless' and to be a forum for democratic debate and the sharing of views across ideological divides.

The frequency spectrum is a public resource that must be managed equitably in the interests of all citizens. The fact that TBN currently utilises part of this spectrum under a CTV licence does not fit with the spirit and ethos of South Africa's CTV environment, which instead favours democratic mechanisms of community ownership and engagement. This awkward legacy of the apartheid era is out of step both with comparable international models and with the regulatory framework established to ensure democratic participation and maximum public benefit for the people of South Africa.

At present, ICASA does not make allowance for any other form of community of interest broadcasting. While the scope for such broadcasting may widen in future with the establishment of digital terrestrial transmission (DTT) broadcasting, which would make more frequencies available for channels on national, regional or local levels, ICASA does not currently favour its inception at the local level. Instead, the regulator has demarcated the terrain of local broadcasting as the exclusive preserve of public access television under the appellation of CTV, and it is this definition that defines the scope of this report.

At the same time, it is essential to recognise that community broadcasting at the local level is centred on the concept of serving various communities of interest within the geographic region defined by the footprint of the broadcast. This is different to the usual conception of community as referring to a geographical grouping located according to municipal area boundaries. Communities of interest often cut across economic and geographical divides, even while certain such communities may locate the majority of their constituents within a particular socio-economic category. It will be vital for CTV in South Africa to leverage this characteristic of communities of interest if it is to serve society on a holistic basis and overcome the perception that is it limited to serving only low-income populations. If CTV is specifically limited to serving low-income populations, it will be subject to the constraints identified by Naidoo (2005b), forcing it into the untenable situation of looking for extensive government support, which is expressly prohibited by ICASA's regulations. This situation would force the CTV sector to lobby ICASA to change its policy to allow for government-supported community broadcasting, which is likely to be a lengthy, highly contested process that would probably set CTV back by a decade.

Current CTV initiatives

There are several current CTV initiatives in South Africa. Three essential models are apparent – the entrepreneurial model, the user-community model and the sector-mobilisation model. These modes of organisation have arisen within the context of the ICASA regulations governing CTV operations and will be analysed in terms of their fit with this policy, together with an assessment of their strengths and weaknesses.

Soweto TV

The entrepreneurial model is evidenced by Soweto TV, a small group that is presently planning a broadcast in Johannesburg. Soweto TV aims to provide a community forum where programming is 'made by Sowetans for Sowetans'. The channel has planned a one-month broadcast to Soweto in December 2005 based on the theme of marking World AIDS Day with programming that raises awareness and explores community issues related to HIV/AIDS.

Soweto TV intends to broadcast for eight hours each day, with programming including live event broadcasts, talk shows, news and locally produced, low-budget documentaries and dramas. The transmission footprint that the station hopes to reach includes Soweto and surrounding communities as far west as Carltonville, including half of Kagiso as well as south Johannesburg. The claimed audience is over 4 million people.

The station is being run by a small group of activists under the banner of a Section 21 company. The concern has a board of directors drawn mainly from Soweto residents. Board members include journalists, businesspeople, a multi-purpose community centre (MPCC) administrator and the managing director of a retail radio and TV company. Chief Executive Officer Tshepo Thafeng is a long-time broadcaster rooted in community radio and specialising in marketing and sales.

Soweto TV was founded at the Ipelegeng MPCC in 2000. Its members and partners have previously participated in the establishment of community radio stations and private television stations. They intend leveraging technology to establish a 'do-it-yourself' television station that will eventually obtain a permanent licence to broadcast to Soweto.

The organisation has expressions of support from various community groups, including the Grace Bible Church, All-Saints Apostolic Church, Katlehong Art Centre, Orlando West Industrial Park Association, Soweto Home of the Aged and the Government Communication and Information System (GCIS).

It intends to engage with other NGOs in Soweto, specifically in the HIV/AIDS sector, through programme production. Soweto TV has been initiating this strategy through engaging with an umbrella organisation called the AIDS Consortium. It has opened negotiations with several key stakeholders in the proposed broadcast, including Sentech, the Film Resource Unit (FRU) and the National Electronic Media Institute of South Africa (NEMISA). NEMISA has responded to Soweto TV's overtures by stipulating an amount for the hire of its broadcast facilities that is more in line with commercial rates than in any way subsidising or supporting a community initiative. It is clear that NEMISA either does not understand the nature of CTV or is reluctant to engage with the sector in a supportive role.

The station appears to have a sound understanding of its target market and defines it in some detail for potential sponsors and advertisers. The channel's business plan lists characteristics such as the youthfulness of the population, historical perspective, residential distribution, educational level and language.

Soweto TV aims to engage the wider community through providing a variety of ways for community members to participate as producers, crew, technicians, editors, interviewers, artists and subjects, and as teachers, administrators and salespeople. The station will rely on live shows to provide the mainstay of its programming, which it describes as 'closer to radio than it is to the other television broadcasters'. Content will include talk shows 'on issues of local importance with local personalities, activists and leaders', with pre-packaged inserts to supplement the format (Soweto TV 2004: 5).

Mobile camera crews will produce inserts and collect views and comments from people on the street, to form small opinion pieces that will enable people to express their opinions on particular topics. Access to cameras and editing suites will be provided for aspiring film makers who will also be afforded training, guidance and support. Special encouragement will be given to film makers who are HIV-positive.

The channel intends to use a dedicated transmitter rather than partnering with another channel for a window. Production options include building a temporary studio in Soweto or using commercial space at a mall in the area. Another option would be to rent NEMISA's facilities in Braamfontein; the drawback with this set-up would be that the studio is not situated in Soweto and, in that case, the station would also want to have another studio in Soweto that would be used for training and production purposes.

Soweto TV believes it can rely principally on advertising support for long-term survival but intends to run fewer adverts than mainstream television. It is targeting a diverse support base, including advertisers, private and corporate sponsors and donors, government agencies and local and international NGOs.

Adverts will be priced at R700 per 30 seconds, running five per hour. If adverts are sold only in prime-time hours, projected revenue over the course of 30 days could be as much as R525 000.

Cue TV

Cue TV is an initiative of the Journalism and Media Studies Department at Rhodes University and is produced by final-year journalism students only. It is run and funded by the institution and is intended to provide students with practical experience in actual production and broadcasting.

Cue TV is a user-group driven initiative and so falls short of being a true CTV project, because participation is limited to final-year journalism and media students and the project is run by departmental staff. These participants decide on the nature of the content and the institution owns the means of production. The course is primarily aimed at enhancing students' production skills rather than training them in community broadcasting (Banzi 2005a).

Cue TV is not limited to covering the Grahamstown National Arts Festival, but is a year-long project that peaks during the festival. Previously, during this period the project would apply for a special event broadcasting licence to cover the festival. This has not happened recently because the department has failed to secure funding for a broadcast and, instead, the channel has partnered with the university's New Media Lab to stream the productions on a website (http://fest.ru.ac.za/cuetv.cfm).

In addition to being streamed on the Internet, Cue TV's productions have been made available to SABC Africa and eTV, and these channels have then had the option of broadcasting them as inserts. The students pay a stipend for their endeavours and the department takes care of tape and equipment costs as part of its annual budget.

In previous years, when Cue TV did obtain a special event licence it broadcast on UHF channel 91. However, the transmission area was limited to the town, and people staying outside the perimeters of town could either not receive it or were unaware of its existence.

History
The first time Cue TV made its appearance in Grahamstown was in 1997, as an initiative by the Rhodes University Journalism and Media Studies Faculty. When it first came out, it was a production that was put onto a tape and narrowcast to different venues around the campus. In 1998 and 1999 the initiative was granted temporary event broadcast licences. In 1999 productions were also netcast and broadcast on the DSTV bouquet and in 2000 Cue TV was only available on DSTV and on the Internet.

The reception was very wide and included the outlying townships. Cue TV volunteers went around the townships telling people how to tune in. The feedback was very positive and businesspeople were keen to advertise on the channel. Reception was a problem because broadcasts on the UHF 91 frequency tended to interfere with other channels, especially M-Net.

Cue TV as a model for CTV
Cue TV is a user-community initiative; in other words, it is based on a community of interest, that being the producers themselves rather than the audience. Although the

project has the benefit of institutional support through Rhodes University and students who are committed to furthering their education through their involvement, it has no relationship with or accountability to its audience and so is not a true CTV initiative.

The people involved in the production are only interested in furthering their academic and career prospects and are merely involved in the production as a formality and for training purposes. Cue TV is not aimed at community broadcasting but at training the students in production. Nevertheless, there are areas of overlap with CTV regulations in that:
- it is run by a non-profit institution (Rhodes University's Journalism and Media Studies Faculty) and is not carried out for profit-making purposes;
- it serves a particular community – in this case, the final-year Journalism and Media Studies: Television Production students;
- its 'community' provides and selects programming content; and
- it is funded by the university and sponsors.

Problem areas
Over the last few years, Cue TV has been producing inserts that have been broadcast by national broadcasters such as SABC Africa and eTV, instead of broadcasting itself. There is a strong sentiment among Cue TV participants that these broadcasters are merely *using* them and not enough recognition is given to their work. For example, Cue TV has to send productions to the SABC in Port Elizabeth for broadcast and, on some occasions, Airtime Outside Broadcasts would refuse to send the productions over the satellite link. As a result, Cue TV had to find its own means of getting the productions to Port Elizabeth. Participants also complain that the commercial channel eTV would broadcast Cue TV productions but the students only received a stipend for their work instead of professional rates.

Cue TV has no community involvement outside of the students and staff of the department. However, there is some sentiment within Cue TV that wider community involvement should be sought and efforts are underway to establish how the broadcast in 2006 could be used to benefit the larger Grahamstown community.

Sustainability is also an issue, as financial constraints have been identified as the cause for the failure to broadcast in the last few years. Cue TV is presently working on drawing up funding proposals timeously and is looking into partnering with other organisations to give the next festival much wider exposure and, at the same time, build new relationships.

The department is sympathetic to the idea of a more permanent CTV broadcasting arrangement for Grahamstown. However, the department's priority is student tuition and it looks at the teaching yield out of a situation, so a permanent broadcast would have to be coordinated with the curriculum. A separate project would have to be established within the department to manage resources, management and equipment booking for an ongoing CTV initiative.

Bush TV
Another example of a user-community driven initiative is the Bush TV project at the University of the Western Cape (UWC). Bush TV made its first appearance at UWC as an exercise in teamwork and life skills for students in 1998. The exercise resulted in a 26-minute programme about student life and issues such as the student riots over financial

exclusions. The project was assisted by the Community Video Education Trust (CVET), which provided video-production training for the volunteers, the Students Representative Council (SRC), which provided the camera, and the UWC Audio-visual (AV) Department, which made its editing facilities available to the volunteers (Banzi 2005b).

After the initial Bush TV production, there was a lull in its activities as some of its main proponents had left the institution. The initiative was revived in 2004 by the African Film Society on campus to raise levels of awareness and appreciation of African films among students and to show students the career opportunities that exist within the industry. The idea was to enable students to control their own media because there were no other student media operating at the university.

Screenings of Bush TV productions were held bi-weekly at the Student Centre and in TV rooms in the residences. Initially, Bush TV did not have any equipment of its own. The productions relied mainly on the goodwill of the AV Department, which made its equipment and facilities available on a somewhat erratic basis. After the eighth broadcast, UWC's rector managed to obtain a donated digital video (DV) camera for Bush TV. This enabled students to shoot at their convenience. A student offered his computer for editing purposes, and for the first time Bush TV was producing content in digital form.

Playback was done by taking VCRs or DVD players to different venues for the screenings. There were three screenings each evening. All of the playback equipment was provided by the Audio-visual Department. At any given time, Bush TV had about 25 personnel ranging from management to technical, marketing and onscreen talent. The whole group was very enthusiastic and tackled their various tasks with vigour. However, the lack of adequate facilities was sometimes a dampener.

The station was headed by the chairperson of the African Film Society, who was the only student in the group who had any training in video and television production, having undergone a short production course through CVET.

Bush TV broadcasts were comprised of 85 per cent in-house productions and 25 per cent short films that were usually about 15 minutes in length. Programming was provided by the volunteers who came up with the ideas and concepts and who then made the items. Programmes included news, sports, entertainment and cultural and academic updates. There were also 'in-depth' discussion shows, magazine shows and film and music reviews. The films were made available by CVET, Sithengi, FRU, Lovelife and a few independent producers.

News was one of the most demanding programmes because it needed a lot of coordination of journalists, editors, newsreaders, camera crew and video editors. Newsgathering was a sketchy affair, given that the team was not well coordinated. There was no team leader but the news team managed to get the production out at the end of the day.

The news team was fortunate in that it was successful in securing a catering sponsor for all its productions and was also on the verge of brokering a deal with On-Campus, a campus weekly newsletter, which was to give the news production team all the equipment it might need.

Bush TV had many types of presenters, ranging from talk-show hosts to newsreaders, film and music review hosts and continuity presenters. Continuity presenters played a major role in the broadcast as links between the different shows, introducing the shows and updating students about projects that the station had embarked on, informing students about happenings on campus, and being the 'face' of Bush TV at events on and off campus.

Bush TV also had a community outreach initiative that drew in participants from high schools and the wider community. As a whole, Bush TV opened doors for many of its volunteers, including participation in other film and video training programmes and careers in the television and film industries.

Because Bush TV was run without a budget, it was not unexpected that it encountered logistical problems. Nevertheless, the students forged ahead armed with only their enthusiasm and a belief that the project could be realised. Despite these challenges, Bush TV was able to achieve its objective of producing 20 weekly productions by the end of 2004. After the departure of the station director of Bush TV in 2004, there was a lull in the activities of the station, but efforts are under way to revive the initiative.

The main problem that Bush TV faces is a lack of formal institutional support within UWC. This situation could change because the university is currently expanding its video production capacity by investing in a recording studio and editing suites. If Bush TV is able to motivate the SRC and administration to provide ongoing support, it will have a far better chance of being sustainable. CVET is investigating the possibility of providing further support for the initiative by making video production equipment available to students but, in the long term, integration with the university's agenda will be vital for the project's sustainability.

GDTV

GDTV was initiated in the mid-1990s at what was then the University of Natal, Durban (now the University of KwaZulu-Natal). The broadcast took place under the banner of the Visual Voice Confest 1995. This conference-cum-festival was oriented around the subject of community access media, with the central theme being 'the role of community access media in reconstruction and development'. The event was aimed at the broader public, media practitioners, the NGO sector and 'the great majority of people who have never had access to media in the past' (Aldridge 1996: 114). It also provided an opportunity to put theory into practice by establishing an experimental community access television station to broadcast in conjunction with the confest.

The GDTV initiative then lay dormant for almost ten years until it resurfaced in 2004 in response to moves by ICASA to address the establishment of the CTV sector. Subsequently, GDTV utilised an agreement between the CTV sector and the SABC, signed in 1998, whereby the public broadcaster committed itself to supporting the development of CTV. As a result of this commitment, the Durban branch of the SABC provided GDTV with a studio and attendant equipment for its broadcasts.

Despite the temporary nature of its broadcasts, GDTV is an ongoing project. Meetings/workshops are held every Saturday and are attended by between 20 and 70 people. The meetings provide a forum for discussion of all GDTV activities, from the broadcast licence application process to report backs on organisational group progress, the introduction of new people, skills development, training and broadcast planning.

GDTV has a management structure that consists of a station manager, assistant station manager and heads of the technical, programming, news and presenting groups. Approximately 100 volunteers participated in the last broadcast (Haysom 2005a).

Content for broadcasts includes a selection of African films and documentaries provided by the FRU. Much of the programming is obtained from volunteer producers. Many of these volunteers respond to on-air invitations to viewers to contribute news items and to host on-air shows.

Access productions made live in the studio comprised some 90 per cent of the programming. Some NGOs responded to the invitation to submit programming and their productions were screened. During the broadcasts, schools are invited to visit the studio and even to join the crew in an experiential learning environment under the technical director's supervision. Six groups of learners visited the studio during the June–July 2005 broadcast and, in addition, groups of about 20 people at a time were shown studio operations on a daily basis.

Funds for the broadcast remained elusive beyond covering the basic transmission costs. Consequently, food to fuel the volunteers surfaced as a problem, which was addressed by donations from individuals, a local business and a religious organisation.

News content was sourced from daily newspapers, the Internet, from community networks and by word of mouth. Events in Durban and its surrounding areas, as well as some events in Pietermaritzburg, were covered. News bulletins consisting of 15 minutes of news items in English, isiZulu, Sesotho and siSwati were aired every day. News coverage included local sports events.

The channel intends pursuing a webcasting model that will run concurrently with the broadcasts to reach viewers via PC networks and cellphones. It has also identified diverse screening opportunities using Internet protocol network delivery mechanisms, such as pavement cellphone businesses, taxi ranks, MPCCs and big-screen public viewing that generates advertising revenue and allows for public service announcements. This mode of distribution can even be extended internationally, and GDTV is considering setting up a video screen in London so that people there can view its broadcasts.

GDTV has relied on facilities provided by the SABC for its broadcasts, and this relationship has been beneficial for the station in that these facilities have been provided free of charge and without them the channel would not have been able to broadcast.

However, some problems have arisen with the relationship between GDTV and the SABC. For one thing, the SABC is moving from analogue to digital linkages with Sentech's transmitter sites, which means that local microwave links are being substituted by a national satellite distribution network. This entails that regional SABC studios feed their material to Johannesburg for uplink to the satellite, from whence it is distributed to transmitter sites throughout the country. The consequence of this for GDTV is that it can no longer utilise the SABC's microwave link to its local transmitter, as well as the fact that the tower on which the transmitter has been situated is to be dismantled. This presents logistical difficulties that will have to be overcome for future broadcasts to take place.

Relations with the SABC have been strained due to the situation of the studio within the SABC premises, where large numbers of people moving in and out of the studio area on a daily basis have caused some consternation among SABC staff (Haysom 2005a). In the past, the SABC has provided its facilities free of charge, but now wants some financial return for their use, particular as some equipment has had to be moved from Johannesburg to Durban for the broadcasts (Lungu 2005). Although SABC technical staff set up the GDTV facilities, lack of pre-planning and finance have resulted in certain inefficiencies such as shortage of equipment and equipment breakdown. Nevertheless, GDTV has developed a sound relationship with the SABC in Durban and continues to enjoy the corporation's support for its activities (Haysom 2005a).

In terms of sustainability, GDTV believes that it has 'moved away from being just a television station into being a brand' and, consequently, is venturing into other areas of activity such as a beach soccer team. The channel has also come up with the concept of 'branding blocks', where the sponsor pays for a production house to make a programme. 'With a branding block, the sponsor team becomes a part of the production crew, comes in with backdrops, etcetera. The MD can speak to company staff around the region.' (Peppas 2005)

GDTV's methodology in terms of staffing is to use volunteers, generally unemployed youth, who train one another in production and broadcast techniques. This is done in the belief that this very basic level of training combined with experience gained during the temporary broadcasts will make them attractive employment prospects for professional production houses and broadcasters. Other volunteers, including students from Technikon Natal's journalism and television production departments, have some video or media training.

Each broadcast has a theme; for example, in June 2005 it was focused on the *Freedom Charter* and the Durban International Film Festival. For the next planned broadcast in December 2005, it will focus on AIDS Awareness Month and the provincial road safety campaign (Mayisela 2005).

The broadcasts have generated considerable interest in the broader Durban community. At one stage, the station broadcast an invitation to people to visit the studio between 12.00 p.m. and 2.00 p.m. and the following day the studio had a full audience during this time (Mayisela 2005).

Analysis of GDTV
About 500 people gained skills and experience from their involvement in GDTV station activities over the 2004–2005 period (Mayisela 2005). The experience they gained in video production together with the insight this gives them into television are undoubtedly beneficial. However, one potential disadvantage of GDTV's current mode of operation is that these volunteers appear to be motivated chiefly by the idea that they will get jobs with the national broadcasters after some experience with the channel's operations.

This expectation is questionable because, as entrants to the professional industry, they will be competing against graduates from tertiary educational institutions for jobs in technical positions. For instance, a National Qualifications Framework-certified video course is offered by Monash University. This is an intensive six-month course taught by experienced industry professionals, after which the learners are placed in permanent and freelance positions as interns with production houses. CTV volunteers should have realistic and appropriate expectations about their involvement with CTV.

The fact that GDTV volunteers are instructed by their peers who have little experience outside of GDTV is not without merit, but the industry is likely to demand higher standards than this in a market that is flooded by freshly trained talent every year. The exception might be presenters, because this skills category requires less formal instruction, but this is a distinct category that cannot be confused with technical positions. The production courses offered by accredited institutions offer a comprehensive view of production activities and theoretical inputs that GDTV cannot match at present. Finding experienced production personnel to act as mentors would be a huge advantage for GDTV.

Despite the above limitations, the enthusiasm and achievements of GDTV volunteers cannot be dismissed. The temporary broadcasts seem to have provided participants with useful skills, experience and insight into television production. However, the notion of on-air training in a 'live, experiential learning environment' (Haysom 2005b) is questionable because, although access to equipment and live broadcasting conditions might spur participants to learn fast, the resulting mistakes, glitches and poor production standards inevitably detract from the audience's positive viewing experience. This situation may be permissible within the ambit of a limited project, for instance a programme about video production or visual literacy, but it cannot support a long-term CTV project that requires buy-in from other stakeholders.

These problems relating to training standards indicate that much attention needs to be paid to improving standards of pre-broadcast training as well as ongoing mentoring of volunteer or access personnel. Another vital need is for CTV participants to have access to production equipment. Such support can be sought from tertiary educational institutions, NGOs, sector bodies such as sports organisations, local businesses and public donations. For a CTV channel to find this level of support will require coordinated marketing and networking campaigns. In view of their operational mandates, organisations like the Media Development and Diversity Agency (MDDA) and the National Film and Video Foundation (NFVF) will have definite roles to play in funding these operational aspects in the longer term.

GDTV needs more community buy-in to be successful. The channel called a public meeting early in 2005, but more extensive engagements with the wider community will be essential to secure the level of representivity required for permanent licensing. This might take the form of successive public meetings or workshops for NGO interest groups similar to those conducted in Cape Town by the Cape Town CTV Collective. Such engagement could generate more widespread and direct community participation to build the sustainability of the channel. For instance, more people can get involved in fund-raising activities, content provision and lobbying support.

The combined GDTV/Durban Film School project will have to find sustainable sources of income. A well-researched business plan is needed to identify these sources and to devise a strategy for accessing sufficient resources to survive. The channel will have to decide what its core business function is and focus on that; for instance, providing sponsors with media exposure over the airwaves has its own complex tensions between commerce, production and access that must cohere harmoniously. The project of giving some people a smattering of video or broadcasting skills is a noble one, but is not in itself sufficient reason for stakeholders to fund a CTV broadcaster.

Other practical problems experienced by GDTV include delays in obtaining a temporary broadcast licence from ICASA, with its last licence being granted only the day before the station went on air. This points to inefficiencies in ICASA's administrative procedures, indicating that the regulator has not improved in this regard since the 1990s when its overly bureaucratic demands were identified as a particular problem for CTV licence applicants (Aldridge 1996).

Funding is a major problem area. This may be partly attributable to concerns about the sustainability of the station, with potential funders being reluctant to part with money on the basis of a temporary broadcast. GDTV has not yet managed to gain a sustainable funding source, although it is in negotiations with the Durban City Council to this end.

The station receives phone calls from areas that are well outside the Durban metropolitan area, as far afield as Eshowe, Pietermaritzburg and Hammarsdale. Some viewers phone in every evening, which indicates that the station is building a loyal viewership despite the limitations of its content.

Conclusion
GDTV demonstrates that it is possible to sustain an ongoing CTV project with very few resources, based largely on volunteers' energy and contributions from local government, NGOs and business stakeholders. The fact that GDTV only broadcasts for limited periods should not detract from the fact that the project has continued over time and has staged multiple broadcasts.

In the longer term, the channel will have to identify a particular value proposition to attract sufficient financial, logistical and representational support for it to be sustainable. Firm commitment is needed from sectoral stakeholders such as local government, educational institutions, NGOs and businesses. To attract this support, GDTV will have to extend its roots into local communities through democratic mechanisms that increase community representation. It must develop its ability to deliver a quality product to stakeholders in terms of training, technical production standards and reliability in programming delivery. This will require investment in the upgrading of training and the establishment of a sound infrastructure of equipment, premises and management resources.

The five broadcasts that GDTV has conducted over the ten years of its history have proved that viewers appreciate local content, despite the relatively poor standards of recording and broadcasting. The station has shown strong levels of viewer support through its live studio audiences and phone-ins, despite broadcasting content from VHS tapes, running mostly live shows from rudimentary studio facilities, making numerous technical mistakes and having elastic programme times and many repeats.

The channel has established a firm relationship with the SABC that could be built on. The disadvantage of this situation is that GDTV is wholly dependent on the SABC for its broadcast capacity. The SABC is also looking to cover its own costs of supporting GDTV's activities and some means will have to be found to address this, together with GDTV's other funding difficulties. At present, GDTV is focused on fulfilling the aspirations of its producer group through training and experience. A broader focus on the communications needs of other stakeholders would build the station's sustainability.

The Cape Town CTV Collective
The Cape Town Community Television Collective (CT CTVC) is a grouping of community media NGOs that began meeting to coordinate a CTV channel for Cape Town in 2004. This configuration was developed by South Africa's Open Window Network (OWN) in

the 1990s and is based on an Australian model (Melbourne Community Television), which sought to bring together NGO stakeholders and their resources into partnership with community groups. Hence, the founding organisations of the Cape Town group (first known as the Cape Town Community TV Consortium) are all engaged in entry-level, audio-visual or arts training, video production, community broadcasting, film and video distribution/exhibition and audience development. The founding organisations were:
- Community Video Education Trust (CVET);
- Workers World Media Productions (WWMP);
- Arts and Media Access Centre (AMAC) (formerly CAP and Mediaworks);
- Bush Radio; and
- Public Eye.

Other organisations, including Molweni Township Productions, the Institute for Democracy in South Africa, the Cape Town Festival and Bush TV, were initially involved but dropped out of the planning process during 2005.

The collective intends building CTV capacity in Cape Town through developing a network of production facilities that coalesce to deliver content to a broadcast point. CT CTVC is very focused on building community support through consultation and awareness-raising in the Cape Town metropolitan area. The group intends to establish a non-profit legal entity to ensure community and stakeholder representation in governance and to apply ultimately for a long-term CTV licence. The resulting channel is intended to serve the information, education, communication and entertainment needs of people living in the greater Cape Town metropolitan area.

CT CTVC initially planned to stage a temporary event broadcast based on the theme of the Cape Town Festival in March 2005. However, these plans were shelved because members felt that they lacked capacity to undertake this task and instead have devoted themselves to building an organisational and community base from which to launch future initiatives. The collective produced a discussion document, originally authored by AMAC Director Karen Thorne (see Thorne 2005), on which it has based its activities. The document provides a background to CTV in South Africa, defines the collective and sets out an action plan for organisational development. It also describes a set of principles and values that the collective has adopted to guide its way forward.

Since the strength of the collective model supposedly lies in the resources and energy that its constituents bring to the CTV table, it is worth looking at the capacity and motivation of CT CTVC participants in order to gauge the capacity of the organisation for engaging in CTV activities. The participants defined themselves in this regard at a meeting on 21 June 2005.

Bush Radio representative Brenda Leonard said that Bush Radio is a community radio station that runs 25 social upliftment and development projects. These range from a children's programme to news programmes involving community learners and schoolchildren. Bush Radio pushes social upliftment messages through its programming and sees CTV 'as a way of bringing our message across'. The station has also been instrumental in aiding the establishment of community radio as a sector in South Africa and elsewhere in Africa.

According to independent consultant Natalie McAskill, who represents CVET in the collective, the organisation is currently repositioning itself and intends to provide video training and skills opportunities to young people from disadvantaged communities. Another project is the visual literacy or media education programme to raise awareness of the educational potential of the medium. CVET's interest in CTV is to develop it as a resource that its trainees can access as an experiential training opportunity. The organisation is also 'concerned with the power of the medium to aid communication and to give a voice to the voiceless' (McAskill 2005).

AMAC has recently undergone a process of change as a result of a merger between the Community Arts Project (CAP) and Mediaworks, a community media training organisation. The organisation includes audio-visual media in its training programmes through a community journalism programme for unemployed black youth. It has a schools programme that teaches media production skills to schools in disadvantaged areas. These learners produce content for a newspaper called *Just Youth*, which will branch out into a multimedia project.

AMAC's interest in CTV is from the point of view of finding a public outlet for content produced by its various learner groups. Some of the school groups are focusing their efforts on video production and the AMAC performing arts programme has a television component. Performing arts are also fostered through a professional development programme that includes a theatre company.

WWMP is a labour media production house that generates mainly radio productions and print media. It has a youth programme and is run with a strong principle of participatory communication. The NGO produces and promotes independent labour media in various forms and it introduces labour views into the mainstream media. It sees CTV as a means of taking these objectives forward.

Public Eye consists of a group of Cape Town artists who facilitate major art projects and events taking place in the public arena. This NGO has been deeply involved in the visual arts component of the Cape Town 'One City Many Cultures' festivals and has also participated in international events. Public Eye has presented successful 'Soft Serve' art events at the South African National Gallery, which involved video and international video conferencing components.

CT CTVC's principles and values
The collective is guided by a set of principles and values that are contained within its discussion document. Because these values underpin the group's endeavours, they are dealt with here in some detail. Each of the points below is taken from the discussion document and is treated individually.

Principle 1 – Preamble: *We recognise that the majority of South Africans, the historically disadvantaged, have been deprived of media ownership, control and production in their own interests. Community TV is one important avenue for redressing this inequality to ensure that the Cape Town community takes ownership and control of this valuable resource for their own empowerment through communication, entertainment and information sharing.*

Discussion: The preamble situates CTV primarily as an empowerment vehicle intended to redress the inequalities of apartheid by placing media ownership, control and production in the hands of historically disadvantaged South Africans. This situates the Cape Town initiative within a particular historical context and lends it a specific political purpose, as opposed to the more general provisions of access and the promotion of human rights for all that are commonly found elsewhere in the world.

Principle 2 – The right to communicate and the communication of rights:
Access to information and the ability to communicate are fundamental human rights in the information age. Community media ensures that all citizens have access to the information and communication channels necessary to exercise their civic rights and responsibilities, to share political, cultural, artistic, spiritual, and individual expression, and to promote a culture of human rights and responsibilities.

Discussion: CTV is different to both commercial and public service television in that it is based on a human rights perspective; that is, enabling the public to express their views and opinions through television as well as to receive information that serves their communication and information needs. The way to sustain these rights through CTV takes different forms, and South Africa will have to develop its own model for doing this on a sustainable basis.

Principle 3 – Equity and social justice: *We believe in the fundamental equality between all people and are therefore committed to redressing the imbalances created in the past, towards the creation of a more just and equitable media and communications environment for all. In the current social, economic and political context, special priority must therefore be given to black, working class communities. This should be balanced against the principle of diversity whereby no group will be excluded.*

Discussion: The statement attempts a balanced approach wherein both past and future are mentioned in terms of the channel's social justice aims. While the black working class is privileged as a beneficiary group, allowance is made for the channel to represent a wide array of interests. The manner in which the black working class is to benefit from its favoured position within this scope has yet to be worked out in practical operational terms.

Singling out the black working class as a privileged sector may be limiting in a sense because it leaves out other sectors of the population who might also be marginalised, for instance women, the disabled and the landless. However, this sector of the population represents the largest collective grouping in South African society to be marginalised by its historical circumstances in relation to apartheid, on the one hand, and capitalism, on the other. Moreover, this class represents the majority of the South African population, particularly if the unemployed are factored into its ranks. At the same time, a focus on this sector presents an economic hurdle to be overcome in terms of drawing funding support, particularly from advertisers to whom this population sector is least appealing.

While the principle of diversity is defined in an open manner, the collective's membership policy confines universal participation to programming, as certain social categories (namely, business, religious and government organisations) are excluded from participation in the governing structure.

Perhaps a paragraph stressing the important role that CTV can play in social development would be fitting, because it would indicate striving to provide a communications channel whereby communities of interest can express their needs and have access to information that will help them to empower themselves. An essential component of empowerment is participation, so this aspect can also be stressed.

Principle 4 – Diversity: *We are committed to engaging a wide range of community perspectives, including those of groups that have historically been marginalised; to promote healing and tolerance and encourage communication across barriers of race, culture, physical ability, language, class, gender, age, and sexual orientation.*

Discussion: This is a wide-ranging, inclusive commitment that once again addresses the concern of rectifying the injustices and imbalances of apartheid. It is also a positive statement in that it asserts the necessity to promote constructive outcomes across social divisions.

Principle 5 – Community cultural development: *Community media has a powerful role to play in Community Cultural Development as a means of enabling alternatives to the cultural values imposed on communities by top-down and commercially driven forms of media.*

Discussion: The notion that cultural values are 'imposed on communities by top-down and commercially driven forms of media' is misleading because there is a dialectical relationship between communities and media, so these values are not necessarily imposed. Perhaps the term 'presented by' (not 'of') the media would be a better phrase.

The term 'top-down' indicates that CT CTV will have a 'bottom-up' approach that opposes the bottleneck found in commercial and public media, where decision-making structures act as gatekeepers that impose their agendas on media producers and media participants.

Principle 6 – Community ownership and control: *A community broadcasting service is defined as a service which is owned and controlled by the community it serves. This includes participation by representative community structures in the management of the station as well as access to training and production facilities.*

Discussion: Because of ICASA's prioritisation of geographic areas for granting single-frequency CTV licences, the community this particular station would serve largely consists of the people of Cape Town. If the definition of geographic community is described by the possible total broadcast footprint, then the channel's community will be constituted from the approximately 3 million people who live in the greater Cape Town area. The potential for reaching this audience will depend on cost and technical factors, including the number of transmitter sites and signal strength. Low-power transmission from a single transmitter, for instance, would cover only a portion of that total population, which would then be the community to be served by a CTV licensee.

By limiting membership to representative organisations in the identified sectors, CT CTV will draw legitimacy from the standpoint of community ownership, provided that it can demonstrate representation that is sufficiently diverse to reflect a credible, broad front of civil society participation.

Access can be defined not just in terms of training and production, but also in access to the airwaves through programme provision and public participation. This suggests that there should be a democratic and transparent means whereby communities of interest within the broadcast area can gain access to the airwaves for their programming. While this process will be mediated by a programming committee drawn from the participating organisations, it should be a process that is open and accountable to the public to maximise community participation.

An additional statement is needed that commits the station to the principles of good governance, including factors such as accountability, transparency and good management practice. Such a statement would advance the channel's credibility and trustworthiness.

Principle 7 – Technology and standards: *CTV shall aspire to delivering the highest quality programming without jeopardising the principles of access and affordability and the space for learning, innovation and experimentation. While every effort will be made to ensure access to 'broadcast quality' formats, participants should be allowed to produce in any formats available to them.*

Discussion: The question of formats is a technical parameter rather than a principle of CTV; but the point is valid in these terms and can guide the implementation of CTV technical standards. The point of aspiring to high standards is a very necessary developmental objective that will further the aims of participants, viewers and funders alike.

Principle 8 – Civic participation: *The media has a powerful role to play in promoting democratic involvement in public life. This is achieved through its ability to provide citizens with access to information. Community media encourages participation in local decision-making by providing services that enable community problem-solving and dialogue with elected officials or decision-makers. This contributes towards social transformation and change as well as people-centred and therefore sustainable development.*

Discussion: This principle promotes engagement with and dialogue between citizens and government structures through the medium of CTV. As such, it is a positive contribution to the role of CTV in society and should be promoted.

Principle 9 – Programming mandate: *CTV programming has a local focus and is directly answerable to the information, education and entertainment needs as articulated by participating groups and in the language of these groups. Cape Town CTV will serve mainly as an access point for citizens and organs of civil society that are non-profit entities to exercise their right to communicate. In doing so it will also ensure opportunities for emerging, independent and progressive producers to develop and air their productions that are in line with the principles and values of CT CTV.*

Discussion: This is a very significant point because it defines one of the most critical areas of CTV operations. The principle articulated here places responsibility for programming in the hands of 'participating groups', which are elsewhere defined in terms of the criteria set by the collective for membership. The collective has defined membership in terms of inviting 'like-minded' people representing public sector organisations with a development orientation to participate in its CTV initiative. Programming would then be responsive to the needs of these sectors, as enunciated by their representatives in the programming forum.

Further exclusions on membership of the CTV channel's governing body, in terms of the collective's policy regarding business, religious and government organisations, do limit representation in programming management. Business was excluded because it was felt that this sector had sufficient communications resources of its own, while religious groups were excluded because of the 'extreme contestation' that existed between sectarian groups. Individuals are also excluded, with representation going to those 'who can represent the broader interests of groups of people' (CT CTVC 2005).

The above criteria and exclusions combined impel the collective towards representing a limited number of community interests when viewed in the context of the overall geographic community to be covered by the transmission signal. However, the collective has made concrete attempts to engage with this aspect of the whole through a democratic process. The criterion of representivity, that persons engaged in channel governance stand as representatives of broader, organised interest groups, is a sound democratic principle. The exclusions are not expected to apply to programming content, where religious programming, for example, is a 'must-have' in terms of ICASA policy. Moreover, the station will have to court some level of involvement from the excluded sectors in order to be sustainable.

The CT CTV workshop

Between April and October 2005, the collective engaged in a process of community mobilisation around the concept of CTV. This led to a public workshop on 18 August 2005, which largely involved representatives from public sector NGOs and institutions and which was sponsored by the Human Sciences Research Council (HSRC). The three-fold purpose of the workshop was to:
- report to representatives of the Cape Town community on the CT CTV initiative;
- generate awareness and support for the CT CTV initiative; and
- obtain and secure the formal involvement of representatives of the Cape Town community in owning and advancing the setting up and establishment of CT CTV.

Invitations to the workshop were sent to organisations involved in different social sectors in order to attract 'like-minded' people to participate in the establishment of CT CTV. The collective decided that this term referred to organisations that were oriented towards social development and included the sectors of education, sport, civic, labour, arts and community media (CT CTVC 2005).

Backgrounds to CTV in South Africa and to the CT CTV initiative were presented together with international CTV models, the ICASA policy framework and the options for CT CTV. Group discussions addressed key questions, including:
- Is there a need for a CTV project for Cape Town? If so, why?
- How would a CTV initiative be sustained organisationally and financially?
- How do we define our community?
- How should CT CTV work and operate in terms of stakeholders and community representation and participation, governance, and ensuring that we are consistent and remain true to our principles and ethical guidelines?
- How would we differ from commercial and public television in terms of content, style, approach and operations?

The political principles and ethical guidelines for CT CTV were discussed in terms of an introductory input on the recommendations of the CT CTVC. CTV and the definition of the Cape Town community were discussed in terms of the following questions:
- Which sections of 'the community' should own and control CT CTV?
- How does the community become aware of, access and get involved in CT CTV? What do we need to do in order to ensure this?

Sections of the community to be targeted, the process for drawing them into the initiative and related concerns were covered. Then followed discussion on the key tasks towards setting up CT CTV and the time frame for this. An interim steering committee was elected.

All of the discussion groups agreed that there was a need for a CTV channel in Cape Town. Suggestions on sustainability and financing included having a low permanent staff component, use of volunteering supported by stipends, use of students, developing accredited learnerships and limiting overheads. Finance could come from sponsorships, advertising, local business marketing and/or sales of airtime.

Among further strategies proposed was the establishment of an independent CTV channel that included a video access centre and a broadcast facility. It was suggested that the City of Cape Town could reinvest some of its income from local filming fees in CTV broadcasting. Local business could be involved not only financially but also through the provision of equipment. There was also a need to look at other models of community broadcasting, including the successes and failures of community radio.

Participants accepted the definition of the community to be served by the channel in terms of those covered by the broadcast footprint, and the disparate communities of interest within that population. The collective's definition of the community to be involved in channel ownership and control was not contested. The collective has defined this community as a sector-based range of interest groups including sport, education, labour, CBOs and NGOs, arts and culture and community media, with the caveat that participants must be oriented towards developmental goals.

It was suggested that CTV deal with membership by NGOs through charging a nominal membership fee. Membership-based organisations must contribute to CTV operations in order to participate and the station would have a strong volunteer component to boost its capacity.

On the whole, the workshop supported the CTV initiative and validated the approach undertaken by the collective. Some debate ensued on the principles and values to be employed in CTV, specifically about the issue of bias towards the black working class. Some participants felt that this was inappropriate in present-day South Africa, while others argued that the needs of society as a whole would be best served by promoting the interests of its most needy sectors. According to the latter position, the effects of apartheid are still being felt by society, and those most affected should be accorded special treatment.

The workshop resolved that the interim steering committee should take the initiative forward and continue to seek ways of encouraging wider community participation. It was decided that a series of sectoral workshops would be undertaken in order to deepen representation in the governing structure. The collective presented on its intention to develop a business plan, form a legal entity to carry out operations and launch test broadcasts during 2006. An interim management committee was duly elected, consisting of the founding organisations and representatives from the sectors identified for participation.

Cape Town audience survey results
Audience analysis questionnaires were distributed to all present at the August workshop, and 17 were returned out of a total of 50. There can be little doubting the support of the representatives who attended the meeting, with 94 per cent indicating a need for CTV in Cape Town and 65 per cent thinking that CTV's growth potential is 'high'. There is a need to research further what shapes these perceptions, as the reasons offered in the questionnaire survey (QS) were too generic. More than 50 per cent of the respondents had not heard of the CT CTVC prior to the workshop.

The QS strongly indicated that a key objective of the representatives was to tap into the opportunity offered by CTV to provide access to TV broadcasting for the community. Some 94 per cent of the responses indicated an intention to be involved in media-related activities in the future (no specific details of the activities were given). The most common objective offered by the representatives was highlighting community issues as a means for 'voices to be heard'. Another priority was 'education and skills development'.

The education sector was the most represented (41 per cent), which is indicative of the priority attached to the training and skills development needs of this sector of the community. The civil society sector was also well represented (24 per cent), indicating the importance for this sector of being able to access the community through community media.

The representatives' common understanding of CTV's role was to access and spread information at grass-roots level and to highlight local community issues – 'people prefer local'. A common benefit was 'promotion of the organisation's message'. Brand awareness was also mentioned. This 'publicity via partnerships' objective, whereby NGOs can increase their profile with their target markets, seems to be an important consideration for many organisations.

Representatives saw operational activity (production of content) as the major challenge. No specific mention was made of financial constraints, indicating a lack of awareness of the financing and funding challenges of CTV. It must be mentioned that 50 per cent of the respondents did not understand the issue of challenges and referred to the challenges facing their own sector rather than those confronting CTV.

The major difference between CTV and commercial TV was understood to be one of 'exclusivity', in the sense that CTV was viewed as being for the 'common person'. The benefits of CTV mentioned were once again access to the media and promotion of the organisation's message, indicating that this conduit to the community is still underdeveloped.

The high level of ideological support for the collective seems to be matched with potential material support. Some 65 per cent of respondents said that they were in a position to offer moral support such as advocacy and lobbying. An equal number indicated that material support such as technical and production skills were available within the collective, but details of the specific skills on offer must be further investigated.

Conclusion
The support for CTV as a community medium was high within the group that gathered for the workshop. There is an indication that community media will fill a gap that current media access cannot or will not fulfil. There seems to be consensus on the important role that CTV can play in community development, particularly in education and training.

There is, however, a lack of understanding of the distinction between CTV and commercial TV, and the direct benefits of CTV to a community. There needs to be more clarity on how the collective will extend its strong ideological support among civil society organisations into tangible contributions in terms of business and operating skills; and a better understanding is required of what the collective means by being involved in future 'media activities'.

National CTV workshop

A national consultation and awareness-raising workshop on CTV was held at the HSRC offices in Pretoria on 27 October 2005. The workshop was organised to present the findings of this HSRC research project and to encourage dialogue around the issues it raised. The stated aims of the event were to:
- subject the research findings to rigorous debate to ensure that they are locally relevant and applicable;
- develop recommendations on models and strategies for the sustainable development of CTV in South Africa; and
- ensure that research and information is accessible and reaches its target group.

The workshop was facilitated by the Media Institute of Southern Africa-South Africa (MISA-SA) and the HSRC. It was attended by CTV activists from around South Africa, including initiatives in Durban, Cape Town, East London and Johannesburg. The keynote speaker, MDDA Chairperson Libby Lloyd, noted the challenges facing the CTV sector and expressed the hope that the sector would mobilise on a national basis to form a united front that could lobby for support and coordinate developmental efforts.

Three CTV initiatives presented summaries of their activities – GDTV from Durban, the CT CTVC from Cape Town and Soweto TV from Johannesburg. The meeting then split into three discussion groups, each of which addressed a different area of CTV operations. The focus areas were sustainability, principles and values, and partnerships. The recommendations of each group are outlined below.

Sustainability group

It is not sufficient to focus merely on financial sustainability; human resources, programming and local content must also be considered.

There are two positions on finances. The one view is that commercial advertising should be completely excluded because it will otherwise influence a channel's editorial independence. This influence can be either overt or covert and sometimes it is reflected in self-censorship.

The other position is that the focus should be on donor funding and building a strong case for state funding, although there is uncertainty as to what mechanisms can be employed in this regard. The HSRC should look at international models of finance from non-commercial sources. It was pointed out that state funding raised the same risk of editorial compromise as commercial support. It was suggested that a combination of these elements could be utilised, especially because donor funding does not last forever. It is important to have the right levels of control in management and board structures to avoid editorial compromise.

Another option would be to get the community itself to provide direct financial support; for instance, every income-earning individual could pay a R1 monthly levy. The question then arises as to how mechanisms can be established in terms of getting people to agree to this and how to effect it in practice. Possibly R1 from each household electricity bill could go towards such funding. State mechanisms to channel money to CTV could also be established. The example was given of union members paying their monthly subscriptions through salary or wage deductions, which provides an integral link between paying subscriptions and controlling the union management. The HSRC should research innovative ways of getting funding.

The issue of human resources was discussed. Volunteering can be utilised in CTV operations, but volunteer energy does not last. People do it for three months and then they fade away, continuing the cycle of bringing in new people all the time while those with experience leave. There is a risk in volunteerism, but when you are dealing with CTV you need to use volunteers to do the work. It is assumed, however, that there would be permanent posts and people would have sufficient incentive to stay in those positions.

To avoid undue influence on programming, no single source of revenue should dominate. Funding should come from government, donors and community donations. Funding from the government could come from various government agencies such as the MDDA, Department of Communications and Sector Education and Training Authorities. We need to identify where all these potential government pots are so that we can approach funders and specify what we would like them to fund.

Principles and values group

The group identified two major issues. One concerned being a non-profit station and the other was about ownership and control of the entity.

Regarding the station's non-profit status, it was noted that Section 21 (non-profit) companies can have two levels of operation, one of which is a profit-making section. Programming can be sourced from independent producers in the community; and they can look for sponsorship for their own programming so that the station itself is not burdened with having to find funding sources.

On the issue of ownership and control, it was noted that community participation should ensure that people will be engaged in the management and production of programmes. In the beginning, people who are passionate about CTV will get involved but in the long run most of them are lost to the sector.

The identity of the people represented in the station must be considered; in other words, the station should ensure that it integrates the culture of the people so that it is not the station that informs the people but the people who inform the station. People must be able to go to the station – it should not be inaccessible to them.

Independent producers are being excluded in the mainstream of CTV worldwide. In South Africa, the station should have a relationship with them. There are many existing training programmes, so there is already a pool of people who have been trained.

Succession planning must be in place within the organisation. Some people overstay their time in the organisation and end up causing trouble. Stations must have a level of internal training so that people can grow and look for opportunities outside of the station. There is a need to balance the individual development and community development aspects.

Community broadcasting should be used as a community development tool. It must engage with NGOs and CBOs. Disciplinary clauses need to be in place.

Where technical standards are concerned, if these standards are raised too high then certain people will not have access to the station and a sector of the community will be excluded.

There is also the problem of 'poaching' of experienced personnel by the commercial sector and this must be managed.

Partnerships group

The group came up with the following main points. CTV initiatives are very reluctant to jump into partnerships with the main broadcasters because they fear being swallowed up, but there is room for sharing equipment and partnering in broadcasting in various ways.

There is a need for solidarity among CTV stations in the various areas. They should support each other and exchange programmes. There needs to be discussion about regional TV and what it might mean in terms of CTV. It was suggested that the National Association of Broadcasters would be a good forum for networking and getting support.

It was proposed that an association of all CTV stations be formed in order to create a strong body for purposes of lobbying and other support functions. The workshop achieved consensus that the CTV initiatives must work together to form a national body to represent the sector.

Funding should be sought to conduct workshops in communities to build support for the CTV sector.

CHAPTER 5

Partnerships

In order to survive, CTV will have to form multi-sectoral partnerships with various stakeholders. These partners might include government, educational institutions, donors, other broadcasters and the private sector. Support from these partners can range from financial aid to content contributions, training and logistical support.

The main competitor for funding will be the proposed South African Broadcasting Corporation (SABC) regional channels. While the Independent Communications Authority of South Africa (ICASA) initially dictated that the channels would be funded solely by grants and donations, the regulator has bowed to pressure from the broadcaster and is allowing it to finance the channels through advertising revenue as well. This overall funding combination means that the regional channels will compete with CTV for funding at every level, including:
- funds directed at social marketing;
- government funding for infrastructure and operational expenditure;
- government funding for transformation;
- international agency grants;
- sponsorship; and
- new regional ad-spends specific to regional service providers such as retailers and manufacturers (De Vos 2005).

In view of the income-sapping potential of the SABC regional channels it may be wise for CTV to form a strategic partnership with the public service broadcaster in order to leverage airtime on the channels in return for developing community production capacity and content. However, such a partnership does carry inherent contradictions; a CTV channel on an SABC frequency might be regulated by SABC editorial policy together with ICASA strictures such as the ban on English on the regional channels. If the editorial integrity of CTV is compromised by SABC influence, the third tier of television broadcasting will be hampered in its democratic mission because the local community will lose its power over programming, so contravening one of the key regulatory provisos for its inception.

The SABC would probably also want to relegate CTV to non-peak time slots, in order for the corporation to maximise the value of prime-time viewership figures for income generation purposes. This would deprive CTV of the opportunity to access these self-same resources by providing programming content in competition with that afforded by the SABC's multiple channels. If CTV does decide that an alliance with the SABC regional channels would be advantageous, a frequency-sharing arrangement should be entered into rather than CTV being simply subcontracted by the SABC to provide content for the public service channels.

The CTV component of such a broadcast would need to run for sufficient time to generate a good income spread from sponsors and advertisers. A short window period of 30–60 minutes, for instance, would not generate much ad-spend, as has been proved by previous attempts at this format (Aldridge 1996; Terblanche 2005).

Funding partners

The government

For CTV to be fully supported by the government, it must not only fulfil the aspirations of the country's citizens, but it must also fit in with broader government agendas. The government has created an enabling environment for CTV through legislation and policy, but it also has the capacity to be an ongoing partner with this media sector. The government has followed this course with the community radio sector by providing capital equipment injections together with ongoing advertising and content inputs (GCIS 2005a).

Government policy-making takes place within the framework of the Constitution, which sets out the country's legislative and normative parameters. The current ANC-led government has committed itself to a programme of development, democracy and unity as its path towards the future. The government's Programme of Action 2005 has the slogan, 'Building a South Africa that truly belongs to all', symbolising a synthesis of the aforementioned concepts. The aim of this programme is to build upon the foundation of the new South Africa that has been laid during the first ten years of democracy in order to create 'national reconciliation, national unity, a shared pride and new patriotism that grows out of building a South Africa that truly belongs to all who live in it, united in our diversity' (GCIS 2005b).

According to the Government Communication and Information System (GCIS), the government is committed to:
- further entrenching democracy and creating a truly non-racial and non-sexist society;
- eradicating poverty with a growing First Economy and a transformed Second Economy;
- opening the way for the fulfilment of each and every South African;
- securing the safety and security of all our people;
- building an efficient, democratic state that truly serves the people's interests; and
- contributing to the African Renaissance and a better life for the people of Africa and the world.

These objectives form part of the government's Batho Pele (People First) policy. Some strategic elements of this policy could affect CTV. The national government has prioritised the provision of further resources for local government and the budget for this purpose has been doubled over the past two years. Since CTV can play a part in bringing the government closer to the people in terms of information exchange between state and citizens, local government could direct part of this spend towards developing CTV.

Local government has the potential to be a strong partner of CTV; in many countries, local government participates in CTV programming. Examples of local government programming include meetings of local government bodies (e.g. metro councils), programmes originating from local government structures (e.g. health, water and electricity) and integration of the station into the local emergency services infrastructure (Aldridge 1997).

In South Africa today, local government has prioritised developmental activities as part of its strategy to uplift previously disadvantaged population sectors within the context of overall regional economic and social development. To do this, municipalities throughout South Africa utilise the strategy of integrated development plans (IDPs) as part of an integrated strategy of planning and service delivery (DPLG 2005). This aims to foster appropriate service delivery by providing the framework for economic and social development within the municipality, and it includes several aspects that mesh strategically with the communication objectives of CTV.

An IDP is a local strategic mechanism to restructure cities, towns and rural areas, and one of its objectives is to provide mechanisms to promote social equality through participatory processes of democratisation, empowerment and social transformation. It pursues specific pro-poor strategies and develops instruments to address sustainability in ecological, economic and social dimensions. In this way, it is intended to contribute toward eradicating the development legacy of the past. In addition, it is supposed to operationalise developmental local government and to foster a culture of cooperative governance. In essence, the IDP is:

> a development plan for a municipal area containing short, medium and long-term objectives and strategies. It serves as the principal strategic management instrument for municipalities. It is legislated by the Municipal Systems Act 2000 (MSA) and supersedes all other plans that guide development at a local level. (DPLG 2005)

Despite its function as an instrument of management, the IDP is intended to include democratic participation by residents through mechanisms such as ward committees; in fact, it understands the concept of citizenship in terms of a responsibility on the part of residents to be actively involved in municipal affairs.

In the light of these factors, CTV offers municipalities a means of actively engaging with their constituencies through programming. Municipal departments might produce their own programming in line with their informational and educational service objectives; they could commission community producers to make programmes relevant to these initiatives, particularly in order to obtain feedback from people on the ground concerning their perspectives on community needs and service delivery; and officials could participate in live talk shows where municipal initiatives and strategies are discussed and debated. Thus, CTV can provide an interactive mechanism that can aid development through communications, as well as fostering government-citizen interaction and democratic participation.

The national government has made investments in the community radio sector by providing content such as interviews with government officials, speeches by government leaders and information regarding government programmes. The Department of Communications (DoC) has also purchased equipment for community radio stations (Letsebe 2005). Despite these investments, the DoC is taking a cautious approach to CTV and the sector cannot expect to benefit automatically from such official favours (Mjwara 2005).

In the case of community radio, the DoC has agreed to fund some aspects of their operations in order to further its own aims. The DoC is aware of the fact that television costs more than radio to produce and intends adopting a wait-and-see approach until it can determine the form that CTV will take in South Africa. If CTV becomes an effective channel to reach the government's key target sectors, only then will the government be able to decide on its relation to the medium.

Another important policy consideration for the DoC is that it is not allowed to interact with broadcasting initiatives that are not yet licensed. In terms of South Africa's regulatory environment, the government may not set up broadcasting structures in order to propagate its own messages, so community radio stations do not get any assistance from government until such time as they are licensed. The nature and type of services that CTV broadcasters provide will determine their audiences and, consequently, what partnerships can be developed with the government.

The DoC aims to aid the implementation of government policy in terms of improving people's lives in four key areas: women, children, health and the disabled. CTV will attract government funding if there are commonalties between its audience reach and government objectives.

The main threat to government funding of CTV is the SABC's proposed regional channels. These indigenous language-based channels will aim to derive revenue from 'social marketing', for example leveraging funds from government departments in need of a regional communications channel (De Vos 2005).

Key sources of regional television revenue will be provincial governments, municipalities and provincial development agencies. Regional and local businesses together with NGOs and community-based organisations would also be called upon to support the regional channels (De Vos 2005). Because these sectors are the potential revenue base for CTV, the regional channels would draw revenue away from CTV broadcasters.

The education sector

The tertiary education sector in South Africa has a limited history of engagement with CTV broadcasting. It can be argued that educational institutions have a 'natural' role to play in CTV, particularly in a country like South Africa that requires innovative means of upgrading the education levels of the wider population. Various educational television initiatives have arisen in South Africa, probably the most notable of which is Mindset Television.

However, another bold experiment in televisual education was initiated by the University of Pretoria, which staged a community-based telematic-learning schools project (TeleTuks), which provided a free educational satellite TV service to secondary schools. The countrywide TV broadcasts were supported by Internet and telephone feedback links and aimed to supplement teachers' lessons with quality educational content (Roodt & Conradie 2003).

The programmes are designed to assist schools in teaching 'problem subjects such as mathematics, physical science, biology, accounting, English, geography and career guidance', and are presented by subject specialists with the intention of reaching a wide base of learners through an information and communications technology (ICT) learning methodology.

The project began in 1997 and by October 2000 about 62 schools nationwide were regularly receiving the broadcasts. This involved approximately 13 schools in Gauteng, 5 in Mpumalanga, 8 in the North West Province and 36 in the Northern Province.

As Roodt and Conradie (2003) report:

> The University of Pretoria's TeleTuks initiative makes use of studio broadcasting to teach many students at the same time. Programmes are transmitted from

a broadcast quality studio on the main campus of the University. Remote-controlled cameras are used in the studio, while computers and a variety of videotape formats are used to enhance the visual quality of a broadcast.

Other universities that have engaged with community broadcasting initiatives are Rhodes University through its Cue TV project and Monash University through its Sector Education and Training Authority (SETA)-sponsored learnerships. Apart from these, South Africa's tertiary educational institutions remain locked in 'Ivory Tower' stasis with regard to engagements with the wider community. Even Cue TV failed to engage substantially with this broader constituency, focusing its efforts on its core community of students.

The problem that these organisations face is that their 'paying customers' are the students, although government institutions are also supported by the state. Universities and technikons have a duty to supply the needs of students before any possible provision of services for those outside the boundaries of formal learning. Nevertheless, we should question this narrow definition of responsibility, particularly in the context of South Africa as a developing nation whose population requires urgent and wide-ranging engagement in the educational terrain to escape the bonds of poverty and related social ills.

Some institutions are beginning to realise that looking after their own interests extends to engaging with a wider audience than those within their walls. The education received by many entrants is often not of the highest quality, meaning that students enter the halls of learning with an inadequate grasp of the necessary skills and knowledge, including life skills. The rationale behind the TeleTuks broadcasts was to stimulate a learning culture among school pupils in mathematics and physical science through the medium of telematics, which should ultimately increase the numbers of those qualifying for university entrance.

Institutions that are willing to participate in CTV activities will have to determine their level of involvement in terms of providing programming, facilitating student participation, making equipment and facilities available to students and even opening their facilities for use by community producers and crews. Engaging with the wider community can be a troubling experience for staid institutions, as evidenced by the conflict that the Greater Durban Television (GDTV) broadcast caused at the then University of Natal in 1995 (Aldridge 1996).

Content provision along the lines of the TeleTuks project, or other educational and marketing material, also has cost implications that institutions will have to consider. However, institutions will find it hard to ignore the needs of society for the types of educational and cultural interventions that they can provide through the televisual medium, not to mention the concrete benefits for media and television students who get involved in CTV production and broadcast activities in order to gain practical experience and hone their knowledge and skills.

Most, if not all, of South Africa's tertiary educational institutions have audio-visual (AV) departments that produce video material, some of which could be tailored to CTV broadcast. Many of them also teach media and AV production, creating their own communities of producers. All of these institutions have the ability to engage with CTV, but it remains to be seen whether they have the will, the vision and the courage to do so.

The private sector

There is considerable scope for private sector investment in South African CTV. While the fundamental imperative of business is to make profits for its stakeholders, a project that may sometimes be at odds with the democratic, development and social-criticism drivers of CTV, there are areas of concern that are common to both sectors. Issues such as enhancing democracy and government accountability, providing quality education to children and adults, adult basic education and training, HIV/AIDS programmes, job creation, crime reduction and social upliftment are all areas of concern to business and CTV alike.

There appears to be a degree of recognition in the corporate sector that social poverty helps to perpetuate economic poverty. Evidence from East and Southeast Asia suggests that the removal of social deprivation can be very influential in stimulating economic growth and sharing the fruits of growth more evenly (Sen in Mdladlana 2000). This principle has been factored into business operations through the King II Report and its insistence on 'triple bottom line reporting', which requires companies to report on their corporate social investment (CSI) activities as part of their responsibilities to shareholders.

South African business has widely adopted CSI practices. For instance, Rand Merchant Bank (RMB) has declared its commitment to contributing to transformation in South Africa by focusing on problem areas where its skills can be used constructively to make a difference to society. The bank uses investment to meet the basic needs of projects aimed at improving the quality of life of disadvantaged people. Programmes include teacher support and development as the linchpins of a programme to remedy the country's educational problems (RMB 2000).

RMB has engaged in media investments such as assisting in the formation of a black consortium bidding for SABC radio stations with Primedia Limited. RMB acted as an advisor in the Perskor-Kagiso transaction whereby the business activities of Kagiso and Perskor Publishers were merged.

Another example is the Absa Foundation, which claims to value partnerships with communities in civil society, international donor organisations and governments. It has partnered with other foundations such as the Vodacom Foundation and the Telkom Foundation to support projects within the framework of a common set of values and areas of concern (Aldridge 2004a).

These initiatives from the private sector occur in a social milieu where great emphasis is being placed on addressing social problems that have arisen as a consequence of capitalism and its evolution through centuries of colonial racial oppression that reached an apogee under apartheid.

Since the inception of the democratic dispensation in 1994, the South African government has stressed policies of social upliftment for marginalised population sectors. It has attended to the transformation of the racial profiles of business, government, education, media and socio-economic stratification within society at large. The government has placed compelling pressures on the private sector to align with its policies in this regard, while transformation of the business and parastatal sectors has contributed to a new sense of social responsibility in upper management echelons.

That being said, it is significant to note that CSI activities typically concentrate on front-line development programmes such as support for formal schooling initiatives (including teacher training), HIV/AIDS programmes, adult basic education and training (ABET) and environmental initiatives rather than secondary or support services such as media.

Nevertheless, there are noteworthy corporate initiatives that do involve media, and television in particular. In the 1990s, Africa Growth Network (AGN), a subsidiary of the ABSA banking group, broadcast educational programmes to business clients, universities and other training institutions from its Johannesburg studio. Lessons in various subjects were recorded and broadcast nationally from this studio to client stations that received the signal via a decoder (Aldridge 1996).

Corporate clients used the service to provide staff training at cost-effective rates, which precluded the necessity of staff travelling nationally to a central point for training, as well as assuring a uniformity of instruction. In addition, AGN aimed to service learning centres based in schools, community centres, churches and welfare organisations (AGN 1995).

Another corporate-sponsored broadcaster with a specific developmental focus is Mindset Network, which broadcasts educational content to schools and health programmes to hospitals and clinics around the country via satellite transmission. Because of its development focus, programming production strengths and national broadcast footprint, Mindset has the potential to be a powerful ally of CTV, as well as setting an example of how private sector and parastatal organisations can cooperate with NGOs to create robust developmental media entities.

Conceptualised by the Liberty Life Foundation and the Standard Bank Foundation, Mindset Network began its production and broadcast operations in 2003. Both of these founding institutions have provided substantial support to the project. The Liberty Life Foundation provided a R35 million grant and in-kind contributions of office space, infrastructure and administrative support. The total value of its contributions comes to about R60 million. The Liberty Life Foundation committed itself to supporting Mindset for an initial period of five years from June 2002.

Key contributions from the Standard Bank Foundation include annually agreed cash grants (R6 million in 2004) and support in developing the network's financial-literacy educational content. The Standard Bank Foundation is also committed to supporting Mindset Network for an initial five-year period.

The Nelson Mandela Foundation has provided R12 million in seed funding for the Mindset Learn Channel and an additional R5 million for its Health Channel. The Foundation has also equipped 250 rural schools with the Mindset receiving infrastructure. The total value of these contributions stands at R20 million, and the Nelson Mandela Foundation has committed to assist Mindset in raising further substantial funds. The Foundation will also integrate the project into its rural clinic initiatives, continue to introduce Mindset to funders and help in the launch of the Livelihood Channel.

The Telkom Foundation is supplying Mindset Network with the necessary funding for Grade 10–12 mathematical literacy programmes on the Mindset Learn Channel, as well as installing the Mindset Network receiving equipment in 500 schools. The total value of the contribution over a five-year period is R20 million.

MultiChoice Africa is providing the educator content component of the Mindset Learn Channel and to this end has made content in maths, science, English and outcomes-based education methodology available to Mindset Network. MultiChoice Africa has provided free bandwidth to the Mindset channels through its DSTV bouquet and is carrying the Mindset Learn Channel into homes on its premium bouquet. It has also agreed to provide Mindset Learn Channel to schools free of any subscription charges. The value of this contribution is R32 million.

PanAmSat has donated access to a transponder, which allows Mindset Network the bandwidth for up to ten channels. The PanAmSat bandwidth facilitates network requirements in terms of content distribution and has the ability to reach every school, home and clinic in southern Africa. The total value of this contribution over three years is R155 million.

The *Sunday Times*, South Africa's largest weekly newspaper, is running a major campaign to support the Mindset Network initiative. The *Sunday Times* carries print supplements to support the broadcast, as well as giving exposure to the founding partners. The newspaper has committed to support Mindset for an initial period of five years, and the total value of the contribution is R20 million.

Sentech is providing wireless connectivity to the project to allow the delivery of a broadcast signal from Mindset Network to its various transmission partners. Sentech will also incorporate Mindset Network content in its roll-out to 500 schools in terms of its multimedia licence. Mindset Network has also been given free channels on the Sentech Vivid broadcast platform. Sentech has committed to support Mindset Network for an initial five-year period, and the total value of its contribution is R20 million.

These investments reflect a combined value of well over R330 million. The range of interests that has combined to secure Mindset as a platform for development programming demonstrates the ability of South Africa's corporate sector to address developmental concerns through a televisual initiative. This could be a good precedent for CTV that demonstrates how an intelligent, strategic relationship between CTV broadcasters and the private and parastatal sectors can result in significant investments for developmental programming and television infrastructure.

Content partners

Film Resource Unit

The Film Resource Unit (FRU) is an NGO that distributes African films in South Africa. The organisation focuses on developing a culture of appreciation for African film in township areas through a network of micro-enterprise entrepreneurs who sell the videos in their communities. The organisation has supported various CTV initiatives in South Africa through the provision of African films.

FRU is engaged in a joint project with the GCIS to launch AV centres in four provinces. These centres are to be set up in Gauteng, North West, Limpopo and Northern Cape and are situated in Multi-purpose Community Centres (MPCCs). The AV centres will consist of a room housing a collection of African films provided by FRU, along with a video projector and mini-screening booths.

FRU Project Manager Desmond Mthembu says that one objective of the project is to encourage an interest in video production among community members (Mthembu 2005). The AV centres can eventually expand their capacity to offer video production facilities that will be accessible to people in the local community.

While FRU and GCIS are piloting the scheme, the centres will ultimately be handed over to local government ownership for long-term sustainability. FRU will remain engaged in the centres by providing content as well as mentorship and guidance to management personnel.

FRU also has a partnership with the Department of Arts and Culture (DAC) to organise film festivals on national holidays at community arts centres in Gauteng, Limpopo, Mpumalanga and the Free State. It is envisaged that this project too will eventually capacitate video production through training and access facilities. FRU intends to have an AV centre located in each province by the end of 2006.

FRU has already run a number of local film festivals on national holidays. The project is now into its market-development phase, which involves training NGOs in how to use African film as part of their community upliftment workshops.

The product-development phase entails channelling young would-be film makers through a video production learnership at Monash University. Four young people from each FRU project area are being trained to make videos about their own communities, which will reflect issues to the community through local screenings.

Mthembu says that FRU will be launching the AV centres from September 2005, with the intention of handing them over to local government by January 2006. The AV centres are intended to be self-sustaining through video sales, the hosting of local film events or workshops, and producing videos for government departments.

Community video producers making use of AV centres will need to find their own means of accessing cameras and video-editing facilities. They will receive six months of training at Monash University and another six months experience in the video industry. In return for this training, they must enter into an agreement with FRU to provide video production services to their own local communities. These community-based producers would be well positioned to contribute to CTV programming if the necessary equipment is available for their use.

FRU's vision for the future is to use computer networks as a distribution mechanism. The organisation launched a multimedia library in Johannesburg seven years ago that houses five Internet-linked computers and a collection of FRU videos. New video acquisitions from FRU are financed by local government library services.

According to Mthembu, FRU would consider buying and distributing well-made products from independent or community film makers. The organisation would sell these products through its distribution network and would pay royalties to the producers. FRU contracts generally give 70 per cent of the income to the film maker and retain 30 per cent for the organisation.

For the past two years, 40 per cent of FRU's income has been from sales and 60 per cent from donors. The organisation wishes to turn this around over the next three years, so that 80 per cent of its income is derived from commercial activities and 20 per cent is donor-funded. FRU was established in 1996 purely to distribute films that were banned by the apartheid government, but economic realities have forced it to move away from donor funding to a situation where the mainstay of support is from commercial activities.

FRU's mission is to create a market for independent African film makers. To this end, it sees a necessity for initiating African cinemas to fill the gap left by unsuccessful township cinemas of the past. The organisation's view is that there is also a need to develop audiences and to improve public appreciation of African films.

FRU sees its role with regard to CTV in terms of supplying African films for screening. Whether this material is provided to CTV broadcasters for free or at a nominal cost will depend on the nature of FRU's distribution agreements with the film makers. Mthembu says that FRU can also interact with CTV broadcasters at an advisory level for programming because the organisation knows and understands what local communities want.

Mindset Network

Mindset Network is an NGO that broadcasts educational and developmental material nationally through digital satellite transmission. The channel has been established with the help of corporate donors and international funders. It not only provides content but also infrastructure, facilitator training and educational supplements.

The broadcaster was established with principal support from the Liberty Life Foundation, the social responsibility arm of the Liberty Life insurance group. Mindset distributes content to schools, hospitals and clinics. It provides TV sets, VCRs, satellite dishes and decoders to these venues, which enables them to receive its content. It also trains schoolteachers in how to use its broadcast material and it has initiated interactive content that is accessed from servers based at the point of delivery.

Mindset produces much of its own content, which it desires to reach as wide an audience as possible and, hence, it has an interest in working with CTV. However, its material tends to be very targeted and selective in terms of treatment and delivery and is sometimes so specialised that it would not be suitable for wider public distribution.

Mindset produces high-school material for the Grade 10, 11 and 12 curricula through its Learn Channel. This material is very specific and it is likely that it will not be appropriate for broadcast to a general audience unless there is a specific learner programme slot, although the information technology (IT) content appeals to wider audiences than scholars alone.

The station also produces a Health Channel that is broadcast to clinics and hospitals. Some of this health content is very specific to healthcare professionals and would not be appropriate for general audiences. However, Mindset does have content for small, medium and micro enterprise (SMME) training and skills development that could be suitable for CTV. It is planning to develop programming on topics related to life skills for unemployed people, as well as higher-education material that could be used by CTV channels. In terms of language, all the high-school material is in English and the health material is in English, Afrikaans, isiXhosa, isiZulu and Sesotho.

Mindset mostly develops its own content for the Learn Channel, although some third-party material is used on occasion. Healthcare material is often sourced from third-party providers, and some SABC content is used in this regard. Mindset is also developing material for primary school curricula.

Mindset is trying to build up material on sustainable development, career development, and arts and culture. Some of this content is commissioned from outside producers such as the Cape Town Film School, where student groups each make two- to three-minute inserts that focus on careers in various industries. Copyright and licensing of such third-party material for CTV use is not likely to be a problem. Mindset obtains content from various sources; some of this is paid for, some is used for free and some is used on a once-off basis only.

Certain content is sponsored by big companies that would expect some exposure (e.g. through adverts or logo display) in return for the material being rebroadcast on a CTV channel. This does not entail 'high-level advertising' but rather takes the form of sponsorship messages. Some generic corporate adverts are flighted but these are not product-specific.

Material such as financial literacy is generic and not lesson-based. It is structured in a way that is both informative and entertaining. Health content uses aspects of soap operas to convey its message to general audiences and includes focused HIV and TB education. Programmes also focus on issues such as personal hygiene, nutrition and how to be a good parent.

The Learn Channel runs from 8.30 a.m. to 8.30 p.m. every Monday to Friday. This will be extended from August 2005, when some material will be broadcast on Saturday. The Health Channel runs from 8.30 a.m. to 4.30 p.m. every Monday to Friday. These hours could be extended if the station has more content; and this presents an opportunity for CTV broadcasters or associated producers to provide such material.

The Learn Channel has about 200 hours of content per month but runs a lot of repeats. Broadcasts are structured into blocks that make it easier for teachers to tape lessons as a coherent unit that they can then use at their discretion in their classes. New programmes are flighted in the afternoons, which also see an hour-long educator slot that presents teacher-related material. Mindset plans to broadcast interesting, non-curriculum material in the late afternoon and early evening. This would not be structured as lessons and could include items such as sport, another opportunity area for CTV to provide content.

Mindset's representatives said the network could consider adding a channel to its bouquet for CTV or it could provide its material to a CTV channel for repackaging. Mindset creates its content in digital segments that facilitate re-contextualising in other programmes.

Nevertheless, the production of curriculum-based educational material is a time-consuming process that entails numerous revisions and a professional cadre of production personnel. To produce a block of eight lessons takes about two months from script commissioning through the consultative scripting process to final production. The production process for non-curriculum material can be much shorter.

One option Mindset has floated for a CTV station is for the channel to use its production resources on a commercial basis. Mindset has its own content development process and has considerable experience in its particular realms of content development that can be tapped for other organisations. Mindset could run a workshop to teach others about the process, or it could take on interns to be trained. Mindset could also partner with CTV organisations to provide the technology platforms necessary to deliver content.

Mindset gets audience feedback for new content through running focus groups with both scholars and teachers. The organisation admits that it has not done sufficient research into its claimed target audience at rural schools but the response that it has elicited has been positive. Two main areas of concern have been programme pace and language level. Consequently, the pace of teaching has been slowed down and language level adjusted. Visual support for educational material is very useful and Mindset attempts to show the school subject material in the real environment.

In terms of providing content for CTV broadcasters, topics on health care and livelihood information offer the best potential. This material is produced as 'edutainment' aimed at a general audience and at addressing particular needs at community level. For example, motor-industry skills are broadcast to the Eastern Cape while agricultural and fishing skills are sent to other appropriate regions. More sponsors are needed to produce this type of content. Nutrition is another useful topic that has been introduced by means of a regionally based cooking programme that focuses on making good food quickly and cheaply.

Mindset has found that for educational purposes live broadcasting is limited because it has to be done at schools that do not have very good facilities. Teachers like to view the material before they use it in class. Consequently, Mindset is moving away from using the live broadcast option to delivering content on demand. This is an asynchronous solution that involves a datacast to servers at the point of access, providing multimedia content in the form of video, web pages and print. This content can be accessed through a computer or television set and is far more useful in an educational environment. The delivery mechanism has been enhanced for educational purposes with the addition of a keypad linked to the television set instead of a remote control.

The Learn Channel is currently viewed in 1 000 high schools and 1 200 primary schools around South Africa. At present, it only broadcasts high-school content but from August 2005 it will also broadcast primary-school content. Mindset is working with provincial education departments to develop region-specific content. The Learn Channel is also available on the DSTV bouquet, enabling anyone with a decoder to pick up the Learn Channel. The Health Channel is viewed in 110 clinics, of which 60 are in Gauteng and 50 are spread across the rest of the country.

Government Communication and Information System (GCIS)

GCIS is tasked with informing the people of South Africa about government programmes, resources and activities that affect their lives. To do this effectively, GCIS employs the services of the Directorate: Local Liaison and Communication, which promotes modes of development communication in order to provide communities with access to information about government projects in ways they can understand. The unit uses various mediums to inform citizens, including Braille, sign language, audio tapes and videos. Subject areas include literacy, women, youth, the previously disadvantaged, and rural communities.

The Directorate has two initiatives that impact on CTV. The first of these is a programme to install MPCCs in every district in the country. MPCCs commonly house at least six government departments, which enables citizens to obtain items such as death certificates, birth certificates, social grants and pensions. The MPCCs can house a variety of other services such as small businesses, NGOs, post offices and church groups. They can also accommodate education and training facilities such as computer labs, ABET classes and tele-centres that provide Internet and telephony access points.

The idea behind the MPCCs is to create a hub to bring government services closer to the people. The site is selected with accessibility in mind. Each MPCC has its own management structure, layout and facilities. Services are varied and are designed to meet local people's needs. The MPCC programme is part of the government's *Batho Pele* policy, and is managed by a national sectoral steering committee. The role of GCIS is to facilitate the programme.

The second initiative is to have a network of community-based communication officers (COs) in every district. These officials coordinate government communication on the ground by engaging in educational and awareness campaigns with NGOs and other stakeholders. This network is intended to identify community needs and to liaise with local leaders and community structures.

Most COs are based at MPCCs. They distribute material from government departments on matters like health and social development. For example, in Youth Month the COs would organise events relevant to the youth and distribute government information material relevant to the youth. GCIS has more than a hundred COs who conduct a minimum of two communications projects each month.

This development communications network presents a valuable opportunity for CTV to work together with GCIS to convey government information to community audiences, as well as to generate feedback to the administration from these communities. The Directorate is responsible for developing content for MPCC distribution in conjunction with various stakeholders and it works with COs to conduct campaigns, facilitating the interface with other government departments.

The Directorate is working with FRU on the MPCC project in using informative African films to educate people about issues relevant to governance. Jacobs (2005) says that people in the rural areas love films and that the project shows all types of African films that have deeper meanings, which can be elucidated through talks by relevant officials – for instance, someone from the Department of Justice could lead discussion about human rights and how to access government services in this regard.

GCIS does have a video unit that shoots footage at government events and which occasionally organises live broadcasts through the SABC. This unit could provide content for CTV broadcasters, and GCIS could build useful links with CTV along similar lines to its relationship with community radio.

Community media are high on the GCIS agenda, and it promotes small media through community radio stations and community newspapers. It also works with the MDDA to develop community media by linking them with the MDDA through its communication officers and by bringing local people to MDDA workshops. There is a special community radio unit in GCIS that markets small media to government departments and private companies wishing to reach community audiences.

GCIS has additional communications strategies that are significant for CTV. Through a partnership with the Umsobomvu Youth Fund, GCIS runs a 35-seater bus that travels the country to deliver life skills through an Internet-linked computer and video screenings. This could provide another outlet for CTV material to reach rural or outlying areas.

The organisation encourages communication initiatives at MPCCs, for example the Community Television Network (CTN), a commercially run project that supplies television set-VCR combinations to MPCCs. CTN screens monthly videos containing edutainment and commercial material along with information about government programmes.

The GCIS research section has established that target communities have a definite preference for radio as a means of obtaining government information. However, GCIS has a strong policy of promoting unmediated information, for instance through the imbizo process, where policy-makers can talk to the people in their constituencies and answer their questions. This presents another potential opportunity for CTV to plug into government communication channels by facilitating the imbizo process over AV media, which could include both broadcast and narrowcast media.

Although GCIS does not have its own financial resources to support community media, it does have facilities, people-power and a directorate called Content Development that collates content from various government departments for dissemination on community media.

In view of people's preference for radio as a means of obtaining information, it is no surprise that GCIS has a strong relationship with community radio. The body works with the National Community Radio Forum and uses community radio stations for live broadcasts at major events, such as Women's Day. It has a toll-free number for people to phone in with comments and queries and it runs interviews with politicians, leaders and policy-makers. GCIS has its own radio studio where it records interviews that are sent out to all the community radio stations. CDs containing interviews and other material are distributed to the stations, which also receive advertising from government departments that GCIS obtains through bulk-buying.

GCIS also has a news service called BuaNews, which is loaded onto its website and sent to the media on a daily basis. Community radio stations make fairly extensive use of that news. GCIS encourages creative methods of communication between the government and the people, and appears to be open to the idea of using CTV as an additional information channel.

Strategic partners

Media Development and Diversity Agency (MDDA)

The Media Development and Diversity Agency Act of 2002 established the MDDA to promote community and small commercial media. It is intended to promote the development of media that benefit historically disadvantaged communities, persons not adequately served by existing media and historically diminished indigenous language and cultural groups. In this context, media must encourage ownership, control, participation and access for these sectors, as well as developing their capacity to engage in these activities with reference to human resources, training and capacity building.

MDDA support for small media includes funding their development and research into their establishment and sustainability. CTV would be an obvious beneficiary for MDDA support in as far as it serves the above purposes.

The MDDA's Manager: Community Media Programme, Harry Letsebe, is of the opinion that CTV may not need to be set up in the same way that community radio stations have been established, with the government funding all the necessary facilities, because existing infrastructure could be used, such as that owned by the SABC (Letsebe 2005). He suggests that CTV could find windows on existing channels and provide programmes for these time slots.

Some CTV initiatives have requested funding from the MDDA for special event broadcasts, but the organisation has declined such funding because it feels that a special event licence does not establish media diversity on a sustainable or ongoing basis. Thus the MDDA has taken the decision to wait until CTV broadcasters are ready to apply for permanent licences before engaging in funding activities.

This stance is somewhat problematic for CTV because of the complex nature of television production – temporary broadcasts are necessary to build capacity in the sector in terms of mobilising resources, testing audience responses and increasing public awareness.

The MDDA's reluctance to engage with CTV on these terms is perhaps understandable in terms of national media development priorities that privilege radio and print media as being the most accessible and cost-effective for reaching mass audiences. Moreover, the organisation has a limited budget of under R20 million per annum to fund all media sectors, including research. Nevertheless, it has agreed to aid this particular CTV research project as a first step to further support for the sector.

From the MDDA's point of view, funding special event broadcasts is problematic because although they serve particular capacity-building functions, the MDDA is looking for sustainable, long-term projects that create the required diversity in the media landscape. However, evidence from the Greater Durban Television (GDTV) initiative shows that even a strictly volunteer effort can be sustained over the long term and that the MDDA's reluctance to support temporary broadcast initiatives is possibly overcautious. Moreover, in order to obtain a permanent licence, an applicant must demonstrate sufficient financial support. Without seed funding from bodies such as the MDDA, it will be difficult for CTV initiatives to obtain licences in the first place, which could then allow funders to decline support for their efforts based on the fact that they do not have a long-term licence.

Letsebe (2005) says that, in principle, the MDDA would like to support CTV; indeed, in terms of its regulatory mandate, it has an obligation to do so. In respect of funding and research, the MDDA is looking to relationships with like-minded bodies like the NFVF, the DAC and the DoC in order to identify the type of support that is needed by the CTV sector. At the same time, Letsebe maintains that it is the CTV sector's responsibility to identify the areas that require support, which indicates a need for the sector to organise itself and to engage with these backers.

The DoC has already established the National Electronic Media Institute of South Africa (NEMISA), which the MDDA believes can provide facilities and support to CTV initiatives. For this reason, the MDDA does not envisage setting up new facilities for CTV in Gauteng, but sees a CTV broadcaster negotiating an arrangement with NEMISA to provide space and facilities. NEMISA has indicated a willingness to engage with CTV initiatives in this capacity, but at this juncture would require an outside agency to initiate the process (Molema 2005). On the other hand, NEMISA does not appear to have a strong grasp of the nature of CTV broadcasting and may have unrealistic expectations of the sector's ability to attract funding equivalent to a commercial venture (Thafeng 2005).

Letsebe identifies content as a potential problem for CTV, as material is required to broadcast and there is an insufficiency of production capacity in disadvantaged areas. Consequently, in the process of establishing CTV, training programmes must be facilitated to equip people with the requisite skills to produce broadcast material.

The MDDA is developing a working relationship with the Universal Service Agency (USA) with the intention of setting up multimedia centres with video production facilities at MPCCs. These facilities would encourage people to get involved in the multimedia sector and could be used as launching pads for people to produce CTV programmes.

Another problem area is that CTV has limited reach as a development medium. Television's penetration into certain priority population segments is limited by factors such as geography (rural areas) and cost (the poor). While the MDDA might commit itself to providing some support to CTV broadcasters, it would not cover all the costs and would not be sustained over time. CTV will have to find its own sustainable financial solution.

The MDDA is prepared to provide support for CTV once the initial research phase is complete. When this has been accomplished, the organisation intends to convene a stakeholders' forum to help develop a framework for ongoing engagement. Letsebe acknowledges that this strategy was not followed with community radio or community print media, but says CTV is a new sector so there is a need for consultation to inform policy. A model of how the MDDA could support CTV requires some level of buy-in from the sector and from the MDDA board, and this in turn demands impetus from the CTV sector.

In order for CTV to gain government support, Letsebe notes that the government's sustainable development programme has identified 14 regional points that hold its development focus. ICASA's licensing priorities for community radio are now based on these points, which include urban renewal areas such as Alexandra, Inanda and KwaMashu.

If CTV can prove itself a viable means of communicating developmental messages in line with government objectives, similarly to community radio, it can win the support of the government. Community programming originating from the nodal development points could be screened by SABC-TV as well as by CTV during special event broadcasts.

Another problem for the MDDA has been the absence of formal CTV structures to liaise with. Now that there are structures establishing themselves as legal entities, it becomes much easier for the MDDA to liaise with them and support them.

Other support from the government for CTV is also a possibility. The DoC has a Broadcast Unit, which has provided R20 million for community radio, much of it to replace equipment at community radio stations. The MDDA's role is to 'fill in the gaps' in ensuring the relevant support for CTV.

Media Institute of Southern Africa (MISA)

MISA is a member-driven advocacy and training network with chapters in 11 Southern African Development Community (SADC) countries and a head office in Namibia. It has five programme areas in South Africa, which include media freedom, media monitoring, the campaign for broadcast diversity, access to information, media support activities and a largely dormant legal defence fund.

According to MISA-SA Director Rene Smith (2005), the organisation focuses mainly on advocacy, and its interest in CTV would fall under its campaign for broadcast diversity. MISA's long-term aim is to ensure the development of local media industries so that more voices may heard in an environment of media diversity and pluralism. To this end, MISA-SA has put a lot of effort into supporting CTV initiatives, following the impetus given to the sector by the 2004 ICASA CTV position paper.

MISA-SA attended the national CTV meeting in October 2004 to find out what was happening in the sector and what the way forward might be. It was asked to participate in some developmental areas, namely the advocacy and research groups. The organisation had also been approached by Independent World Television (IWT) to see whether it could be involved in the IWT initiative. A meeting was held with MISA-SA where a range of interested parties discussed the IWT project and its possible relation to CTV in South Africa. Because Smith is in charge of the broadcast diversity project, she felt she should find ways of merging the IWT initiative with the CTV project, believing that IWT could provide content for CTV and vice versa.

MISA-SA put energy into developing the Gauteng CTV consortium from late 2004 to early 2005 but made it clear that its role was limited to advocacy and lobbying and that it was not in a position to drive the process. The Gauteng consortium subsequently lapsed but MISA-SA has elected to continue its involvement in CTV through supporting research and advocacy strategies.

In MISA's view, CTV serves a positive function as part of the overall media landscape. The organisation's position with regard to regional television is that the issue of exclusive African language programming is problematic and that the money being invested in the regional broadcasts would be better spent on propping up public service television.

MISA has a strong focus on supporting public service broadcasting, following the SABC's television licence amendment process. The organisation believes that with proposals for increased African language content on the SABC 1 and SABC 2 television channels, the idea of regional television channels should be re-examined. However, Smith suggests that regional TV could provide windows for CTV and that at present the CTV sector does not have the capacity to broadcast on its own.

There is also a need for CTV to obtain a public mandate, because it has to demonstrate demand on the ground for its services in order to be licensed, as does community radio. There have not been any preliminary studies around what people want in terms of CTV, why they would want it and how it is different from public service television.

MISA's role in the development of CTV will continue to be through advocacy, lobbying and research. It played a key role in organising the October 2005 national CTV workshop which it co-hosted with the HSRC.

Southern Africa Communications for Development (SACOD)

SACOD is a network of film producers and distributors in the SADC region. It has a fluctuating member base of about 60 organisations from all SADC countries except Malawi, Mauritius and the Democratic Republic of Congo.

Director Tambudzai Madzimuri (2005) says the NGO works with its members around issues of training, advocacy, information and services. It informs members on issues such as film markets, festivals, funding, training and partnership opportunities, and encourages members to be in touch with each other outside of the forum.

To help members economically and to advance developmental communications, the organisation seeks alternative film and video distribution channels outside of the broadcast arena. African countries face challenges in terms of lack of film and video production infrastructure and limited audiences due to the absence of TVs in most homes. Consequently, one of SACOD's objectives is to bring socially relevant video content to people who do not otherwise have access to television. To do this, it uses mobile video units in Lesotho, Mozambique, Zambia and Zimbabwe, and it works with the FRU in South Africa.

African people have found other means to view videos. In Zimbabwe, they have viewing events where temporary structures are set up on which to screen films. In Mozambique and Zambia, they have video canteens in spaza shops, which are run off corporate sponsorship for indigenous language programmes. The Mozambican model focuses on African film, while in Zambia content is unregulated and videos are mainly Hollywood movies and pornography. These examples demonstrate modes of video access that are peculiar to Africa and that CTV can take note of where there is a need to reach audiences that otherwise have limited exposure to television.

SACOD's advocacy programme revolves around policy issues to ensure a sound environment for socially relevant video production. Advocacy is really the core of what the organisation does, and it engages with broadcasters to promote local content and social message films. It has partnerships with other industry organisations such as professional associations.

SACOD has a training programme to encourage skills development. The organisation runs country-specific training courses and, where possible, it uses its own members to conduct the courses (failing this, it identifies outside experts).

On the issue of CTV, SACOD's view is that video production is an expensive but effective way of communicating social development messages. CTV can fill a particular gap in the market in terms of conveying developmental messages, which fits in with SACOD's agenda. Furthermore, SACOD members use participatory communication methods in dealing with social development issues and they work with communities to compile productions that are relevant to community needs, an aim that aligns with CTV objectives.

CTV could be a resource for SACOD members to communicate with their communities. SACOD members would have a platform for distributing their material, while audiences could learn from the developmental material they produce. Communities can work with SACOD members to gain a voice through participatory communication. This would happen in a context where CTV is owned by the community and community members run the station, with professional SACOD producers backing up community production efforts.

Madzimuri believes that if CTV is done properly it can generate income by addressing developmental issues, although it faces challenges such as ensuring proficient management. SACOD questions whether CTV needs to be run on its own broadcast channel or whether it should find alternative means of content distribution.

SACOD sees its role as working with independent content providers. The organisation can bring existing productions to CTV broadcasters. Its members have expressed an interest and willingness to get involved and most of them run training courses or learnerships. SACOD could encourage its members to run courses for CTV initiatives on relevant issues. The organisation can also play a role in lobbying and engaging with various structures to ensure support for CTV.

National Electronic Media Institute of South Africa (NEMISA)

NEMISA is a tertiary educational institution specialising in multimedia production disciplines ranging from Internet to broadcast mediums. It was set up by the DoC with the aim of producing a new generation of black multimedia, film and video producers.

Acting-Director Stanley Molema (2005) says that NEMISA has been involved with community radio broadcasting. The institution has engaged in internal discussions on the issue of CTV but has had doubts about its viability in South Africa and has not taken the issue further. NEMISA takes the view that there is a skilled television industry in South Africa that is dominated by public television in the form of the SABC; hence, it focuses its efforts on training students to become professionals in the public service and commercial broadcasting arena.

While NEMISA welcomes initiatives to establish CTV, it believes there are several challenges to ensuring its viability. One such challenge is that the station will rely on the community for sustainability; for example, a CTV station in the Johannesburg metropolitan area would rely on the city government for its existence. Secondly, NEMISA believes that television is driven by advertising, to a large extent, and how CTV is funded will determine its nature as a commercial or local government sponsored entity.

NEMISA's interest in CTV would revolve around training people to participate in the broadcasting, and it would be prepared to provide content through the activities of its students. The institution's participation in CTV could involve collaboration with other training institutions and with independent producers.

In terms of support for CTV, NEMISA has the technical capacity to get involved in CTV broadcasting. Molema describes the institution as being 'almost like a television station in waiting', but NEMISA would want funding for a CTV broadcast.

NEMISA certainly has the all the facilities that would be required for broadcasting. It has a range of digital cameras and post-production facilities that include three digital non-linear edit suites and three analogue edit suites catering for formats that range from Betacam SP to digital video (DV). Non-linear editing is accomplished using the Avid, Avid Express and Adobe Premier software applications. Twenty PCs are available for other applications and a Nuendo audio lab takes care of any sound requirements. The institution has a microwave link to the Sentech transmitters on the Brixton tower.

Courses begin at entry level and continue for 18 months to provide 'a complete value chain of television production'. Specialist skills are not taught in great depth because the intention is for students to understand how the different areas of production affect one another. Course components include television scriptwriting, camerawork, studio production and audio elements. A total of 20 students make up an intake for the television course. The institution has capacity to accommodate more and intends expanding student numbers in the future, in addition to offering more specialist courses.

At the end of the course, student groups produce a seven-minute production that is used to assess their level of expertise.

Molema believes that a CTV initiative would be a good training platform for NEMISA students, because a live broadcasting situation would provide added motivation, differentiating the event from the simulated environment of the classroom. He adds that the trainees would not necessarily have to be NEMISA students, but could be from other training institutions; however, NEMISA would want to be the lead partner in such an arrangement.

NEMISA may be in a position to provide content in partnership with other institutions, independent producers and training providers. Still, some investment would be needed for the institution to support a CTV initiative. Molema says that the provincial or local government would need to be a partner and for that to be sustainable, the legislature would require broadcast exposure.

In view of the new opportunities that convergence provides for content distribution, NEMISA could be one of the leading institutions to test its capacity. The institution has ISDN (integrated services digital network) connectivity and has capacity for Internet-protocol streaming, particularly if partners such as Eskom could be induced to share their fibre-optic telecommunications infrastructure. Skilled people would be required to work for the station, and skills-transfer to students would have to be ensured.

Production facilities at NEMISA are currently in use only about 20 per cent of the time, but Molema stresses that use of the facilities would require income to cover costs as well as to make a profit for reinvestment.

South African Broadcasting Corporation (SABC)

South Africa's public broadcaster, the SABC, has spearheaded television development in this country. The broadcaster runs three television channels that have programming structured to reach separate national target audiences. The institution has recently applied for revised licensing conditions that will allow it to run two public service channels and one commercial channel.

The Corporation entered into an agreement with CTV representatives in the late 1990s to lend support to CTV initiatives. This declaration of intent, entitled SABC and Community Television: the Natural Partnership, was negotiated between the SABC and the Open Window Network (OWN). Since then the broadcaster has given strong support to the GDTV initiative in Durban by providing studio space and equipment free of charge for GDTV special event broadcasts.

Apart from this agreement, the SABC does not have any policy in place regarding relations with the CTV sector, according to Head of Regulatory Affairs Lara Kantor (2005). It would consequently wait to be approached by CTV broadcasters rather than initiating contact itself. The SABC would nevertheless stand by the goodwill expressed in the declaration; it would be a matter of exploring what form of partnership is expected and how it could practically come about.

The SABC recently reorganised its business and commissioning processes. Instead of each channel commissioning its own programming, the Corporation has formed a unit known as the Content Hub where all commissioning has been centralised. There is now but one head of genre in each department (i.e. drama, education and factual) and each of these chiefs has the services of commissioning editors. The rationale behind this is to achieve operational efficiencies and a seamless approach to content development across SABC channels. The Content Hub is now responsible for relationships with the production industry.

The SABC is at a point where its content delivery is being driven in particular directions because of the amendments to its television broadcasting licences. ICASA has proposed draft licence conditions that include significantly increased levels of factual programming and African language programming. These licence conditions are additional impositions on anything the Corporation does in terms of regional broadcasting (i.e. the proposed regional channels).

The SABC has replied to ICASA's position by declaring that an 80 per cent Nguni-language quota for SABC 1 is unreasonable and perpetuates apartheid language divides. The SABC adopts a multilingual approach to its editorial policy for a number of reasons, including nation building. If it implements an 80 per cent Nguni quota on SABC 1, together with an 80 per cent Sesotho and Afrikaans programming quota for SABC 2, it would only have about six hours per day of English programming on these channels, measured over a 24-hour period.

The SABC's counter-proposal entails an incremental approach to increasing indigenous language content to the point where it would reach a maximum of 65 per cent African languages in prime time on SABC 1 and 35 per cent on SABC 2. The Corporation is hopeful that ICASA will accept this proposal, which already places a significant burden on the broadcaster to source African language programming. Nevertheless, Kantor believes that increased local content will expand opportunities for content producers.

The issue of regional broadcasting is another driver of SABC policy and development. ICASA has agreed to grant licences for the regional, language-driven SABC 4 and SABC 5 channels, but this has been suspended until the Corporation finds sufficient funding to set up the channels. According to the regulations, the onus is on the state to fund the channels, and the state has made no provision for this yet.

If state funding is forthcoming and the channels are established, they will comprise of regionally focused, African-language programming, including Afrikaans. The SABC has committed itself to begin with daily four-hour broadcasts, building up to an eight-hour window in the fifth year of operations. The regional channels are to be set up to cater exclusively to indigenous language groups despite the fact that ICASA has now substantially increased the African-language quotas for the SABC's two public service channels.

The SABC sees the channels not only as a conduit for African languages but also as a means to reflect regional issues in a way that national channels cannot. Content will include regional sports, news and 'a much more grassroots, developmental approach to programming'.

The challenge faced by the SABC in this regard is that there is not much African-language programming available – not many of the current generation of directors are fluent in African languages and the Corporation foresees many practical problems in fulfilling the heavy African-language quotas demanded by the regulator. Moreover, the ban on English content will inhibit the channels' ability to communicate regional issues to all citizens, and large English-language groupings will be left out in this regard.

To fulfil its new licence conditions, the public service broadcaster must increase the amount of African-language and factual-content programmes. ICASA wanted to impose a stringent documentary quota of seven hours a week. While the SABC has a long-term strategy for growing audience interest in the documentary genre, it told ICASA that it could achieve no more than four hours of documentary a week over the next eight years.

The SABC estimates that the regional channels would require R200 million per channel per year to run. Once government funding is received and the licences granted, it would take the SABC another 12 months to develop the channels' infrastructure sufficiently to begin broadcasting. The bulk of regional channel content would be produced by independent producers, with news, actuality and some sport programmes being produced by the SABC.

The government initially wanted public-private partnerships to raise the regional channels' funding, but the broadcaster is sceptical of this idea because most of the content would be outsourced, so a private partner would not see any particular benefits from its involvement. Consequently, the SABC is of the view that development is best left up to the broadcaster itself, supported by state funding and advertising revenue. The fact that ICASA has now allowed the channels to receive advertising revenue is a little surprising, given its previous opposition on the grounds that this would further fragment the television advertising market to the detriment of the other players and entrench the SABC's market dominance.

Nevertheless, the SABC believes that the regional channels will not significantly increase its commercial income opportunities; instead, the channels represent an opportunity to extend its reach in a way that has not been done before. While it is hoped that the channels will draw audiences, it is expected that these audiences, falling mainly within the lower Living Standards Measures (LSMs), will not be very attractive to advertisers.

The SABC recognises the need to develop the capacity of previously disadvantaged groups in the independent production sector. The Corporation has been criticised in the past with regard to its relationships with the independent production sector, and it is focusing on improving this interaction in terms of empowerment, parity and development schemes.

The broadcaster intends to begin implementing the new African-language quotas from 2006. It will be issuing its commissioning briefs at the Sithengi Film Market in September 2005. In terms of local-content regulations, the SABC is given incentives to invest in particular kinds of programming that count towards its local-content quota. Incentivised programming includes arts, drama and programmes produced outside of Gauteng, the Western Cape and KwaZulu-Natal.

The SABC's counter-proposals for language quotas include making additional contributions (of about 10 per cent) to African-language programming on its commercial channel, SABC 3. The broadcaster suggested that African-language content be measured particularly over prime time.

Implementing increased African-language programming will be expensive for the SABC. If ICASA's proposed quotas are implemented, it will cost the SABC R1.3 billion in the first year, while advertising revenues would decline by about 20 per cent. This figure is arrived at by calculating the costs of cancelling existing programme contracts and increasing investment in independent productions. With the present plans in place, a slight revenue decline is envisaged and the SABC is of the opinion that the way in which it will introduce African-language content will elicit a positive audience response.

ICASA did not propose quotas for the marginalised African languages but the SABC is prepared to submit itself to a quota for marginalised languages in prime time. A major driver for the regional channels is that the SABC cannot deliver all 11 languages in prime time, although it will be increasing marginalised language delivery on its national channels.

The mainstay of African-language programming will be original South African content. The SABC has found that audiences do not respond well to dubbed entertainment, so only some children's and educational programming will be dubbed.

In terms of direct support for CTV, the SABC intends adopting a wait-and-see policy. It will respond to applications for support from community broadcasters and, if there is a need, it will appoint someone in the organisation to deal with these requests. Kantor suggests that CTV broadcasters should approach local SABC offices with requests for support in order to avoid overly bureaucratised procedures.

The public broadcaster is looking at the possibility of forming an SABC foundation that would coordinate its social responsibility programme. The concept has been approved in principle by the board and will probably be set up within the next two years. This body could then act as an interface with CTV.

The SABC's current direction represents both opportunities and threats to the CTV sector. The Corporation's increased African-language and factual programming requirements can provide opportunities for community-based producers and production collectives to create content. This will provide a boost to the independent production sector in general, with particular benefits for black producers.

The SABC's regional channels could offer opportunities for CTV by providing windows for CTV broadcasters, instead of CTV using its own broadcast frequencies with the attendant cost implications. However, the ICASA ban on English content for the regional channels would limit CTV's potential to become involved through contributions or 'windows' in their programming in terms of providing English content.

Where CTV broadcasters attempt to strike out on their own with a dedicated frequency channel, the regional stations will present significant competition for funding and content. The channels will attempt to attract viewers with indigenous language programming that addresses local and developmental issues. The requirements of producing such programming will draw in producers who might otherwise provide content for CTV, and those who gain training and experience through CTV activities could be lured away by the increased professional opportunities available through the regional channels.

The SABC stations will also be hungry for advertising revenue and will present attractive options for advertisers (including the government and NGOs) aiming at market segments in the lower LSMs, which CTV will also be targeting. Consequently, CTV will have to secure local advertisers with smaller budgets who cannot afford to access the regional channels, or offer more innovative and cost-effective packages for reaching local audiences. However, this will lower the amount of income that CTV will be able to derive from commercial, government and NGO funding.

Training partners

Monash University

Monash University is a private, Australian-owned tertiary education institution. One of its departments is the Film & TV Unit run by industry professionals Dr Melanie Chait and Nikki Tilley. Monash runs professional development courses for the film and television industries as well as entry-level video production learnerships. The Film & TV Unit aims to challenge stereotypes by being innovative, experimental and 'thinking out of the box'.

All positions on the learnership and other courses are sponsored by bodies like the Media, Advertising, Publishing, Printing and Packaging (MAPP) SETA, the NFVF and the DAC. Monash University also subsidises the Unit. Dr Chait claims it is very difficult to do this kind of training on government funding alone. The SETA provides funds for only one year; just the entry-level courses are supported in this way, and last year the SETA funding was cut by a third. The Unit also runs video courses for other institutions such as Defence TV and M-Net.

The Film & TV Unit emphasises training in developing interesting, challenging and creative television content. Students are afforded an overall understanding of the broadcast landscape. Courses are run at various levels ranging from entry to intermediate and advanced. The course duration can be from five days to ten months and are intensive, accelerated, full-time courses involving hands-on training. The entry-level course is six months in duration and once students have completed this phase the institution attempts to find them places in professional production activities on either a full- or part-time basis.

The Unit monitors students doing their internships, as well as ex-students, by phoning them every month to ascertain what their mentoring needs are and what shortcomings they are experiencing. When interns are between freelance jobs they can use equipment from the Unit for their own projects. These post-course students can hire the equipment for a nominal fee if they have a budget to make the video, otherwise the unit sponsors equipment for those wanting to develop their showreels. These individuals can access the Film & TV Unit's five PD 150 cameras, three high-definition (HD) cameras, three HD G5 edit suites and ten Apple Mac G4 digital editing platforms. Camera kits include lights, tripods, sound kits and gaffer bags.

Chait and Tilley (2005) suggest that the best route for CTV is to use windows of one or two hours a day on existing or regional SABC channels, which would be cheaper than setting up infrastructure. They point out that broadcast infrastructure requires enormous resources and skills, especially in management and financial management. They believe that there is no shortage of content that can be provided by film makers and that the essence of CTV is to ensure sufficient capital and skills to sustain the project. According to this view, CTV management staff should be differentiated from film makers and there should not be an overlap between these disparate groups. Moreover, those involved should be paid in order to ensure the sustainability of the project.

The Monash learnerships are an opportunity for community video producers to obtain a high standard of training in a relatively short time. Learners can enter into agreements with sponsors to do video work in and for their communities on completion of the course and internship period, and so would be well positioned to participate in CTV broadcasts and to provide content for CTV.

The disadvantage of the Monash course is that it emphasises training for the industry rather than the human rights and non-professional aspects of CTV. The Monash trainers are suspicious of CTV, because they feel that training requires an intensive, full-time commitment that is incompatible with the demands of broadcasting. They also believe that video production is a specialised discipline that is substantially different from the activities involved in running a broadcast channel; consequently, their trainees would be better positioned to produce content rather than manage a broadcast.

Community Video Education Trust (CVET)

CVET is a training and capacity-building organisation based in Cape Town. It is presently in a 'transitional stage' (McAskill 2005) with its operations being run by its board members assisted by an independent consultant. The organisation intends to run an entry-level production training programme that covers the knowledge areas required for a basic level of video production. The aim of CVET is to provide a learning environment that affords people an opportunity to learn basic techniques, implement theory and try out their own ideas. It also wishes to provide low-cost visual-literacy programmes for people from disadvantaged communities and for those engaged in community development.

CVET focuses its efforts on training but occasionally supports independent production initiatives; however, production activities sometimes put a strain on its resources, which causes internal conflict over continued support for this type of engagement.

Instead, CVET aims to bridge the gap between those who wish to obtain basic video skills and the training and equipment necessary for this purpose. It can provide opportunities for people to make videos in order to gain experience but does not allow general access to its resources. CVET aims to partner with other organisations for production purposes and has considered supporting the Bush TV initiative at the University of the Western Cape as well as the possibility of establishing a video access centre.

CVET sees its association with CTV in terms of building capacity for previously disadvantaged film makers. The organisation could support CTV by taking CTV material in physical form to communities at libraries, schools and organisations.

Arts and Media Access Centre (AMAC)

AMAC is a Cape Town-based organisation that provides training to NGOs. It has several programmes that could by synchronised with CTV training. AMAC's high-school media programme could use CTV as an outlet for video clubs at schools producing content for children's programming. The video clubs currently produce short, five-minute 'video diary' pieces, but once participants have been through a full training programme they could produce youth actuality programmes.

At present, AMAC has five media clubs consisting of ten students each. These clubs have trained 50 teenagers who have gone through two weeks of basic training. For CTV purposes, the training programme would have to be shaped in order to produce a youth magazine programme for television, which would entail youth identifying issues of concern to them in their communities.

The journalism programme functions as a MAPP SETA-accredited learnership for unemployed youth and school leavers. It currently focuses on print journalism but wants to add a video and a broadcast-journalism component. AMAC students publish the *Just Youth* newspaper, and could be positioned as news journalists for a CTV station.

AMAC is interested in providing a news service for a Cape Town CTV station. It is examining the community video access centre (C-VAC) model, where community news-gathering units utilise video access facilities to produce news programmes. The organisation has a training programme and a fully functioning newsroom that can be utilised for this purpose, as well as a news agency (African Eye News Services) through which it sells articles produced by learners to mainstream media around southern Africa.

The organisation is also open to the idea of drastically transforming its community journalism programme to become a full-time print and broadcast news service, which could be utilised for part of a CTV channel's news requirements; alternatively, it could provide the entire news service for the channel. The organisation's news training programme will be accredited through the National Qualifications Framework as a level-four programme and could be run as a skills-development programme through the MAPP SETA.

AMAC has adopted an operational approach that synergises with the activities of other organisations; for instance, both the schools programme and the learner programme recruit people who are already involved in community organisations such as school clubs or community groups and NGOs. This strategy positions AMAC to interact with a CTV channel in a manner that draws on strong organisation-based links within the wider community.

AMAC's drama and performing arts programme is in the process of becoming a two-year learnership. The second year is on a practical level, during which students produce dramas written by young people. A scriptwriting course will be introduced in 2006 and the programme intends to produce youth-oriented drama such as a youth soap opera or drama series. These programmes would be written, performed and videoed by young people participating in the AMAC learnership programme. The organisation wishes to develop skills in studio productions, and to develop a methodology for shooting community theatre on video.

AMAC also has an NGO media programme that provides media training to non-profit organisations. This training programme consists of short courses for NGOs and includes print and AV media production. The AMAC art, crafts and design programme is inviting experts in television graphics to talk to learners about the field and to inform them on what technologies and skills are required.

The organisation also functions as a video access centre for NGOs. It intends offering a short course in video production specifically for NGOs and activist groups, providing skills training for those who will use them outside the ambit of the professional video production industry.

AMAC is a strong proponent of CTV and is looking at positioning all its programmes in relation to CTV, which it sees as a major opportunity to combine its community training programmes with real production activities. The organisation has a sound base of video facilities including cameras, lights, tripods, microphones and video editing platforms.

Despite its strength in facilities, programmes and training ability, AMAC wants to prevent competition and duplication in terms of the services that it offers; consequently, it is willing to relinquish specific training or production areas to other organisations that wish to occupy these spaces.

National Film and Video Foundation (NFVF)

The NFVF was set up by the government to support the development of the film and video industries in South Africa. According to the NFVF's Dimitri Martinis (2005), the organisation is currently funding an industry census to survey activity within the film and video production sector together with the provincial film offices. The objective is to determine baseline information for setting sector targets in terms of a transformation charter, information that can be of use to CTV initiatives and which should also include them as part of the overall production landscape.

Martinis observes that the NFVF is 'delighted to see CTV becoming a reality' and believes that it is very important to have as many state initiatives supporting it as possible now that the policy framework is in place.

In terms of how the NFVF could become involved in developing CTV in South Africa, Martinis points out that the organisation's mandate is quite specific in terms of the areas it is permitted to fund. The organisation needs to develop a position paper on CTV, which must then be approved by its council before it can adopt an approach that is specific to CTV's needs.

The NFVF currently has four funding areas. The first of these focuses on script development. There is a special focus on attracting scripts in the nine African languages, in other words excluding English and Afrikaans. CTV scriptwriters could then apply for funding from the NFVF to develop scripts for broadcast. Funding decisions are only made by NFVF council members, not staff. The scripts are first recommended by a peer-review system of industry experts. Those that pass scrutiny are then referred to a script editor and recommended for development funding.

The second area of NFVF activity is a production fund for feature films, short films, documentaries and animation projects. Producers in these genres can access the NFVF fund to gain finance for a pilot programme. The NFVF's mandate is primarily to develop film, so television series are not considered for production funding. Because CTV could be an outlet for programmes, producers wishing to create material either specifically for CTV or that can be sold to other broadcasters could apply for this kind of support.

The third funding area is the marketing and distribution of film or video products. Funding is granted when a film is invited to a competition or film market, and usually covers the cost of the director and producer attending the event. The idea behind this is to encourage film makers to leverage the hype at the event to arrange distribution deals. Sometimes the NFVF also pays for the lead cast members to go to such events in order to promote South African stars and film makers.

People may also apply to this fund to attend film markets and film festivals, even if their film has not been accepted in the competition. The NFVF works closely with the Department of

Trade and Industry, which has an export marketing incentive assistance (EMIA) fund. This fund pays 80 per cent of the film maker's travel and accommodation costs.

The fourth NFVF funding area is training, which falls under the Department of Human Capital Development. There are two types of funding here – bursaries and a scholarship fund (the Lionel Ngakane Fund). The NFVF pays course fees to the bursary holders rather than supporting the training organisations directly. There are exceptions to this rule, however, and the NFVF does support the Audio-Visual Entrepreneurs of Africa (AVEA) centre. There are two programmes running at the centre, the Sediba (Sesotho for 'fountain') programme for script development and the AVEA producers' programme. There is also the Kevin Harris Fund that supports entrepreneurship training for emerging film makers.

The NFVF also compiles skills development programmes like the MultiChoice Vuka awards, a joint venture with the Department of Labour and Create SA to train learners to enter the film industry. The role of the NFVF is to ensure that the skills development programme meets the needs of the film industry.

All of the above training initiatives can be of use to CTV in producing trained personnel who can gain further experience either by working on CTV broadcasts or by producing content. A stronger relationship can be built between the CTV sector and the NFVF as the former gains organisational strength over time.

Martinis suggests research into the MAPP SETA funding arrangements to get a sense of how the skills development levy is being used. This levy can be used to generate opportunities for full-time staff at CTV stations and for freelancers. Most people in the film and video sector are freelancers who never get the benefits of the fund, but that is where it is most needed. The Information Systems, Electronics and Telecommunications Technologies (ISET) SETA, which deals with the IT industry, could also be a source of funding for CTV training and skills development.

In terms of the NFVF's founding legislation, one of the things it is instructed to do is to commission a feasibility study into launching a national film school. The legislation was enacted in 1996, before the implementation of the national skills development strategy. Now the NFVF is developing a strategy for film training in South Africa in conjunction with the government. This strategy was jointly developed by the NFVF and the Departments of Communication, Labour, Education, Trade and Industry and Arts and Culture.

In the absence of a national film training strategy, the NFVF is working closely with the MAPP SETA, which has to publish a sector skills plan (including film and video) once a year. The sector skills plan is developed by all who pay a levy. It takes into account the types of employee that are needed in an industry sector and their consequent career development paths. In areas of skills scarcity, the SETA uses money from its discretionary fund to either create a training programme or find accredited training providers that can offer training to redress the problem.

At present, the SABC draws about 70 per cent of the money from the film and electronic media sector fund. Possibly CTV could have representation on the MAPP SETA as a special interest group and so receive funding from this same fund to establish training facilities.

The NFVF bursaries are freely available to all who qualify and who are registered at a film school. The idea of training covers a wide array of activities, although commercial advertising is specifically excluded; otherwise, funding is available for any aspect of motion picture production as long as it includes a training function.

Certain institutions accredited by the NFVF as film schools are funded. Purely advertising studies are excluded. There are between 15 and 20 NFVF bursary holders at Tshwane University of Technology, Wits TV, the South African School of Motion Picture Medium and Live Performance (AFDA), City Varsity, Boston College, the Cape Film School and Monash University.

Martinis believes that a CTV station would probably not be accredited by the NFVF as a training institution. Such organisations have to prove that they are capable of training, have qualified trainers, the necessary equipment, facilities and so on.

The NFVF is not a funding institution, but its mandate is to develop the film and television sector and it has money to do this. Where a need is identified by the industry, it has to respond to it. The NFVF has a total budget of R26 million a year, 75 per cent of which goes into the four areas identified above and 25 per cent into administration. The organisation has great potential to be a strategic ally of CTV as the sector develops.

CHAPTER 6

Signal distribution

In order for viewers to receive a television signal, it must be transmitted from its point of origination at the station to the viewer's television set. There are two stages in this process; firstly, to get the signal from the station to transmitter sites and, secondly, from the transmitters to the receivers. In addition, there are two types of technology used in signal distribution, analogue and digital, and two licensed signal carriers to provide these services, the parastatal Sentech and the privately owned Orbicom.

Television transmission in South Africa is mainly based on analogue technology, using land-based transmitter installations – a methodology known as terrestrial broadcasting. The national terrestrial broadcasting infrastructure is owned by Sentech, which provides the signals for the SABC channels and for eTV. Orbicom provides signal distribution through digital satellite technology, chiefly for MultiChoice Africa.

A means of getting the programme broadcast to the transmitter is required and here one could consider a microwave link or a telephone line link. A problem that has cropped up for CTV broadcasters is that the SABC has changed its signal distribution methodology; instead of delivering broadcasts to local transmitter sites from regional production hubs, now all SABC content is sent from the regions to Johannesburg, from whence it is delivered to terrestrial transmitters via digital satellite transmission. This means that the SABC no longer has the infrastructure in place to deliver local broadcasts from its local production facilities.

The economics of broadcasting boil down to cost versus coverage. In commercial television terms, this translates into cost per head; in other words, the fewest transmitters covering the largest possible area. CTV broadcasters will have to figure out the economics of their particular target coverage area in terms of the number and cost of transmitters relative to their potential income.

Sentech

Broadcast planning

Sentech is the main signal carrier for television and radio in South Africa, a position that sets it in a good strategic position to partner with CTV broadcasters. The first step that a would-be broadcaster has to take is to establish the signal coverage area that can be provided, based on existing transmitter sites and the power of the transmitter that will be needed for the signal to reach viewers in this area.

Sentech's initial task with regard to broadcast planning is to ascertain which areas the broadcast would cover. This entails a process of reverse engineering where the target coverage area is identified and Sentech's planning department then uses the necessary models to determine what coverage is attainable in terms of Sentech's existing 220 transmitting facilities across South Africa. Once the coverage area has been identified, the planning department would determine what strength of output power is needed and from what transmitter. The CTV broadcaster would then use this information to apply to the Independent Communications Authority of South Africa (ICASA) for a frequency allocation, carrier characteristics and a licence.

Sentech prepares the technical parameters for the licence application on behalf of the broadcast licence applicant and would advise the latter on which frequency should be used. Once a CTV broadcaster has obtained its licence from ICASA and the technical parameters from Sentech's planning department, Sentech would then enter into a broadcasting contract. There are two types of contract, depending on whether the licence is a long-term or a temporary (or special event) licence.

In the case of a special event licence, Sentech requires an installation fee because it does not have the opportunity to recover installation costs in the long term. Should the licence be for one year or longer there is no installation cost. The monthly rental fee covers maintenance costs, and Sentech guarantees 99.5 per cent on-air availability. Should this uptime not be attained, the broadcaster would get a tariff rebate. The monthly fee also covers the use of equipment, electricity, stand-by maintenance personnel and broadcast monitoring.

Although short-term special event licences pose a problem for Sentech because of the difficulty in recouping costs, Greater Durban TV (GDTV) was the exception to this rule because Sentech had equipment available that was deployed for GDTV's special event broadcasts. Sentech does not usually have spare transmitters on account of the large capital cost involved, which could inhibit the ability to conduct temporary event CTV broadcasts.

However, since Sentech is continuously in the process of servicing its equipment, it is possible that it would have equipment available for such transmissions. Permanent licensees must bear in mind that Sentech purchases transmitters from other countries, so permanent broadcast applications require three to four months lead time to implement. It is necessary for broadcasters to get requests for transmission capacity in early so that the service provider can advise as to what equipment it has available.

After the service is on air, Sentech provides the broadcaster with a coverage map that delineates coverage areas that are ascertained by measuring reception. Sentech can also provide demographic information about how many people are covered and in which population groups they fall.

The broadcaster must assess key target markets to be reached so that the appropriate transmitter parameters can be identified to provide the requisite coverage. The smaller the area, the cheaper the transmission costs. Smaller coverage areas receive lower tariffs, and transmitter power can sink to as low as one watt. For instance, Sentech has a one-watt installation in Amanda Glen in the Western Cape that is rented for R4 600 a month, but it covers a very small area. Low-power transmitters can be set up on existing structures such as water towers. Sentech has even rigged up a 100-milliwatt transmitter in a rugby stadium. Better cost efficiencies can be gained at the small scale by co-locating a studio with the transmitter.

Broadcast frequencies

There are two frequency bands that are used for television broadcasting – very high frequency (VHF) and ultra-high frequency (UHF). Because UHF frequencies are higher than VHF, they require a greater power input to generate adequate signal strength and also impose line-of-sight restrictions. Consequently, UHF transmission should be over-engineered in terms of television signal strength to ensure that viewers receive it.

UHF is the frequency band 475–850 MHz, VHF is 175–240 MHz and FM is 87–108 MHz. The lower the frequency, the longer the signal path; for example, if a 1 kW transmitter is used on each of the FM, UHF and VHF frequencies, UHF would be the shortest wavelength, VHF next in length and FM the longest. UHF is the only available frequency band for CTV and, within this spectrum area, there are currently 13 frequencies available but they can cause interference if they are too close together. There are guard bands in-between the different television channels to prevent interference between broadcast channels, and this conservative bandwidth allocation exacerbates frequency scarcity.

In order to receive the broadcast signal, viewers must have an aerial type that is appropriate for receiving the required signal frequency. For UHF reception, those who are able to view M-Net terrestrial and eTV broadcasts already have the necessary aerials. Sentech also staggers its broadcast in the given bands. UHF requires double the power of VHF in order to achieve the same coverage, and this is particularly true in the higher end of the UHF spectrum. The UHF signal is split into two, and this is why the cross bars on fixed TV aerials are closer together to receive UHF frequencies.

Sentech's DTM (Digitised Topographical Map) facility has a digitised representation of the whole country and can calculate transmission reach to within two metres. The higher the frequency, the smaller the area covered; thus, it is necessary to know exactly what obstacles stand in the way of signal reception when siting a station. The DTM shows only guaranteed coverage in terms of Grade A and Grade B coverage areas. The signal does not stop after Grade B, but the service is degraded from there on.

Satellite transmissions can cover the whole country with one frequency, but audiences then need satellite dishes and decoders to receive it. The nature of the transmission medium is determined by the broadcaster's target audience. Satellite costs stand at R111 000 per month to cover the whole of South Africa and its neighbours with the PAS 7 satellite. Sentech currently runs a satellite-based system for business television.

In rural areas, self-help stations use low-power transmitters of between one and two watts, covering up to two kilometres, to rebroadcast the SABC channels for small communities outside the range of Sentech's terrestrial analogue transmissions. There are about 500 of these community stations that have their own transmitters. Sentech does not guarantee the quality of signal received by viewers and does not guarantee service for these transmitters. The service provider makes sure that these subcontractors stick to the frequencies supplied by ICASA and it compiles the licence applications on their behalf without profiting from that service.

The picture regarding Sentech's level of service commitment changes with a station that is reliant on signal availability. Sentech has built-in redundancy so that if one transmitter fails another is available, with generators providing standby power. The company's tariffs might seem expensive, but they ensure 24/7 availability. A broadcaster can apply to ICASA to have its own transmitter. This can be installed by Sentech or by other private operators or it can be self-installed, provided that the installation and transmission conform to certain standards. However, technical back-up and know-how are essential to maintain a constant service. When Sentech owns the equipment, it takes on the risk; if the transmitter is disabled, Sentech will replace it with no knock-on effect for the broadcaster.

Digital versus analogue broadcasting

The difference between analogue and digital terrestrial transmission (DTT) is that an analogue transmitter can only broadcast one channel per frequency, whereas a digital transmitter can broadcast up to eight channels simultaneously on the same frequency.

Analogue also suffers a disadvantage in that the same frequency cannot be reused within an radius of 300–500 km, specifically with high-power transmitters of 10–20 kW. Sentech's tariff will be cheaper with digital transmission because more channels will use the same transmitter, so spreading the cost.

Sentech is engaging actively with the government on digitisation, which is a worldwide trend forcing analogue transmission into obsolescence. When digital terrestrial broadcasting will come into play in South Africa hinges on government policy. The 2010 soccer World Cup is influencing developments in this sphere, because there are certain expectations on broadcasters to cater for multiple-channel coverage. With the 2010 event in mind, the government has extended funds to the SABC to upgrade its digital infrastructure.

A problem with digital broadcasting is that viewers need a set-top box to decode the signal. Set-top boxes cost between $60 and $80 in Europe, a price that has gone down from the $200 mark a year ago. As demand increases worldwide, the prices will be driven down further.

The process of switching from analogue to digital transmission is another problem that has to be considered. In Germany, analogue TV broadcasts were switched off entirely two weeks after digital transmission came into effect. On the other hand, the United Kingdom decided to run analogue and digital broadcasts concurrently for ten years. Here in South Africa, the Department of Communications (DoC) will have to determine what will be most suitable for the local scenario.

Digital broadcasting cuts down on a broadcaster's monthly costs; in addition, value-added services can be introduced such as Digital Video Broadcast Hand-held (DVB/H), a combination of traditional broadcast and data broadcast to cellphones, which assumes that viewers have access to cellphones that can receive the broadcast signal. This reception could be of another channel produced by the same broadcaster and repackaged accordingly. Digital transmission relaxes the constraint of analogue in terms of the number of broadcasters that can access the airwaves. Sentech is instituting two multiplexes at each transmission site that will combine transmission signals to enable up to 16 broadcast channels.

It is possible to encrypt the digital signal, which would allow only a specific subset of people to see the information. Sentech can roll out two digital channels in the future without affecting the frequency plan, and expects DTT to achieve significant penetration within a two-to-three-year window.

Orbicom

Orbicom is a signal distribution company for a small group of clients, with its primary customer being MultiChoice. Orbicom is part of the MTN group and is currently being sold back to MultiChoice. It has 165 analogue transmitters in southern Africa and is used by M-Net in conjunction with Sentech to distribute M-Net's analogue signal around South Africa.

The company brings in satellite channels from overseas and transmits them in Africa. It has satellite earth stations transmitting signals to PanAmSat's PAS7 and PAS10 satellites. It also has a satellite earth station in Cape Town that broadcasts the parliamentary channel. Orbicom also provides satellite signals to many smaller towns that have their own local transmitters. The bigger sites are called professional sites because they have higher-powered transmitters.

Orbicom believes that digital broadcasting is the best way of creating a 'future-proof' technology platform. However, one problem is that viewers require a decoder, although set-top boxes can be bypassed with a converter.

Satellite distribution has the advantage of national availability; on the other hand, it is relatively costly to use and digital transmitters are far more expensive than their analogue counterparts. Moreover, location plays a role. For instance, if content is produced in Cape Town, it has to be sent to the satellite uplink facility in Johannesburg and to do this using an electronic network is expensive. It used to cost R300 000 a month to get the parliamentary coverage up to Johannesburg.

The Mindset Network broadcast is part of Orbicom's corporate social investment programme. Orbicom uplinks the Mindset service to PanAmSat using bandwidth sponsored by the satellite's owners. Mindset's Health and Learn Channels are sent to Sentech via this satellite for redistribution via another satellite.

From a signal distribution perspective, digital terrestrial networks offer an optimum medium because of the advantage of spectrum efficiency where up to eight channels can be carried on a single frequency. Orbicom has launched a digital terrestrial broadcasting site in Windhoek, Namibia. This is the first commercial digital terrestrial site for MultiChoice and it runs six subscription channels (instead of just one) on one frequency. Electronic programme guides provide viewers with broadcast schedules and the channels are received on the viewer's set-top box.

Analogue and low-power transmission options

In Orbicom's view, analogue transmission technology is becoming outdated but still has many advantages. For one thing, analogue equipment is much more cost-effective than digital. This means that a broadcaster does not need large-scale coverage in order to offset costs against market penetration, so low-power transmitters can be set up in local areas. This means that broadcasters can opt for a once-off capital investment for a transmitter. Access challenges are reduced because viewers only need a normal television set, without any additional decoders. For instance, Orbicom operates a 40 watt transmitter that covers the whole town of Hermanus, so one could argue that a 5 watt transmitter could cover local areas such as Khayalitsha. Coverage depends on the power of the transmitter, the transmitter's pattern of gain and the height of the mast.

With digital broadcasting, buffer channels are not required, although this qualification is subject to power specifications because digital transmissions can interfere with analogue transmissions, although the reverse does not hold.

The scarcity of available broadcast frequency in South Africa is exacerbated by the fact that rural telephony requires a broadcast spectrum in which to operate. There is a big push in South Africa for universal telephone access, with a consequent need to provide telephony services in under-serviced areas, and this will use up frequencies that may otherwise have been available for broadcasting.

Analogue space at a distribution level has significant advantages because it can empower people at the local level for low-power transmitter set-ups. Orbicom recommends analogue broadcasting services as the best solution for CTV broadcasts over the next two to three years.

CHAPTER 7

Production

Production requirements for television broadcasting involve balancing the quality of the finished product against factors of cost and expertise. CTV is substantially different from commercial or public service television because, as the third tier of licensed broadcasting, it has different parameters of methodology, programming input and revenue base. In the first instance, CTV is conducted for non-profit purposes, so the motivations for introducing programme types and standards are not driven by the demands of commercialism. Many of the programming staples of the first two tiers will be absent from CTV, for instance the US-made sitcoms, police dramas and Hollywood movies that characterise the offerings of the current television incumbents.

Because CTV programming is community-driven, programmes will tend to relate to the information needs of specific communities of interest within the local geographic area served by the station. This does not exclude programming that relates to more general audiences, but the fact that CTV has a smaller income base than national channels means that less money will be available for content acquisition. These factors mean that suitable levels of local and foreign programming must be sought to accommodate community interests and budgets.

Where programming results from public access, student and NGO production, low levels of expertise and equipment quality may result in standards that are substantially different to those of the high-quality, professional productions seen on existing channels. Budgetary constraints and lower levels of personnel expertise will restrict the station's equipment base, which will have implications for comparative product quality.

The challenge for CTV broadcasters will be to find the appropriate level of equipment that enables the channel to produce content to a standard sufficient to meet the information and aesthetic requirements of audiences. As with any medium, economics of scale are vital to broadcasters' survival, and programming must meet the demands of achieving optimum cost-per-viewer to justify support from funders, advertisers and communities.

Broadcast tape formats for CTV

Addressing the question of video formats for CTV broadcasting requires image quality to be measured against cost-effectiveness and accessibility. Each format has its own particular cost implications, with improved image and sound quality coming at a premium. Video cameras have varying degrees of sound-recording capability depending on their level of sophistication and attendant price range. More expensive cameras have better sound controls and inputs than their cheaper cousins. The higher the quality of the final image in terms of factors like screen resolution, range of recordable light frequencies and absence of visible faults, the higher the cost of the equipment and associated magnetic tape products.

The quest for better image quality has been going on ever since the first images were recorded by pinhole cameras. Since then, the technology of both optical devices and recording mediums has progressed, first through film and then through video into the current digital age. Until the advent of high-definition (HD) video, film was a far better medium than video to record high-quality images because the range of light frequencies recorded by optical and chemical processes on celluloid exceeded what was recordable on magnetic tape. While lens optics are the same for both mediums, the technology for recording light frequencies on these disparate mediums has differed in sensitivity.

Magnetic tape has not managed to capture the same range of gradations of light picked up by celluloid, and it is only with modern digital technology that the medium is catching up with its cinematic counterpart. HD technology employs high-powered computer processing chips to capture large amounts of light information in each frame, reproducing this data on screen at a resolution of 1 920 X 1 080 pixels, a significantly higher resolution than its nearest rival. This increased processing power results in a picture that is sharper and has better colour rendition than any other video format.

Television-screen resolutions are usually measured in the number of horizontal lines scanned by the cathode ray tube of a television set. Standard-definition systems with a resolution of 525 lines have a pixel resolution of 480 X 720 pixels, and 625 line systems have a resolution of 576 X 720 pixels.

The quality of data received through a broadcast transmission depends to some extent on the quality at input. The rule of 'garbage in, garbage out' is often cited in this regard – if poor-quality video is input at the point of origination then it worsens with progress through the transmission chain (Emerich 2005). The chain should start off with as good a quality video as possible because each link in the chain degrades the quality further. For instance, if a microwave link is used to get the signal up to the facility, this degrades the service. The worse the quality of the signal input into the chain, the worse the picture received by the viewer. This is the rationale for the notion of broadcast-quality video relying on high-resolution video formats such as Betacam.

Betacam

Until the advent of the modern digital formats, the international broadcast standard, at least among developed nations, was based on the analogue Betacam format. Betacam is a family of half-inch professional videotape formats developed by the Sony Corporation from 1982 onwards. This analogue component format stores the luminance on one track and the chrominance on another. This splitting of tracks provides a crisp, broadcast-quality product with 300 lines of horizontal resolution.

In 1986, Betacam SP (for 'Superior Performance') was developed, which increased the horizontal resolution to 340 lines. Betacam SP became the industry standard for most TV stations and high-end production houses until the late 1990s. Betacam SP uses metal-formulated tape, as opposed to Betacam's oxide tape.

The Betacam format is roughly equivalent to other proprietary formats, which are not always compatible across proprietary recording and playback platforms. These diverse types differ in factors such as materials used in tape manufacture, thickness of data-recording strips for video and audio, recording-track pitch and recording-chip technologies.

It is not necessary, for the purposes of this discussion, to go into the technical minutiae of these disparate formats; suffice it to say, the image quality and usability of Betacam equivalents fall within the same general range of quality and cost parameters that define the professional broadcast range as a whole and, thus, can be considered as a group rather than being compared as individual formats.

The Betacam format has now moved into digital terrain with the advent of digital video (DV) technologies that record data onto magnetic tape in digital rather than analogue form. This progression has given rise to the format known as Digital Betacam (commonly abbreviated to Digibeta or d-beta or dbc), which was launched in 1993 and supersedes both Betacam and Betacam SP. Digital Betacam is capable of outperforming cheaper digital formats such as DVCAM and DVCPRO. Panasonic offers the competing DVCPRO 50 format, which has similar technical abilities.

Digital video

A major benefit of DV is its ability to store, copy or transfer digital content with minimal loss of quality, while analogue formats suffer considerable degradation, resulting from editing and transfer processes, at each new generation. With digital formats, loss of image and sound quality occurs as a result of compressing the digital content across platforms; that is, as the material is transferred from the camera to the non-linear editing (NLE) or digital storage system, and again if it is further compressed for transmission.

DV formats vary according to proprietary systems that differ in factors such as encoding algorithms, tape characteristics, colour sampling rates, recording modes and data transfer rates. The DV range includes Mini DV, a sub-format that uses a narrower tape and is associated with smaller camcorders for recording purposes. One effect of digitisation is that magnetic tape is now becoming obsolete as recording technologies encode data onto storage mechanisms such as optical laser discs and hard drives in the camcorder.

There are two proprietary DV formats used by high-end broadcasters: DVCAM (Sony) and DVCPRO (Panasonic). Both use 4:2:0 (PAL) compression sampled at 25 MBps. A standard DV recording system can record up to 276 minutes of high-quality 8-bit, 13.5 MHz DV component digital images. Mini DV tapes can record up to 63 minutes.

SABC news teams now use the DVCPRO 25 standard for electronic news gathering (ENG) recording (Joubert, in Stead 2005). DVCPRO, introduced by Panasonic in 2004, is a professional DV format especially tailored to ENG applications. It features tapeless (non-linear) recording of DVCPRO or DVCPRO 50 streams on a P2 solid-state flash memory card. The system includes cameras, digital recording decks that replace VCRs, and a special computer drive for random access integration with NLE systems. The cards can also be used directly where a memory-card slot is available, as in most notebook computers.

Solid-state memory is not subject to tape-related problems such as drop-out, and it provides superior resistance to impact, vibration and temperature change. Recorded data cannot be accidentally overwritten and, unlike videotape, no fast-forward or rewind is required – clips can be found and reviewed immediately through representational thumbnail images that are visible on the liquid crystal display (LCD) viewfinder. Lower-end video cameras use solid-state flash cards to record footage. This is a small, reusable digital recording device that records data on a chipset. It offers similar advantages to the P2 card but has less functionality.

Consumer formats

Generally, all of the above formats are considered acceptable for broadcast purposes in developed nations, although lesser formats may be broadcast when absolutely necessary, usually in news bulletins when no other footage of a newsworthy event is available.

While Mini DV was barely tolerated by major broadcasters in the past, this is changing as camera technology evolves and cost-efficiency factors make themselves felt in the industry.

Camcorder technology is another factor that impacts on formats, because different cameras within a particular format group have varying recording capabilities that depend on factors such as lens type and number and size of data-processing chips. While lens type can be limiting in terms of optical range, focal depth and refraction index, the main measure of broadcast-standard compatibility is the number of chips used for processing light frequencies. Cameras with three chips allocate one chip to process each of the red, green and blue frequencies refracted through the lens and are generally considered to produce acceptable broadcast-quality footage, while single-chip cameras must perform this colour encoding with only one chip, leading to a lower quality recorded image that is generally rejected for broadcast purposes.

Compared to these broadcast formats, other format types produce images of lesser quality in terms of factors like screen resolution, colour range and sharpness. These formats include Digital8, Hi8, VHS and S-VHS, which are generally referred to as 'non-professional' or 'consumer' formats because they are used mainly for non-broadcast purposes. However, such formats do find quite widespread use by broadcasters in developing nations, although digitisation is bringing about a confluence in recording technologies around the DV standard.

The most ubiquitous of these non-broadcast standards is VHS, which is widely used for video distribution purposes despite being the lowest quality of all the formats. VHS stands for Video Home System (or Vertical Helical Scan), and is a consumer-oriented videotape format using half-inch tape on cassette. Both VHS and S-VHS (Super VHS) were developed by the video equipment manufacturer JVC. VHS offers 250 lines of horizontal screen resolution, while S-VHS provides over 400 lines.

There are problems with using VHS as a recording medium. It is an analogue medium, and where analogue equipment is used for editing purposes there is a loss of quality at each generation of the recording process. Quality also erodes over time as tapes age, and there is a further loss of quality through the broadcast process as the signal is transmitted across the airwaves.

Although VHS is scorned by most broadcasters, it can provide adequate picture quality for television viewing purposes. As the Greater Durban TV broadcast in 1996 showed, it was the strength of the broadcast signal that made the most difference to picture reception, rather than the quality of the originating tape (Aldridge 1996). The most recent GDTV broadcasts have also had to cater for widespread use of VHS as a broadcast format because so much material has been provided in this format by community participants.

The VHS format has been the most accessible of all formats for community producers because of its ubiquity as a consumer medium – there are still many VHS cameras in circulation and many video programmes and films have been distributed worldwide in this format. This scenario is changing as cheap digital cameras are replacing VHS as a recording medium, using instead the Mini DV, DVD and flash-card formats that have come to replace it as a consumer-level recording medium.

Because of its relatively low quality, VHS is not recommended for broadcast purposes; however, a CTV broadcaster would have to allow for certain material provided on VHS being broadcast because of the value or relevance of its content.

Mini DV

Camcorders using the Mini DV tape format range in size, sophistication and price, with three-chip 'prosumer' cameras offering the best quality. This range of Mini DV cameras encompasses the overlap between the professional and consumer production levels. These cameras (marques such as the Sony PD170, Panasonic DVX100 and the Canon XL2) are expensive relative to consumer models, but cheap compared with the Betacam and professional DV ranges (see Figure 7.1).

The advantages of Mini DV make it a popular format for low-budget video productions. Cameras are smaller and lighter than the larger DV or Betacam camcorders, while tapes are small but have high storage capacity. Most cameras in the Mini DV range allow for digital effects and have a still-picture or photographic mode, and some models include analogue to digital conversion capability. Mini DV may have slightly better image quality than Digital8, but this is usually due to the use of better lenses on the Mini DV models.

Digital8, on the other hand, is cheaper in terms of camera and tape prices. On the downside, cameras are larger and heavier, and tapes are physically bigger but hold 50 per cent less video. Fewer models support digital stills and effects.

The video quality provided by camcorders using the Mini DV format is determined by factors that include the size of the charge-coupled device (CCD) elements, how colour is processed, lens quality and compression methods. Because the format is digital, it can be transferred directly to computer for editing purposes without significant loss of quality, although this step requires that the video data is compressed for transfer, storage and editing purposes. No further degradation occurs through the generation-loss problem of analogue editing and reproduction, although degradation may occur through subsequent compression, depending on the medium used for reproduction (recording onto CD, Internet protocol (IP) streaming, etc.).

Its widespread popularity among video amateurs and professionals alike, together with its cost and quality advantages, make Mini DV an ideal format for cost-conscious CTV broadcasters. Mini DV has also progressed into the HD realm with manufacturers bringing out prosumer-level HD camcorders that record high resolution images onto Mini DV tapes.

Digital data formats

There are other storage formats that a community TV broadcaster will have to consider, these being digitally encoded material made available on CD, DVD (Digital Versatile Disc or Digital Video Disc) and flash cards or through IP streaming. These digital formats are proliferating today as technology lowers barriers to entry for video producers who use low-cost cameras and PCs to produce digital content.

DVDs are high-capacity optical storage discs that store much more data than CDs. While a CD can store 650 to 700 MB of data, a single-layer, single-sided DVD can store 4.7 GB of data. This enables full-length movies to be stored on a single DVD. There are also advanced DVD formats that use a two-layer standard to almost double the single-sided capacity to 8.5 GB. These discs can also be double-sided, so the maximum storage on a single disc can go up to 17 GB, 26 times more data than a CD can hold. Manufacturers are now producing consumer-level digital cameras that record directly onto DVD. Video that is processed and stored on computers is generally available in three main proprietary formats, these being Apple QuickTime, Windows Media and Real Media. These formats are used for digital non-linear editing, storage and streaming. The quality of these file formats depends on factors that include compression algorithms and data-transfer rates. It is important to bear in mind that non-linear digital editing applications are based on a single proprietary format (usually QuickTime or Windows Media) and, consequently, are not inter-operable; material produced in one format cannot be edited on another platform using a different digital format. This has implications for content-sharing arrangements, archiving and collaborative production initiatives.

Because DV comprises vast amounts of data, varying compression/decompression algorithms (or codecs as they are known) have been developed to transcribe the data in digital form for storage, editing and streaming purposes. CTV will have to cater for these formats for ingress and streaming output, in addition to the tape-based formats mentioned above.

High definition

There has been a recent surge of interest internationally in HD television, with the format receiving more attention than ever before in its ten-year history. HD is finding more widespread adoption among broadcasters in many First-World countries, such as Japan, the US and several European countries.

For South Africa, widespread adoption of HD is still a long way off. Although the SABC has to beef up its HD capacity to cater for external broadcasts of the World Cup football tournament in 2010, the Corporation is not contemplating broadcasting in HD for at least the next five years (Joubert, in Stead 2005).

The HD format must be distinguished from other broadcast standards because it demands specialised playback and viewing equipment capable of reading and delivering data at high transfer rates. HD is best viewed on a large, wide screen capable of displaying its 1 920 X 1 080 pixel resolution and 16:9 aspect ratio to best advantage. Large plasma display screens are currently considered optimal viewing, while television viewers in Japan, the US and certain European countries are increasingly adopting widescreen HD TV sets as broadcasters move to this standard.

HD television depends for public distribution on the availability of higher scan frequency reception sets. These sets are able to display progressive signals or include a line doubler to convert the incoming viewable NTSC or PAL signals at 480i (interlaced) to 480p (progressive). HD sets must have ATSC tuner/decoders and meet the widescreen specifications of a 16:9 aspect ratio, as opposed to the 4:3 ratio of standard definition (SD) formats. The foundation of HD TV is the ability to display the high resolution image defined by the ATSC standards of 1080i or 720p.

HD is hailed for its ability to emulate film in its chromatic sensitivity and image sharpness. For this reason, it is being used by film makers who desire the cost advantages of working with video as well as the convenience of non-linear editing. While HD is best viewed on a big, high-resolution screen, it can be dropped down to SD formats and still retain some of its cinematic quality in finer gradations of colour and shade.

The significance of HD TV for CTV is that it is a very expensive medium that will not see significant consumer uptake in South Africa for some years to come. Despite the current surge in popularity that HD is undergoing in the professional broadcast community, HD is an upmarket consumer phenomenon that is out of reach for the majority of the South African population.

The 2010 Soccer World Cup is being heralded as a milestone for South Africa in terms of HD broadcasting, because the SABC will be hosting global distribution of footage to foreign networks, many of which will be demanding HD capacity. Even then, however, HD will be more the prerogative of affluent home-theatre enthusiasts in foreign countries than the staple of the African masses. This situation will change gradually as time progresses and HD becomes the de facto broadcasting standard, especially once reception technologies like LCD TVs achieve dominance in the marketplace.

Content production on HD is also expensive. Despite the entry into the market of low-end HD camcorders based on the 3-chip prosumer Mini DV cameras, HD production still requires expensive playback videotape recorders (VTRs) and large hard-drive storage space. Non-linear digital editing packages are bringing out HD plug-ins to upgrade their capacity to handle this information-heavy format; and the ability of HD to mimic cinematic quality means that high-end cameras, tapes and editing set-ups find a market among only those with the big money necessary to pay for them.

All of these factors suggest that HD is largely beyond the scope of CTV broadcasters but, at the same time, we must recognise that the format will gain increasing adoption according to market forces. This means that film makers, video producers and their more affluent audience sectors will increasingly invest in HD for production and viewing purposes.

While HD is on the cutting edge of production, it will remain an expensive technology until large-scale adoption reduces overall costs. Although HD is a long way off for most viewers in South Africa, CTV broadcasters may choose to leverage certain aspects of HD technology, such as the low-end prosumer camera ranges.

For example, the JVC GY-HD100 compact shoulder camcorder is priced in the prosumer market range and can record in DV and HD formats. This model has the advantage of a detachable bayonet-mount HD zoom lens that can be swapped with various other wide-angle and zoom lenses, which makes it versatile and enhances its capability where long-range shooting is required, for instance in recording sporting events. The shoulder platform allows for more stable shooting than the handycam type of camera that must be supported by the operator's arms in non-tripod shooting situations.

Field production and outside broadcast

The area of field production assumes that the CTV broadcaster has content-acquisition crews that go out into the field to record footage and conduct interviews. The mainstay of field production is the camera, as it records both images and sound, while other peripheral equipment supports this central device. Associated production equipment includes microphones, lights, tripods, batteries, battery chargers, camera lenses and filters. There is a wide variety of such items on the market, differing in price, quality and functionality, but they will not be considered in detail here.

Cameras

Camera types differ hugely, ranging from low-end consumer palmcorders to prosumer handycams and professional shoulder-mounted camcorders that consist of a recording back end and variable clip-on lenses. Camera prices in this report are quoted in rand values as they stood in November 2005.

There are several criteria that determine the relative merits of video cameras. These factors include chip number and size, recording format, lens quality, sound apparatus and connections, interface functionality and data transfer rate.

Video cameras today are an accessible resource that has undergone dramatic improvements in quality and functionality as the technology has matured. Digital technology has enabled the development of small handycam cameras that utilise the advantages of digital recording to produce video images that are superior in terms of resolution and colour retention to analogue formats like VHS, Hi8 and Video8. Consumer cameras range in price from just a few thousand rands to below R20 000, and are generally defined by having just one CCD chip.

As camera prices reach the R20 000 mark, they enter the prosumer range, which is generally defined by three CCD chips and XLR (as opposed to RCA or mini-jack) audio connections. Camera microphones in this range tend to provide better audio quality in terms of digital sampling rates and frequency sensitivities than their consumer-sector counterparts. This is a significant feature for broadcasting, because cameras that are used often in the field are stressed, particularly at their weakest points, and the RCA and mini-jack audio connections are very vulnerable to wear and tear.

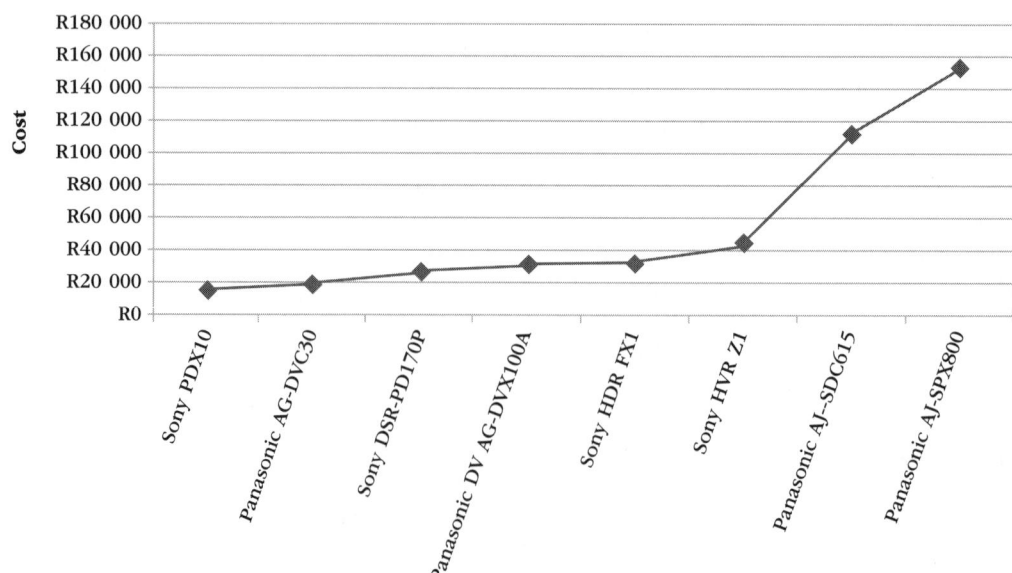

Figure 7.1: Prosumer to professional camera price range

Figure 7.1 shows comparative camera prices ranging from prosumer to professional levels. The prosumer cameras are typically used by national broadcasters wishing to leverage their compromise between cost-effectiveness and quality. These cameras are robust and functional, giving the operator sufficient control over light and sound-acquisition factors to produce material of internationally acceptable broadcast quality.

The Panasonic AJ-SDC615 DVCPRO camcorder offers good value for money as a professional-standard camcorder, but its price is significantly above that of its nearest prosumer competitor, the Sony HVR Z1. Priced at R44 460, this HD camera offers a robust design that is capable of recording in DV and HD formats, as does its close cousin the Sony HDR FX1 at a slightly lower price.

The Sony DSR-PD170P (R22 530) and Panasonic DV AG-DVX100A (R32 410) are mid-range prosumer cameras. At the lower end of the prosumer range are the Panasonic AG-DVC30 (R18 700) and the Sony PDX10 (R15 000); these cameras are positioned at the margin of the top-end consumer/bottom-end prosumer market. These 3CCD digital cameras are very affordable options for CTV purposes; they utilise the Mini DV tape format and XLR microphone connections with volume controls.

Figure 7.2: Low to medium camera price range

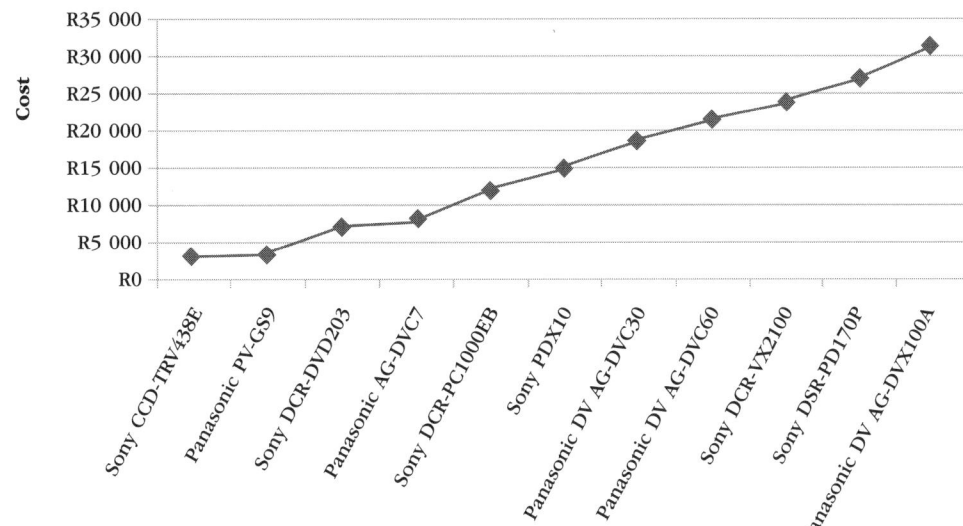

Figure 7.2 shows the relative pricing of the lower-end consumer cameras compared with the prosumer range. The three-chip range starts with the Sony PDX10, while cameras below this point have only one CCD. The Sony DCR-DVD203 records onto DVD, but all the others record onto Mini DV tape.

Cameras that fall below the R15 000 mark may be used by community-based video producers, but the station itself should use the prosumer range and it should encourage outside producers to use this level of equipment. We must also bear in mind that camera prices have been dropping, as supply and demand factors drive down production costs (in terms of increased market demand and supply availability), which means that prosumer range cameras are becoming ever more accessible. This trend is intensified by cameras becoming available on the second-hand market, making them easier to acquire.

Studio cameras should be seen as separate items because of their specialist function. Some studios use field cameras like the Sony PD170 or Panasonic DVX100, which are adequate for the task. The problem with these cameras, however, is that they are not genlocked and, consequently, do not synchronise at the vertical, horizontal and chroma phase levels that enable cross-camera cuts, mixes and cross-fades without noticeable roll, jump or chroma shift in the picture.

Purpose-built studio cameras have many advantages, despite their relative expense. Cameras with half-inch CCDs offer better light-recording capabilities, which is an advantage in generating clear image quality. Typically, studio cameras have features that enable ease of operation, such as handle-based remote controls, large viewfinders that are well situated for continuous viewing and dolly-mounted tripods that can move around the studio. However, currently priced at over R100 000, such cameras are significantly more expensive than the prosumer range. An alternative would be to use remote-controlled cameras in the same half-inch CCD quality range, which has the advantage that on-camera controls and viewfinders are not necessary, so reducing cost; on the other hand, this limits the manoeuvrability of the camera and does away with the training function for studio camera operators.

Camera accessories and peripherals

Basic-level consumer cameras can be used with few accessories. The camera-mounted microphone is usually of the rifle type that picks up sound in a relatively narrow cone of reception from the receiver. However, these microphones tend to pick up ambient sound as well, so they are not optimum equipment for precision recording. Specialist microphones may be added to consumer equipment, but the mini-jack inputs that are usually employed are not robust and are a point of vulnerability for mechanical breakdown and sound distortion.

Microphones of various types are important for field and studio operations in order to obtain optimal sound quality. These items include boom, rifle, interview, lapel and radio microphones. On prosumer and professional-level cameras, microphones connect to the camera through XLR connections that are robust and stable. Microphones on the prosumer cameras tend to be more sensitive than consumer versions and provide good sound quality on their own.

Tripods are very useful for video operations, but they vary tremendously in quality and price. Lower-end tripods may be too light for video-camera operation, although their lightness can be helpful when transporting them. These tripods generally have single-strut supports, while the higher-end tripods have three-strut supports. A fluid head is essential to mount video cameras on tripods.

Lights are another item to consider. There are various ranges of lightweight ENG lights on the market that can effectively replace the larger 'Redheads' that have been standard equipment for the professional broadcast sector. It would only be necessary to invest in larger lights such as 'Blondes' if serious outside shoots are undertaken (e.g. for dramas or special events), so these would be an unnecessary expense for initial CTV set-ups. Studio lighting should consist of cold lights to minimise ambient heat build-up in the room.

Additional camera batteries must be purchased and these must be 'long-life' batteries, which provide up to five hours recording time. A camera light can also be an advantage in the field, although modern camcorder technology has improved low-light capabilities that enable fairly good image capture without this aid. Headphones are an essential item for monitoring sound even though most cameras come equipped with a camera speaker, in order to give the camera operator a good idea of sound quality. Prosumer cameras are equipped with sound-level meters but these can only measure the loudness of the sound and not its overall quality and freedom from interference.

Technical requirements for ingest and broadcast

Television broadcasters generally have set technical standards for the material they accept for broadcast. For public and commercial broadcasters, these standards are set according to factors that include screen resolution, chrominance and luminance range, audio levels and audio setting. Other technical factors would relate to quality in terms of the stability of the signal on tape (i.e. the picture does not roll, distort or disintegrate) and absence of artefacts such as picture break-up or pixellation. These factors are defined partly by the quality of equipment used for recording and editing the footage, as well as by the skill of equipment operators in selecting and manipulating the footage when compiling the content.

Public and commercial broadcasters generally rely on expensive, professional-standard equipment to record images at the highest possible resolution on tape or digital recording formats that provide stable, artefact-free images and undistorted sound levels. They also require 'professional' standards of production that include factors such as clarity of focus, absence of untoward camera shake, matching chrominance and luminance values between shots, narrative value of shots and correct lighting levels. There should be no blank frames between shots, a correct white balance and absence of digital noise due to shooting on excessive gain. There may also be specific requirements for audio settings such as shooting with the Dolby setting either on or off.

The question that faces community broadcasters is whether the notion of access means that any and all submissions should be broadcast as a matter of course, or whether certain technical standards should be imposed on producers as a prerequisite for broadcasting their material. Community producers may not have access to good equipment and some material may only be available on low-quality formats such as VHS. Moreover, producers may not have much in the way of production skills, resulting in poor quality or incorrect methods of recording, composition, editing and narrative. It is essential that production personnel be required to undergo at least a basic course in video production before they contribute material.

From the channel's point of view, it relies on viewer support and appreciation of its programming, and sustainability may be undermined by delivering poor quality material, where technical glitches and production errors distract viewers during their viewing experience. Advertisers and sponsors will also want their messages to be carried within a framework of sound production quality. These factors put pressure on the channel to demand good technical proficiency and quality from contributing producers. Each CTV station will have to weigh the demands of access and production quality in instances where they mitigate against one another; however, the station should encourage producers to deliver material of the highest possible technical standards, given the production environment in which it exists.

The technical specifications for Triangle Television in Auckland, New Zealand, are instructional as a basis for setting technical parameters (see Triangle Television 2005). Triangle has a funding model that stresses self-funding for programme producers, who may be community-based volunteers or commercial entrepreneurs. This puts the onus for origination in the hands of the producer and, while the broadcaster caters for various ingest tape formats, all footage is then transferred to the channel's internal format of

DVCAM. Any programmes that are submitted on DVCAM or DV tapes (large format cases, not Mini DV) are played out directly to the transmitter. Technical requirements for DVCAM and DV tapes that go straight to air include:
- one show on one tape, to ensure the correct programme gets aired;
- pre-roll of at least 20 seconds before the first frame of the programme to be aired;
- post-roll of at least 20 seconds after the last frame; and
- studio levels averaging -20dB (levels above that are compressed by the system and may result in sound distortion).

Technical requirements for all other tape formats (VHS, SVHS, Mini DV, DVCAM, Beta SP) are:
- one show on one tape, recorded in short play;
- pre- and post-roll of 20 seconds; and
- audio levels averaging -20dB.

These requirements indicate that while the broadcaster prefers digital formats it also caters for lower quality analogue formats. The latter formats require special facilities for analogue-to-digital conversion, although this can be effected through low-cost PC video cards.

Production and broadcast studios

The heart of a broadcast operation is the studio. Here live programmes are transmitted, others are pre-recorded and, along with other pre-recorded material, are played out to air. While it is possible to stage a television broadcast with minimal equipment, as shown by the GDTV broadcast from the University of Natal in 1995 (Aldridge 1996), this route is not recommended for a sustainable CTV channel. Firstly, the resulting low standard of production quality is likely to have a negative effect on viewer perceptions of the channel where it competes against the slick, high-quality standards of other broadcasters. Secondly, a low-budget set-up is difficult to manage in terms of tape handling (tapes get mixed up and lost), logging (of music and adverts) and continuity (slip-ups in cutting from presenters to programmes, blank screens when a tape jams or the wrong button is pressed, etc.).

The minimum recommended standard for a city broadcast would involve setting up a dedicated broadcast studio that includes the following components:
- a studio floor with multi-camera set-up, mid- to high-range prosumer DV cameras on standard tripods, and portable lights;
- autocue, VCRs for analogue and digital formats, PC, vision mixer, audio mixer, and monitors;
- manual final control when tapes or live broadcasts are played to air;
- subsidiary editing booths with digital editing suites and VCRs;
- a repair room for equipment maintenance; and
- a microwave or high-bandwidth landline link to the transmitter site.

This scenario assumes that studio equipment such as cameras and lights could also be used for field recording, although this is not an optimal set-up because of the resulting risk and wear on these items that are central to live studio broadcasts.

A medium-range solution would follow the example set by the type of facility commonly found in tertiary education institutions where video production is taught. It would include the following additional features:

- a soundproof control booth with vision mixer, audio control panel and multiple monitors;
- camera-operator to control-booth communications;
- dedicated half-inch 3CCD studio cameras with genlock and mobile tripods (alternatively, remote-controlled half-inch 3CCD cameras);
- a cold-lighting grid;
- automated digital final control that schedules digital content for playout;
- a digital storage area that ingests content from various sources (optional); and
- a dedicated sound-recording studio with separate control room and sound booth, multi-channel audio mixer, communications, speakers, digital sound-editing platform (PC), audio players, VCRs and monitors.

It is important to give attention to the sound dimension of video production in any reasonably sophisticated production facility. Sound is a dimension that may be easily overlooked in a video production facility, but it is important that sound be accorded its true status in building a facility capable of producing quality output. It is then necessary to have dedicated sound production tools, including a digital sound-editing platform and soundproof recording facilities that can be used for recording voice-overs and music.

Figure 7.3: Manual broadcast workflow

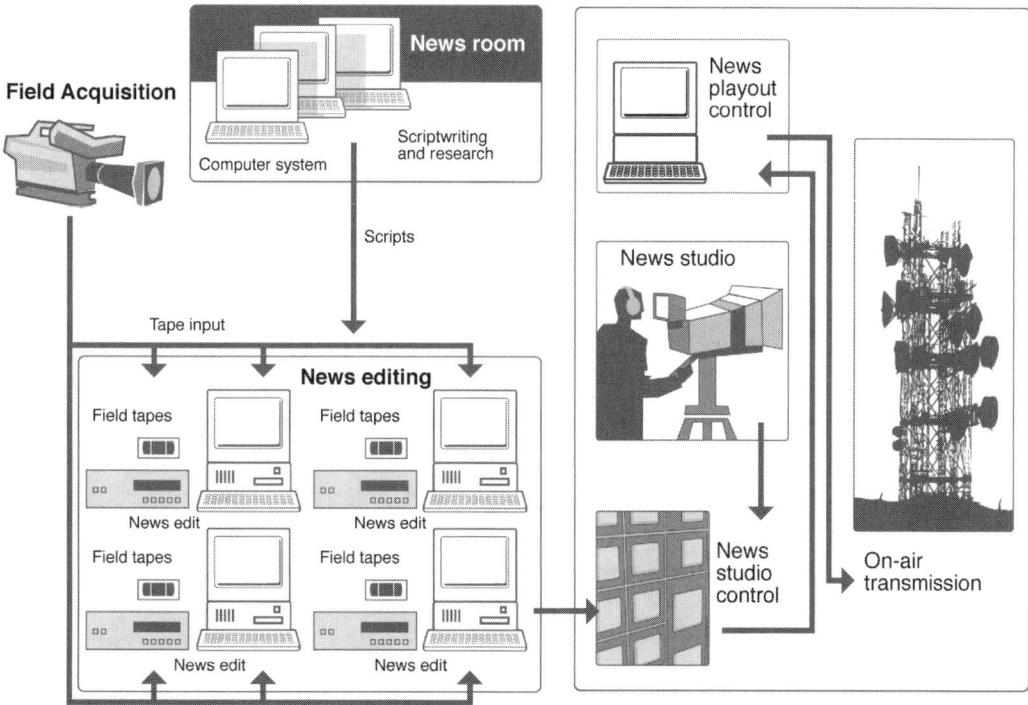

Source: System based on Grass Valley technology (www.thomsongrassvalley.com)

Figure 7.3 describes the relationship between field acquisition, scriptwriting, editing, studio, control room and final playout in terms of news production, but this can be applied as a general broadcast workflow. This set-up is scalable in that other components can be added to make it more sophisticated; for example, a digital storage area can easily be networked between the edit suites and final control to automate the broadcast process.

At the high end of the spectrum lies a fully automated digital workflow solution that combines the different production silos into an integrated unit. In this scenario, material is ingested into a digital storage area from which it is accessible for editing and playout. Journalists or scriptwriters have access to a low-resolution copy of the footage that they can perform a basic edit on as they compile their script. The edit decision list (EDL) is then sent to an edit suite where the programme or insert is compiled. This material is then available to the studio or final control for insertion in a live broadcast or scheduled playout. The major disadvantage of such a system is cost, with one estimate putting it at about R12.5 million (Wainer 2005).

Figure 7.4: Automated digital workflow solution

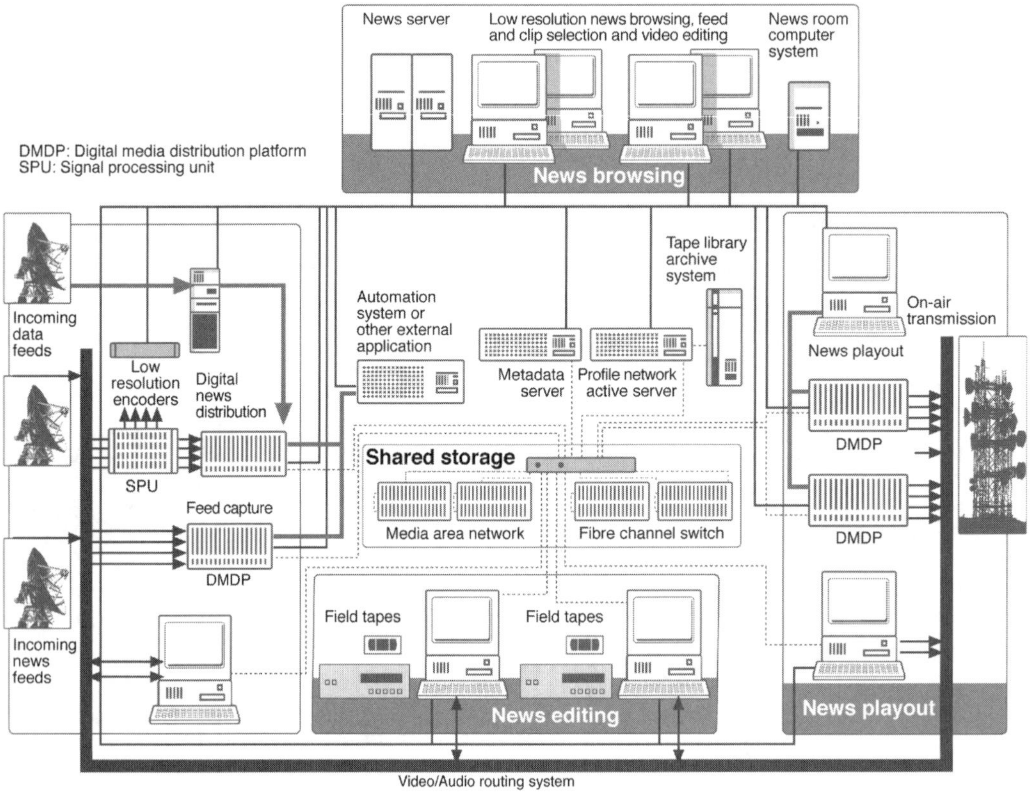

Source: System based on Grass Valley technology (www.thomsongrassvalley.com)

It must be noted that, in terms of ICASA regulations, whatever programming is played to air must be archived and stored for a period of 30 days after broadcast. Storage could be on tape (VHS would be adequate for this purpose) or on a digital medium such as DVD. Unedited content or edited clips can also be stored for retrieval by producers who need such archive material in their programmes. Archive material can be sold as stock shots, so it is necessary to keep this material in a good-quality format, which could mean that the original tape is kept and not reused or that the material is dumped onto another tape or DVD.

This scenario locates some production capacity at the station itself, which will not necessarily be the case if the model of stand-alone broadcasting is followed. In that case, production capacity would be located outside the station and the broadcast facility would consist simply of a playout and transmission set-up. Given the nature of the South African situation, with the majority of the population unable to afford production equipment, and the scarcity of such equipment among NGOs, it would probably be best to incorporate production capacity into the station. As the GDTV experience shows, live studio broadcasts can form a mainstay of community access because they are cheap to produce, but such productions require an appropriate studio set-up.

Additional features would include a back-up generator and an uninterruptible power supply. Logging commercials for billing purposes would be done manually because automated billing systems are expensive, costing about R2–3 million. Air conditioning and high-speed network connections to link computers would also be needed.

Qualified personnel would be required to run and maintain a broadcast system. For instance, a high-level system would need at least one technician with a national diploma in electrical engineering and at least two years' experience in broadcasting, at a salary of approximately R150 000 a year.

Outside broadcast

The basic idea of an outside broadcast (OB) is the transmission of video material from a location outside of a television studio. In the course of normal broadcast operations, the television signal is conveyed from the television studio to the transmitter site; an outside broadcast would route the signal either to the studio, from where it would be sent on to the transmitter, or directly from the outside location to the transmitter.

OB essentially involves replicating studio equipment in the field, ranging from cameras to communications links, editing platforms, monitors and transmission capacity. These facilities are usually housed in OB vehicles, which may vary in size from large trucks to a minivan. Signal transmission is usually effected by means of a satellite or microwave link to the studio. Satellite links are expensive, particularly given the high bandwidth required for live broadcasts, and microwave links are limited by the necessity for a line-of-sight relationship to the receiving station as well as by distance.

Because of these factors, OB is usually an expensive process. For example, the SABC's Airtime facility in Cape Town has an eight-camera vehicle that is equipped with graphics facilities and VTRs, and another smaller four-camera unit. Transmissions from these vehicles are by satellite or microwave link. SABC Airtime hires out the large OB unit for R30 000 per day while the small OB van goes out at R15 000 per day. Better prices can be gained for longer hire periods but in the summer months there is a great demand for the OB facilities and personnel; more favourable rates are available from May to October (Terblanche 2005).

In terms of signal transmission, transfer speeds differ according to the quality of broadcast required. For sports, typically a 9 MBps connection is used, whereas news can get away with just 4.5 MBps. Satellite transmission paths are fully digital, so if analogue recording equipment is used then the signal must be converted to digital prior to transmission. Satellite bandwidth is 270 MBps, which can be compressed down to 9 MBps (Terblanche 2005).

A microwave link can be hired from Airtime at R2 500 per day. A dual microwave link can be set up to ensure uptime, but this costs 30 per cent more and is generally not necessary because the equipment is fairly stable. Long-term broadcasts (for instance, for a month) work out cheaper than the daily rate for hiring equipment and may be charged for only 15 days on a month-long hire (Terblanche 2005). Nevertheless, these costs would probably prove prohibitive for a community broadcaster, which would then have to find alternative solutions for OB if it is to be used at all.

One solution would be for the CTV broadcaster to equip its own small-scale OB vehicles with basic production facilities. These could include prosumer cameras and accessories along with laptop PC editing platforms. The major problem in this instance would be signal transmission, because only a few operators (such as Airtime) are licensed for satellite connectivity and because satellite transponders and airtime are also expensive.

Television journalists in remote locations do make use of satellite phones to send their stories to their home stations, but these are short-duration pieces of about two minutes in length, which then take several hours to transmit. Another option would be to stream video over telephone or wireless networks, but because of the relatively low bandwidth currently available over these mediums this would generally result in low-quality reception for live material.

Video streaming

One option for delivering video content to a CTV station is to stream it over an IP network. This mode of delivery is currently constrained by the limitations of compression technologies and bandwidth availability; however, as time goes on, these factors are bound to improve due to the nature of technological progress and the demands of the market for converged products that can provide AV communications over various networks.

To stream full-screen, full-motion video over an IP network requires bandwidth in excess of 1 MBps. This can be achieved by multiplexing eight 164 KBps ISDN lines together, but this requires an ISDN fixed-line set-up, which would only be feasible in locations such as sports stadiums or music venues. Wireless networks are another option, but these networks have a limited presence and are found only in certain parts of South Africa's major cities; they also provide only limited bandwidths, and bandwidth availability fluctuates according to network congestion.

However, advances in compression algorithms have dramatically reduced the bandwidth requirements for delivering broadcast-quality video. Compression rates today give between 3.5 and 4 MBps per video stream, and MPEG-4 has cut the bandwidth even more, squeezing high-quality video into bandwidths of about 1 MBps. MPEG-4 AVC (video codec) and MPEG-4 AAC (audio codec) represent a huge step forward in compression efficiency, offering broadcast-quality SD video at bitrates between 800 KBps and 1.3 MBps (Bray 2003). Advances in telephone bandwidth are coming with the latest generation of asymmetric digital subscriber line (ADSL) chips with new standards such as S=1/2 and ADSL 2+, which can also enhance fixed-line connectivity if they are implemented in South Africa.

Streaming options for OB purposes could be effected by making use of a PC equipped with encoding software such as Windows Media Encoder, or a sophisticated mobile streaming server such as the Sony Anycast Station. This device provides a built-in streaming encoder and streaming server. The streaming encoder function allows the high-quality programme output of the Anycast Station system to be streamed in real-time, with minimum degradation and through very simple procedures for distribution over the Internet, local-area networks (LANs) or leased lines (Sony Electronics Inc. 2005).

The problem with streaming video over IP networks is that it does not yet provide full television resolution. Picture sizes are based on PC monitor resolutions of up to 320 X 240 pixels. Nevertheless, streaming can be successfully combined with television for content delivery, especially as the technology advances to provide greater bandwidth and screen resolution.

Post-production

Video editing systems have evolved from tape-based analogue to digital solid-state, hard-drive devices. While digital VTRs are still employed to play or record tapes, whether digital or analogue, the actual video editing process takes place on a PC. A DV editing solution consists of an assembly of components including hard drives, processors, motherboards, monitors and software.

The most commonly used video editing applications in the broadcast and broadcast training environments come from manufacturers such as Avid, Adobe and Sony. Other systems such as Pinnacle, Discreet and Canopus are also in use in the industry but are not popular among institutions. Those facilities that have Apple Macintosh computers generally use Apple's Final Cut Pro editing software.

The most commonly used editing packages in the industry are the Avid and Adobe systems. Avid produces packages such as DV Express, while Adobe has the Premier range. The Avid systems suffer the disadvantage of a non-intuitive interface that has various esoteric symbols indicating particular function buttons, and the system is based on analogue editing techniques that insert defined clips into the timeline, with no timeline editing functionality; in other words, the system does not make use of the flexibility afforded by a non-linear platform.

Consequently, the Avid systems require intensive instruction before an operator can really get to grips with how they work, and it takes a long time (up to a year) for an operator to become really proficient in using the software (Mindset Network 2005). Avid uses the Apple QuickTime (.mov) DV format.

On the other hand, Avid offers comprehensive data-flow solutions in high-end IT-based systems that allow different categories of users such as journalists and video editors access to different levels of information. Thus, journalists can use low-resolution versions of the footage stored on a server to compile a script and do a basic edit, while the video editor can then use the resulting EDL to work with high-resolution footage in compiling the final product for broadcast.

Adobe Premier suffers the disadvantage of being relatively unstable, especially with the differing types of video card found on Wintel PCs. This can be a huge problem when deadlines have to be met and system crashes interfere with the editing process. On the plus side, Premier has an intuitive interface and makes good use of the flexibility afforded by non-linear systems. It also has a good depth of functionality for advanced editing techniques and effects. Premier systems use the Windows Media (.avi) DV format.

There are other options that CTV producers can explore, an example of which is the Sony Vegas Video software, an affordable video editing package that is stable, has a wide-ranging and robust functionality and which makes good use of non-linear functionality. Vegas Video is often used for DVD authoring but is a reliable video editing package that is suitable for beginners and professionals alike. There is a wide variety of video editing software available on the market and it may be that CTV is a good forum for experimenting with different programmes in order to find the most suitable ones for effective, low-cost production and access.

Another system that has been recommended for newcomers to video production is the Casablanca Aveo editing system. This consists of a digital device that outputs video and audio to a TV monitor. It is a menu-driven, rather than a graphical user interface, system that is operated with a mouse. Transitions, titles and sound can be added to the final product. It is priced at about R12 000 and users do not need computer skills in order to use it (McAskill 2005).

The disadvantages of the Casablanca system are that users do not acquire PC skills that will help them with other editing packages or other applications, nor does it have the flexibility of timeline editing and other advantages of PC systems such as drag-and-drop and cut-and-paste. The Digital Storytelling group teaches people without any computer skills to edit video in NLE packages in just three hours (Hill & Weinshenker 2005), which shows how easy it is to master the basics of such programmes in a short space of time. Moreover, to spend R12 000 on a dedicated editing system that can do nothing else is by no means a cost-effective investment when that amount would buy a very sophisticated PC with far greater functionality.

In terms of hardware, PC platforms should be specifically designed with video editing in mind because working with video requires a machine capable of dealing with high rates of data throughflow and storage. Consequently, the machine must have fast processor speeds, fast access hard drives with large amounts of data storage space, a dedicated video card and a high-capacity graphics card. Large, high-resolution monitors are also a necessity and a television set is useful for monitoring the television quality of the output.

In many ways the Apple Mac G5 machines are ideal for video production purposes. The Mac offers stability as well as a 64-bit processing capacity that is an exponential enhancement in terms of computing power over 32-bit systems. On the downside, Mac hardware and software are expensive relative to Wintel PCs and fewer applications are available.

Open-source options

The availability of open-source software (OSS) products for CTV is another factor to consider in terms of finding cost-effective solutions. Despite the cost advantages of OSS, which is free of licensing or even purchase costs, it is not in evidence in professional or institutional video production environments.

Although OSS is beginning to make significant inroads into IT infrastructure in the corporate, government and NGO sectors, it has not yet made its mark in video or television production. Nevertheless, it is a useful option to pursue for non-production purposes such as office applications and could be integrated into CTV operations in this way as a cost-saving measure.

Critics of OSS note that efficient software systems are generally built by a professional designer or software architect who has a clear design concept in mind. By adhering rigorously to this, the designer is able to fashion an effective product, while the collective, non-professional approach leads to piecemeal development that results in inefficient software systems. The conceptual integrity approach is based on a strong architectural vision that is not found in the community-based method of software development, despite the strength of the peer-review methodology applied in OSS software development (Marshall 2005).

It may be for reasons such as these that OSS has not yet come to the fore in the video production industry. However, there are some open-source video applications that can be experimented with in the CTV environment. These include systems such as Video4Linux, a programme that digitises video and is compatible with most computer TV cards.

Open-source tools accept and export data in common, open formats. It is possible to add these tools together to create a powerful non-linear post-production system. For example, Broadcast 2000 is an open-source video editing application that works with any size of frame, any frame rate and any number of audio tracks (Fulton 2000). These developments suggest that OSS applications should be further studied and developed for CTV broadcasting. Firstly, there are cost advantages to be obtained by using OSS; in addition, there are philosophical similarities between OSS and CTV in that both involve a community approach to their operations within a context of aiming for freedom from commercial constraints.

Office equipment

In addition to the equipment required for video production, a CTV station will also have to consider the equipment and furnishings required for support activities such as administration and journalism. Apart from furnishings like desks, chairs and tables, the organisation would have to consider the nature of its computing requirements in terms of hardware, software and networking.

Hardware requirements

It is useful to view the information environment of the CTV station as an interlinked whole, where silos of production, support and administration connect with one another to facilitate communication and information sharing. Taking this kind of holistic view suggests that certain sectors of the network be transparent to one another, while the necessity will remain for other sectors (for instance, finance) to be securely partitioned. This does not mean that such sectors cannot draw information from the others; for example, a finance department should be able to keep track of aspects such as advert flightings or sponsored time on air through connections with other data centres. This viewpoint suggests that while production, administration and support might seem to be entirely different sectors of operation, they do in fact overlap in certain areas; thus, journalists might send their copy through the network to an editor, who could send a video clip to the legal department or station manager for legal clearance, and so on.

There are other issues that affect the station's functioning in terms of overall computing resources, these being factors of performance, maintenance, equipment renewal or upgrading and software licensing.

There are two types of PC that dominate today's computing environments, the Wintel PC based on Microsoft Windows and Intel chips, and the Apple Macintosh based on Apple's proprietary technology. When considering the so-called Wintel PC, it must be borne in mind that OSS is coming into increasing use and would also be run on this type of machine; however, for the sake of differentiating it from the Macs, we will term them Wintel PCs in this document.

Macs appear to be superior to Wintel PCs in many respects. Firstly, while the purchase price of Macs is higher than that of comparable Wintel PCs, they generally require less support than PCs and, thus, are cheaper and easier to run and maintain, resulting in a lower total cost of ownership.

For students embarking on the process of learning how to use computers, a report by John Droz Jnr argues that:

> ...the Mac OS is easier to learn, requires fewer keystrokes for similar tasks and results in much higher user productivity than PCs. Macs can also run a Windows or Linux operating system simultaneously with only a modest additional investment, essentially providing two computers for the price of one...Macs also experience hardware/software problems...[but] are very reliable and are easier to support than PCs. And when properly maintained, they experience fewer problems. Furthermore, Macs are much less prone to virus attacks and are more secure. (Droz 2003)

For some years, Macs have been the industry standard in terms of hardware in sectors like graphics, desk-top publishing and video editing, although Wintel PCs are making significant inroads into this dominance.

While there is no industry-standard measurement that gives a real-world indication for an average user as to which computer is faster or more powerful than another, one accepted way to measure computer processing power and performance is by looking at MTOPS (millions of theoretical operations per second). Here Macs outperform comparable PCs, and other system speed tests seem to bear this out.

Arguments in favour of Wintel PCs include the allegation that the Mac is a niche market where there is very little selection and high premiums are charged by resellers. Other problems include being unable to upgrade features such as graphics cards unless newer Macs are purchased. PC cards will not work in Macs because Apple adds a proprietary basic input-output system (BIOS) code to make it exclusive. With PCs there is a greater choice of products and compatibility.

Price comparisons in the US appear to favour Macs over comparable PCs, but while Macs may be slightly more expensive in dollar terms, this price differential assumes far greater proportions when translated into rands. Unfortunately, Macs in the South African market are significantly more expensive than Wintel PCs, and this price differential may well offset the support costs that would otherwise favour Macs.

Moreover, despite the arguments in favour of the Mac-user experience, the fact of the matter is that there are far more PCs than Macs in use in South African NGOs and government. To summarise the case for PCs, they are cheaper and more amenable to upgrades than Macs, and a greater variety of applications can be run on them. CTV broadcasters and producers will have to select their editing platforms based on these factors. PCs also have the advantage of running OSS such as Linux, which does not require licensing, although critics argue that it is less secure than Windows and requires more maintenance.

Thin-client solution

Another option for running Windows applications is the so-called thin-client solution, where the intelligence of the network resides in a central server. All of the applications software is on the server and individual computers are used only to communicate with the server.

In this approach, the reliability of the network becomes critical. If the network is down, none of the terminals will work. Some experts believe that applications that rely heavily on multimedia are not well suited to this kind of environment, and thin-client solutions require high levels of network bandwidth to work well. The trade-off is that with such tight centralisation, the costs of support can generally be controlled more easily.

Because the functionality of the server is the most important component of the system, a high-performance server is required. This can mean a high initial purchase cost, although a reasonably fast, modern PC can suffice, given sufficient random-access memory (RAM). The life cycle of such servers is more limited than individual PCs that can easily be upgraded when necessary; the life cycle of a server is about four years while PC workstations can 'live' for about seven years. Another cost factor is the number of users (clients), because software licences must be purchased for each client, unless OSS is used.

The advantages of the thin-client solution lie mainly in administration, because the administrator can effectively limit the control each user has over the applications and operating system. There is a danger in normal operating environments that users may change settings on the machines they are working on, resulting in increased maintenance costs. Instead of performing maintenance on every computer in the network, all configurations and software installations are performed only once on the thin-client server.

A thin-client solution would not work for applications that require heavy processing because this would overload the server. It would be useful for office and administrative applications but not for video editing, sound editing and graphics.

Network

An office network would be essential for a CTV station. It would allow information to be shared by all personnel, as well as enabling the interface with the outside world through the Internet or other networks. The network would serve to link all CTV personnel and could carry data traffic, including voice and video, for conferencing or production purposes; and, as Metcalfe's law states, 'the usefulness, or utility, of a network equals the square of the number of users' (Hill 2004).

There are two main types of network infrastructure – cable and wireless. The latter is a newer technology that is finding increased adoption because it is more cost-effective to install and can be easily moved.

Wireless has been called 'the networking technology of the future', and it is becoming increasingly accepted, as standards for wireless telephony are developing apace. Wireless bandwidth now stands at 2 MBps, and 54 MBps connectivity is on the horizon.

A television production and broadcast system based on a digital workflow solution would require a network capable of delivering high-quality DV. Optimally, this would require an optical-fibre network infrastructure capable of carrying data flows running at 2 GBps (Leitch 2004). Lower-end systems can get away with smaller data flows, but this will reduce functionality and slow down delivery times to the broadcast server.

CHAPTER 8

Programming

Programming committees

In terms of ICASA's regulations, a CTV licensee must enable community participation in programming through the selection and provision of programmes. This task is the responsibility of the programming committee, which must be representative of different sectors within the community served by the station. These committees must select the types of programme to be shown and acquire them.

This places an enormous responsibility on the committee, as well as conferring great power. The committee is responsible to the community it serves, in this case a geographic community, for providing content that is educational, entertaining and informative. The role of CTV, according to the Independent Communications Authority of South Africa (ICASA), is to act as a 'responsible civic custodian' in ensuring that anyone who chooses to appear on television does so in a responsible manner (ICASA 2004). For programming, this could mean that any programme submitted by a community or community-sanctioned source must be broadcast.

This is the approach taken by some CTV broadcasters internationally; one example is Triangle Television, a non-commercial, regional TV station in Auckland, New Zealand. It delivers content 24 hours a day, 7 days a week, on a government-owned frequency, and combines aspects of access, public service and ethnic television programming into its own unique format. The channel aims to reflect the diversity within the city of Auckland. All individuals are allowed to produce their own programmes and book a time slot to have them aired. The channel does not have its own facilities for programme production; instead, it connects would-be producers with community members who have the necessary skills and facilities to help them produce their own shows. (See Triangle TV 2005)

In Brisbane, Australia, the Briz31 channel has a programming policy and guidelines that are governed by the Australian Broadcast Services Act of 1992 and the Codes of Practice of the Community Broadcast Association of Australia. The Australian model of CTV involves selling airtime to those who can afford it, through community support or programme sponsorship. The Briz31 CTV station has a programming committee that previews pilot episodes to determine their eligibility for broadcast. The channel sells airtime to organisations and individuals seeking the broadcast of their programme or concept. Briz31 receives hundreds of proposals every year but only a small percentage make it to broadcast. The channel works closely with programme providers to secure sponsorship and to increase the percentage of proposals that obtain sufficient production support to be created and broadcast. (See Briz31 2005)

The responsibilities of programming committees vary from station to station, even within a single national policy framework, and these differing functions can inform the inception of programming committees in South Africa.

In view of the democratic imperatives of South African CTV, it is clear that the function of programming committees must not be to act as gatekeepers in preventing citizens from expressing their views through programmes, but instead should be to ensure equitable access to the airwaves. While programming committees should be able to object to content on technical or legal grounds, they should not act as censors or manipulators who deny people information or who limit points of view to those that are acceptable to the powers that be, whoever they are.

Despite the democratic imperative of CTV, there are still various ways in which a programming committee can suppress or marginalise the voice of a community. Programmes can be turned down for broadcast on unreasonable technical grounds or can be allocated time slots when very few people would be watching (for instance, very late at night); or it might be decided that screening the programme is not in the interests of viewers. Whatever the relative merits of such decisions, there should be mechanisms in place to balance the power of the programming committee and to subject its decisions to review, particularly if a dispute arises with content providers who believe their programme has been unfairly marginalised or suppressed.

One way of loosening the editorial control of programme committees is for the station to remain separate and independent from programme providers, allowing them to book slots on a first-come, first-served basis while at the same time privileging access material. This is the model followed by Triangle Television, which has a structure that ensures its independence from particular social interest groups. As the channel's website notes:

> The station acts independently from all programme providers. This independence ensures that Triangle Television cannot be controlled by individuals or groups with their own agendas. The station's independence ensures that editorial control remains with the programme provider. Air time is allocated on a first-come, first-served basis bearing in mind the need for equitable representation of all groups. (Triangle TV 2005)

This raises the question of the relationship between the broadcaster and contributing producers. In East Africa and in parts of southern Africa, broadcasters often demand that the producer pay them to broadcast the show rather than paying a licence fee for screening local productions. In Tanzania, for example, broadcasters share advertising revenue with the producer and allow the producer to use their equipment; then both parties sell the sponsorship and advertising space and retain the income accordingly, an arrangement that enables local producers to make videos. However, this type of arrangement is still rare because the East African broadcasters tend to rely on cheap foreign content (De Vos 2005).

There is also the possibility of developing key content focus areas that will ultimately provide quality content for regional, national and international markets. For example, animation is one area where Africa has the potential to compete globally because of the non-specificity of language on animation projects (De Vos 2005). It is much easier to dub an animated show into multiple languages than it is to dub other genres, and it is for this reason that a lot of animated productions are made for the international children's TV market.

South Africa could follow the Reunion Island model in establishing low-cost animation production units. Home-grown animation content has become a source of employment and revenue for Reunion Island, because the government financed the start-up of the industry through purchasing equipment and subsidising the animators' salaries. Once the industry had been established, the Reunion islanders began to compete internationally for both servicing work and the creation of home-grown content (De Vos 2005).

Programme acquisition and syndication

South African CTV broadcasters can draw on programming from various sources, both local and international. Cartoons might be a popular genre and could be acquired at relatively low cost (Auret 2005). On the international front, there are numerous CTV stations that produce their own indigenous programming. Much of this programming is pertinent to local communities and will not be suitable for South African audiences, but there are programmes such as documentaries that will be of interest to international audiences. One obstacle to obtaining programmes from these stations is the issue of copyright, where it resides with the producer rather than with the station.

For instance, the Downtown Community Television Centre (DCTV) is a non-profit organisation that creates and distributes social-issues documentaries. This media centre and its team of producers, film makers and broadcast journalists have won a variety of awards in the field of television since its inception in 1972.

The DCTV catalogue contains a range of videos that will be of interest to international audiences as well as to Americans. These videos cover subjects such as drug addiction, crime, Asian Americans, Latin America, disabled people and youth. Although many of them relate to the experiences of Americans in the US, their subject-matter will find strong resonance among people in South Africa confronting the same issues.

Some DCTV videos are available on VHS only, while others are also available on DVD. These videos demonstrate the fact that well-made content is an internationally saleable product. Where South African CTV producers are able to create compelling content, they would be able to sell this product locally and internationally. This could be through sales to organisations, individuals and other community broadcasters.

Questions of copyright ownership and the sales mechanism then come into play. DCTV sells its products through its website and a print catalogue and it also makes footage available for use in the compilation of other programmes. Fees range from minimum payments of $250 for industrial (non-broadcast) purposes to $2 000 for a feature film. Units charged range from $50 per second for industrial to $200 per second for feature film usage. Per minute charges are also available, except for commercials and feature films. The producer levies a minimum charge of five seconds per cut to all broadcast and non-broadcast material, with the exception of commercials and feature films, which are charged at a ten-second per shot minimum.

Fees for broadcast material are calculated on the basis of a variety of factors including the broadcaster's commercial or non-profit status, the kind of licence applied for (single use, multiple airings in a set time frame or unlimited airings over a specific period) and territory description (market, number of viewers, audience profile, etc.).

There is also free and at-cost programming that would be available to a CTV broadcaster (see, for example, www.alliancecm.org). Contributors to this service include the Weather Channel, the US Environmental Protection Agency, the Air Force News Service and Army Newswatch. Programmes range from professional development to the Classic Arts Showcase and Free Speech TV. Specialist categories include the aeronautical science series from the National Aerospace Agency (NASA) and Peace Works, a half-hour TV programme of ten poems and videos for peace created for the recent Nobel Peace Prize Forum.

This indicates that funding is available from state institutions and special-interest organisations for their own brand of community programming. South African CTV could tap into the same band of content production for its programming and production purposes if it is able to stimulate state bodies and NGOs to increase their output of video products.

In addition to the above programming sources, there are national CTV syndication and broadcasting organisations that eventually may provide some of their programming for use in South Africa. However, these organisations appear to be reluctant or uninterested in forming relationships with South African CTV at this stage, and did not respond to emails sent during the course of this research.

One of the best known North American networks of this kind is Deep Dish TV. The channel derives its name through combining the ideas of a parabolic satellite receiver dish and an apple pie or pizza dish. It was the first national satellite network in the US to link local access producers and programmers, independent video makers, activists and other individuals who support the progressive television network.

Deep Dish claims to offer an alternative to the 'homogenous and one-dimensional view of society' provided by the commercial television networks by catering to a diverse base of producers and viewpoints. The channel aims to distribute creative programming that educates and activates instead of encouraging passivity. Its programmes are shown on over 200 cable systems around the US and on some public television stations. Programmes are also received by thousands of satellite-dish viewers nationwide. They are also used by teachers and community groups for group screenings and discussion (Deep Dish TV 2005).

Another progressive US broadcaster, Link TV, aims to broadcast programmes that 'engage, educate and activate viewers to become involved in the world' (Link TV 2005). These programmes provide a unique perspective on international news, current events and diverse cultures, presenting issues not often covered by the US media. The channel seeks to connect viewers 'with people at the heart of breaking events, organisations in the forefront of social change and the cultures of an increasingly global community' (Link TV 2005).

The station's programming aims to educate American viewers by offering what it calls in-depth programmes on issues of regional and world importance. These programmes are intended to provide a global perspective on world issues and culture offering alternate viewpoints that are not US-centric. This is achieved through the presentation of other nations' newscasts that reveal US domestic issues in relation to global affairs. The channel aims to give voice to people without a voice, from communities that are under-represented in conventional media. Programmes connect viewers not only to the 'movers and shakers' but also to the 'moved and shaken' (i.e. people affected by the news).

Link TV broadcasts via direct broadcast satellite (DBS) television as a basic service to more than 22.4 million US homes. The DBS broadcast rights for Link TV were obtained under Federal Communications Commission guidelines, which require DBS operators to allocate 4 per cent of their channel for non-commercial, public-service programming. This legislative requisite is analogous to ICASA's stipulation that subscription broadcasting services in South Africa must make a channel available for community-owned broadcasting. In this sense, it provides a model for how a national CTV broadcaster in South Africa could provide a similar service.

Link TV is operated by Link Media Inc., a non-profit organisation formed through a partnership between Internews Network, a leading supporter of independent television around the world, the Independent Television Service, a supplier of independently produced programmes for public television, and Internews Interactive, a specialist in participatory TV programming.

Link TV also fosters collaboration through coalition building with partner organisations and grassroots organisations around specific-issue programmes, and could be a useful partner for South African CTV. This example of a collaborative partnership mode of operations could be followed by a national South African CTV organisation that could obtain content on behalf of various CTV initiatives, which would afford economies of scale that would help local stations to receive international content without bearing excessive strain from overall costs.

The danger of forming a national organisation, however, is that it can dilute the power of its individual constituents. The structure of any national body tasked with content acquisition would have to conform to strict levels of accountability to its constituents in terms of what content it acquires and distributes, its screening obligations and its governance. If South African CTV broadcasters have access to a national footprint, the implications of this in terms of how access and governance would be structured will be open to contention.

Audience reach is another issue, with satellite transmission favouring those recipients affluent enough to own a digital TV decoder. This drawback could be overcome by digital-to-analogue conversion and terrestrial retransmission or through IP netcasting, but such details would be subject to negotiation among the various parties concerned. Some means of providing low-cost set-top boxes or transcoders to viewers could also be investigated. For instance, the TBM Network subsidises IP video installations at client sites in return for a share of advertising revenue (Aldridge 2002a).

There are other Internet-based initiatives to spread CTV programming around the world. The International Community TV & Video Exchange (ICTVVE) is the first stage of a service for CTV and video makers internationally. Their website (www.ozemail.com.au/~catman/ice/) contains information about programmes made by community video workers that are available for exchange between organisations and individuals. As this service develops, users will be able to access a database on-line to search for programmes that they may want to screen through their organisations. They will also be able to place information about programmes that they have made.

ICTVVE notes that CTV exists on all continents and in nearly every country. As technology has become more accessible, there has been a dramatic increase in the amount of local video documentation. Over the past decade, international organisations have slowly developed to bring together community video makers to increase cooperation and information dissemination. As part of that development, there has been a need for a systematic approach to exchanging programmes, and ICTVVE is an attempt at setting up an international programme exchange system. It is hoped that in the near future this service will be available in several languages. Also, this service will be mirrored in Europe and the US to provide easier access.

The Global Village CAT website has links to 700 community and public access television sites worldwide, and other links related to the movement for freedom of speech.

A pan-European organisation, Open Channels for Europe (OCE), was launched in Berlin in November 2004. The OCE began with a membership of 18 organisations from six countries (Germany, France, the UK, Poland, Norway and Sweden), and is committed 'to building a European coalition for citizen's media as part of a global movement for media equity and democratic communication structures' (Berlin Declaration 1997). It has called upon the European Parliament and the European Commission, as well as national parliaments and governments in Europe, 'to recognise that people's direct access to information and participation in community television and radio and open channels are indispensable to democratic societies'.

In these aims, OCE echoes the intentions of South African CTV and could be a good partner in acquiring and disseminating progressive content that supports its democratic and humanistic objectives.

Another option that CTV channels can explore is to link up with or partner with CTV stations in other countries. For example, C31 Melbourne in Australia has expressed an interest in establishing relationships with South African CTV channels and is open to obtaining programming content from South African producers. Although at present C31 does not purchase programmes, it intends to do so in the future, and would then look for programmes that would appeal to an Australian audience or to members of the South African community in Australia. Documentaries about South Africa and its culture, food, environment and so on would be of interest to the channel (El-Khoury 2005).

Independent World Television

South African CTV channels can look to other progressive television initiatives around the world for content. One example of such a network in the process of establishing itself is Independent World Television (IWT), a Canadian initiative that aims to create a new global television network. The concept is similar to CNN in some ways, but it aims to create a news and current affairs network that will be funded primarily by its viewers, and that consequently will be independent of government or corporate support.

The project has been formalised into an organisation that employs four full-time staff, based in Toronto, Canada. A group of independent South African film makers has come together as a forum to further the African arm of the IWT project, and they see the CTV movement here as providing a possible partnership for content sharing (Aldridge 2004b).

The potential for this viewer-funded initiative has been demonstrated by a web-based organisation called MoveOn.org, which started during the Clinton presidency in the US. The organisation's mission was to raise money for television adverts with a progressive political message – at the time, opposing the media frenzy concerning the Monica Lewinsky scandal in order to refocus public attention on issues of real political significance.

MoveOn.org now has 1.7 million members. The organisation has proven itself to be very successful in fundraising; for instance, in just three days it raised some $12 million to oppose Arnold Schwarzenegger's conservative gubernatorial campaign. Over a six-month period it raised $58 million to counter George W Bush's Iraq adventure. As MoveOn.org shows, it is possible to harness people's energy and money in order to create an institution that will outlast the wave of energy that rises (and later falls) in response to world crises such as the Iraq war.

IWT is built on the belief that an independent global broadcaster is needed. The criteria for the proposed global news channel are good, honest journalism and courageous debate. In essence, it is a movement for democracy that will be funded by viewers, web-based fundraising and funding organisations.

The concept of the network is to have a centralised newsroom operation based in Toronto, with an international board of directors. Journalists around the world would report on the situations in their respective regions, necessitating a network of professional station representatives in each region. Because the station will (at least initially) broadcast in English, the English-speaking nations are the first targets for IWT operations. The station would form companies in different countries, but these would have a common board of directors (i.e. that of the international body).

News is the heart of the operation, and a deal is being negotiated with Associated Press (AP) to use AP's worldwide footage. Teams consisting of a veteran and a junior reporter, armed with digital cameras, would cover local stories. The station's programming allows anyone to be a reporter – an idea that is based on the concept of OhMyNews in Korea, where independent videographers send in footage that is vetted by professional journalists. Good material would go into a show called J-Pop; the really outstanding material would be broadcast on the IWT news, while other material could be posted on a website.

IWT has launched itself as a website and continues to seek public funding and to find international carriage partners for television broadcasting. It may be a useful content partner for South African CTV if the concept takes off.

African content

Another potential source of low-cost content is programming made for broadcast in other African countries or films from this continent. According to Sithengi Film Market CEO Michael Auret, most African films are made with low budgets, are very slow-paced and are often more appealing to Europeans than to Africans, so many young people do not much like them (Auret 2005). Auret feels that it is doubtful that South African audiences would prefer to watch poorly made programmes from other countries rather than the far more sophisticated South African material. For instance, Zambian soap operas are not as well-made as their South African counterparts. Low-cost programmes bought from elsewhere in Africa are unlikely to win local audiences.

The Sithengi Film Market has experimented with screening Nigerian films in the townships of Guguletu and Nyanga, but these audiences were not very enthusiastic about the films. However, Nigerian films are popular in other southern African countries such as Zimbabwe and Zambia. Kenya and Zimbabwe make about 10 to 20 films between them each year, whereas Nigeria produces about 600 films annually.

M-Net recently bought the rights to a large number of African films, acquiring broadcast rights over a period of 25 years for US$25 000. The channel based its acquisition on the expectation that a pay-per-view model will be instituted in South Africa, which means that people will pay to download these films. M-Net shows African films on the African Magic channel and pays producers US$250 per film.

Nigeria has 40 small-scale broadcasters. The capital, Lagos, has about six television broadcasters with various operational approaches. The most popular of these is a commercial, free-to-air channel, much like South Africa's eTV, which shows foreign, mostly American content. Galaxy TV is the next most popular channel, and it shows mostly local content; the station has moved up in the popularity rankings by improving its production quality.

Some Nigerian operators buy films 'off the street' on VHS tapes that they then rebroadcast. This is not legal but the anarchic state of broadcasting in the country allows this very entrepreneurial approach to continue. Distribution and publicity networks for Nigerian films, however, are highly developed. Every Sunday the radio and TV broadcasters interview the film makers about the movies that are about to be released the next week, so building public awareness of the product.

The Anglophone African countries are all making cheap content, but Ghanaian and Kenyan producers have less money than their Nigerian counterparts and struggle to produce films. In terms of acquiring African content, there is a programme market in Nairobi and a programme exchange project in East Africa, although this has not been working very efficiently.

Television stations in Ghana, Zimbabwe and the former Zaire went through periods of showing no foreign material. Audiences in other African states enjoy their local programmes, but South Africans are spoilt for choice in the range of content offered by the country's national broadcasters.

Auret (2005) points out that producing local television content can be very expensive and language dubbing is costly. At the same time, advertising support is low and the government is committed to investing in regional TV. The SABC's hugely increased local content and indigenous language quotas will make it very difficult for CTV to compete against it.

Covering local events that do not get exposure on national television is one way of producing cheap local content. Events such as film festivals, conferences, exhibitions and sports occasions could provide content.

Programming profile

The following schema indicates a possible structure for weekly broadcasting based on a sectoral approach. Categories in Table 8.1 where no 'hours per day' are given reflect the supposition that these items would not appear every day of the week; for example, educational programmes relating to school curricula might not be shown on Sundays, hence the six-hour-per-week figure is not stated as a per day ratio.

Table 8.1: Weekly CTV programming

Genre	Hours a week	Percentage	Funder
Education – schools	7.0	4.17%	Mindset TV
Education – ABET	3.5	2.08%	Sponsor
Education – Adult	7.0	4.17%	Sponsor
Children	7.0	4.17%	Sponsor
Local music	7.0	4.17%	Advertising
Health	7.0	4.17%	Mindset TV
Local documentary	7.0	4.17%	Advertising
Drama	7.0	4.17%	Community
Government – provincial	1.0	0.60%	Government
Government – city	1.0	0.60%	Government
News	3.5	2.08%	Funder
Commercial	7.0	4.17%	Sponsors/ads
Access	14.0	8.33%	Funder
Community-owned	5.0	2.98%	Community
Foreign community	5.0	2.98%	Funder
Foreign news/actuality	3.5	2.08%	Funder
Foreign documentary	3.5	2.08%	Advertising
Sport	7.0	4.17%	Advertising
Films	14.0	8.33%	Sponsor
Other	51.0	30.36%	Sponsor
Total	168.0	100.00%	
Hours in a week	168.0	100.00%	

The assumptions underlying this model are as follows:
- Some programmes will be repeated (e.g. a local documentary can be shown twice in a week).
- At least one hour a week of school curriculum and one hour of health programming could be obtained from Mindset Network. Adult and ABET educational material can be obtained from educational institutions, NGOs and live studio work.
- The commercial segment refers to programme space that is sold on to private production companies or production collectives, which then raise their own production fees through the sale of advertising or sponsorship messages in their programmes. These contributors might also pay a broadcasting fee to the CTV licensee. This sector could include commercial programmes that have been made specifically to generate profit, such as advertorials.
- Access programming includes social or NGO sectors such as youth, women and schools. Much of this could be done live in studio, so two hours a day is not unreasonable.

- Community-owned programming consists of programmes produced by particular communities; for instance, a Christian programme on Sunday or a Muslim programme on Saturday. These programmes would be produced by the communities concerned and provided to the station on tape or DVD. Such communities might also pay a broadcasting licence fee to the channel.

Figure 8.1: Weekly programming hours

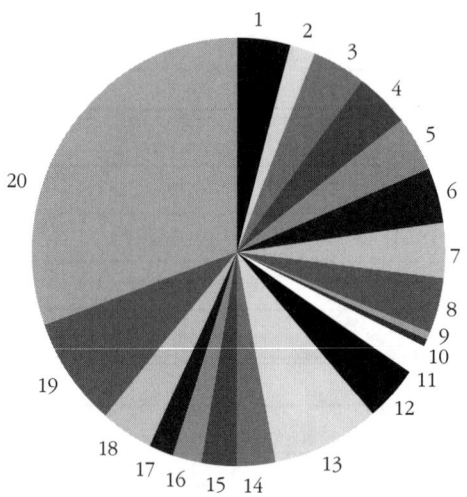

1	Education – schools
2	Education – ABET
3	Education – Adult
4	Children
5	Local music
6	Health
7	Local documentary
8	Drama
9	Government – provincial
10	Government – city
11	News
12	Commercial
13	Access
14	Community-owned
15	Foreign community
16	Foreign news/actuality
17	Foreign documentary
18	Sport
19	Films
20	Other

- Foreign community would be programmes produced by other community stations or producers around the world; the station would probably have to pay to get these programmes, although the costs are not high relative to regular commercial programming.
- Foreign news/actuality would be sourced from other news broadcasters internationally (e.g. IWT).
- Foreign documentary would be obtained from international sources that can include CTV broadcasters, NGOs and independent producers.
- Seven hours of sports programming can be obtained by shooting important local sporting events; for instance, a soccer match takes 90 minutes to complete, so just shooting a few different sporting events during the week can make up a lot of time.
- Films can be obtained through the Film Resource Unit and local production and distribution agencies. For instance: AFDA produces many student films each year; South African commercial and 'alternative' films would be desirable options; and content could also be sourced from Bollywood (India) and Nollywood (Nigeria).
- Music videos are freely available from record companies, and live studio sessions with local musicians and recordings of live performances at local clubs can also be used. The issue of music rights payments would also have to be taken into account.
- For local documentaries, existing productions from independent producers can be licensed for broadcast rather than bought outright. Small-scale budgets can be afforded to emerging producers to generate new content. New content endeavours could be supported by a video access centre attached to the station.
- Drama is a difficult genre because it costs so much to produce local television drama. Possibly, plays produced by community drama groups could be recorded, or low budgets made available to emerging production groups.

- Government programming can be provided by the national government through the Government Communication and Information System (GCIS), and provincial and local government can either provide ready-made material or their own live shows.
- News is a problem area. We have made allowance for half an hour of news per day, taking into account the resources necessary for producing TV news as well as language considerations. One idea is to link crews with the operations of community radio news, although this would present its own set of logistical problems. News is an area that should be explored in a temporary event broadcast, although it can be noted that few CTV stations internationally have daily news broadcasts and rely instead on community news and actuality programmes.
- The category 'Other' could consist of various source material such as Internet streaming, multimedia adverts or locked-off camera images like a fire burning in a hearth (used by a US campus channel) or a city scene (used by GDTV in 1995).

Figure 8.2: Daily programming, Monday to Friday

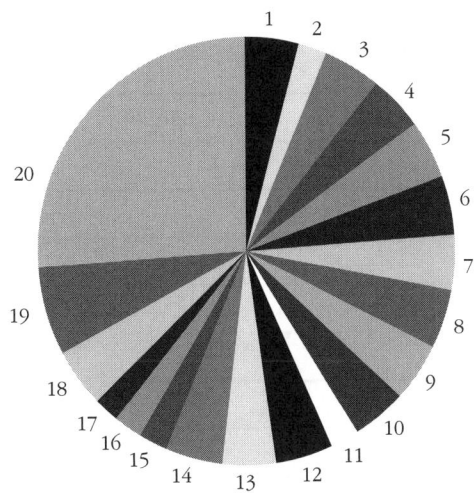

1	Education – schools
2	Education – ABET
3	Education – Adult
4	Children
5	Local music
6	Health
7	Local documentary
8	Drama
9	Government – provincial
10	Government – city
11	News
12	Commercial
13	Access
14	Community-owned
15	Foreign community
16	Foreign news/actuality
17	Foreign documentary
18	Sport
19	Films
20	Other

This programming model splits production funding between different sources depending on programme type. Mindset could provide CTV channels with content free of charge, in return for branding and carrying the sponsor messages of its programme funders; the basis of this arrangement would be that CTV is providing a service to Mindset by extending the reach of its programming, and so adding value for Mindset funders and sponsors.

Some programming, such as drama, could be community-funded. Various programmes might be paid for by sponsors, while others may be supported by advertising sold by the station or by a national CTV advertising and content-acquisition organisation.

The Australian model reflects a more commercial approach to funding, where airtime may be sold to commercial interests or to programme producers who then raise their own finance by selling airtime within their programmes for advertising or sponsorship messages.

Table 8.2: Daily programming, Monday to Friday

Genre	Hours a day	Percentage
Education – schools	1.0	4.17%
Education – ABET	0.5	2.08%
Education – Adult	1.0	4.17%
Children	1.0	4.17%
Local music	1.0	4.17%
Health	1.0	4.17%
Local documentary	1.0	4.17%
Drama	1.0	4.17%
Government – provincial	1.0	4.17%
Government – city	1.0	4.17%
News	0.5	2.08%
Commercial	1.0	4.17%
Access	2.0	4.17%
Community-owned	1.0	4.17%
Foreign community	0.5	2.08%
Foreign news/actuality	0.5	2.08%
Foreign documentary	0.5	2.08%
Sport	1.0	4.17%
Films	1.5	6.25%
Other	6.0	25.00%
Total	24.0	100.00%
Daily	24.0	100.00%

For instance, Triangle Television fills programme time not used by community programme providers with local programming and public service television programmes aimed at a wider audience. Triangle Television hosts a range of satellite feeds from other television broadcasters around the world, including Deutsche Welle TV from Germany and Voice of America Television. However, it must be borne in mind that the Australian stations target middle to upper income groups that are attractive to advertisers, which is very different to the development-focused model aimed at the lower income earners that South African CTV broadcasters tend to aim for.

Programme producers make use of time slots that they book with the station. A standard half-hour time slot is 29 minutes, with the remaining minute used by the channel for programme and station promotion. Most of Triangle Television's programme providers produce or import their own shows and materials. They use their own production and post-production equipment, although Triangle Television does offer a limited amount of technical assistance, including camera and studio hire.

Programme providers can utilise up to six minutes of their allocated time for advertising or sponsorship messages, which they sell to assist in meeting their costs. Programme providers set advertising rates for their own shows. It is up to the programme provider to source advertisers, and any arrangement for advertising is a business deal between the programme provider and its advertisers.

Triangle charges producers broadcast fees that vary between prime and off-peak time. Prime time is from 6.00 p.m. to 11.00 p.m. daily. Off-peak or standard time is from 11.00 p.m. to 6.00 p.m. daily. The broadcast fee charged by the channel depends on the type of programme (non-commercial or commercial), its length and broadcast time (prime time or standard time).

The broadcast fee for a half-hour time slot in prime time is Au$440 plus sales tax, and for standard time it is Au$260 plus tax.

Commercial programmes are defined as programmes that have been made specifically to generate profit, such as advertorials or programming where products are sold or endorsed in order to make a sale. These profit-driven programmes may be screened in any time slot not booked by community programme makers, who have priority access to time slots. Commercial programmes are subject to the same broadcasting standards and advertising rules as all other programmes, and broadcast fees are set at Au$1 200 plus tax per half-hour.

Time slots are allocated on a first-come, first-served basis. Applications for time-slot bookings are made directly to the programme manager, who will discuss available time slots and content issues with the programme producer to ensure an appropriate time for broadcast.

This model is useful in considering the economic structure of South African CTV. It demonstrates that CTV airtime has value and that people are prepared to pay for it. The example also balances the imperatives of commerce, on the one hand, with the prerequisite of public access, on the other, in order to find a viable solution for economic sustainability. South African CTV licensees should be wary of transferring funding responsibility to the programme producer because, unless strict guidelines are applied, the producer could exploit either the licensee or the advertisers in order to extract greater profit at the expense of these partners in the transaction. When it comes to any sort of commercial transaction, strict standards of corporate governance and accountability will have to be applied to monitor the licensee's transactions and to prevent abuse.

News

News is one of the most important programming aspects of television. Of all programme genres, news programmes typically receive the highest viewerships as well as the most criticism in terms of journalistic reporting standards and norms. News is also considered to be one of the most expensive genres, because it requires constant daily production by travelling news crews backed up by editorial newsroom teams and foreign programming inputs.

The logistics of news operations must be considered separately from other production facilities, because of the daily demands placed on them and the pressurised, deadline-driven nature of news production. In the context of CTV, there are different ways of addressing the nature and demands of news production in order to create news broadcasts that are relevant to the communities served by the station and that circumvent or alleviate some of the pressures that news production may place on the station's resources.

The primary task of television news is to present noteworthy happenings of the day or week in a visual manner. There is no point in simply replicating radio news by having a presenter read news items with no visual backup, and the onus is then on the station to acquire relevant images to amplify the narrative of the newsreader or voice-over.

In terms of the regulations governing CTV, ICASA has stipulated that licensees must provide regular news programmes and that it is up to the Authority to determine the duration of daily news bulletins in the licensees' licence conditions. This raises the question of how much news can be produced on a daily basis, assuming that news programmes occur on a daily rather than a weekly basis; indeed, there seems to be no directive that news be produced with this frequency, although it is probably in the broadcaster's interest to do so, given the popularity of news and public expectations with regard to the frequency of news programming by other television and radio broadcasters.

There are also particular regulatory requirements regarding the standards and norms to be applied in newscasts. These are elaborated in ICASA's Code of Conduct for Broadcasters, which is dealt with in the regulatory overview in Chapter 2 of this report. These stipulations mean that news must be dealt with in a thoroughly professional manner and that there will be little tolerance of news programmes that do not meet the exacting standards expected of broadcasters in terms of the regulations. Thus, while CTV channels may make use of young, inexperienced or semi-professional personnel in news operations, stringent editorial control by experienced editorial staff will be essential. There are many tricky situations that arise in news programming that pertain to matters of political bias or outright propaganda, misleading information and legal issues such as slander, misrepresentation and sub judice information. These matters require a level of expertise to be dealt with in an appropriate manner that does not leave the station open to public outcry, legal action, fines or licence revocation.

These considerations aside, it is worth noting that CTV news productions need not follow the path established by national broadcasters and that there is scope for innovation in their methodology. A case in point is the news programming of the 1995 GDTV broadcasts produced by Rob Greaves, an employee of Natal Newspapers, who single-handedly provided innovative daily news programmes that ranged from 5 to 20 minutes in length. Greaves went out with reporters from the *Daily News* newspaper to cover stories in the Durban area. Events covered included a police car chase, a ship being painted in the harbour and even a 'music-video style' story about a local surfing contest. These items were very different from national news programming in terms of camerawork, narrative style and insert length; at the same time, they were informative, locally relevant and entertaining.

Despite such achievements, there are certain problems with this mode of news production. During a presentation on CTV to ICASA during the regulator's public hearings on the Local Television Discussion Paper in 2003, ICASA's Michael Markovitz raised the question of editorial independence, noting that use of the *Daily News* reports did not add to diversity in the media landscape of Durban. Another problem was that *Daily News* reporters were concerned about the additional workload imposed on them and indicated that were such procedures to be followed in future, they might demand additional payment.

Nevertheless, there is merit in considering this partnership mode of news production for CTV, because it could reduce the economic impact of hiring news reporters, paying for news-wire services and running a newsroom. One idea would be for a CTV broadcaster to partner with the news teams of community radio stations, locating news resources such as camera operators and editing stations at these remote venues and coordinating news operations from the central station. This solution would pose its own set of problems, including issues of distance, coordination and accountability, and would need to be carefully considered and perhaps even tried out during temporary event broadcasts prior to its implementation at a permanent station.

Another consideration for news bulletins in the South African context is to make allowance for multiple-language newscasts to cater for the country's language diversity. Separate newscasts could be run in English, Afrikaans and locally dominant African indigenous languages. At the SABC, this approach leads to duplication of news personnel with different language bulletins having their own news staff to compile the bulletins. A CTV station could use a single pool of production personnel but have different presenters for each particular language, or even presenters capable of speaking multiple languages for different bulletins.

Other methodologies of news production can also be explored. For instance, news items could be subcontracted to independent community crews; news bulletins could be of flexible duration, depending on the amount of material that is ready for broadcast at the specified time; and different approaches to news content can also be explored, such as lengthier news items that investigate situations in greater depth than is the case on the existing channels.

Following the logic of station complexity outlined in Chapter 7 of this report, three tiers of news gathering can be envisaged for CTV news operations. At the most basic level, community volunteers gather news from particular communities of interest represented amongst the channel's participants; for example, volunteers from sporting communities would contribute sports inserts, labour volunteers would investigate labour issues, and youth would come up with stories relevant to young people. These personnel would use equipment owned by themselves or by their communities to produce material, and production would be tape-based rather than digital.

The GDTV broadcasts have adopted a limited form of this concept, where a small group of volunteers mimics conventional news operations by reporting on general-interest news items. Since GDTV does not have its own cameras, visual news inputs are limited; and, in the absence of an autocue, presenters memorise the text of news stories, using live or pre-recorded interviews to enliven the newscasts. This is more of a radio style of news production that would certainly be improved by the addition of cameras to the equation; however, travel costs are a considerable burden on news production teams and this also has to be taken into consideration when costing a news operation. A solution to this problem would be to use networked communications, through which geographically dispersed production centres could contribute to news programmes, but this requires a high bandwidth availability only barely present in South Africa at this time.

The second tier of news production would be a semi-professional operation, with teams of volunteers and interns running a permanent news production environment. These personnel would produce news of general interest rather than merely community-based material, using the station infrastructure to do so. Production could be tape-based in the field but digital in the newsroom environment, and play-out to air would also be based on a digital network.

In the high-end scenario, a semi-professional or professional news staff would conduct city-wide news operations. They would use digital technology for live broadcasts in the field as well as a fully digital production environment in the newsroom. The station would own its own fleet of vehicles and would have sophisticated news-gathering capacity in terms of drawing feeds from national or foreign sources through various high-speed data networks. This would be a news operation akin to City TV in Canada, a commercial channel that conducts local television operations in various Canadian cities.

Case study: GDTV programming

GDTV has staged a total of five broadcasts to date, four of which were in the period 2004–2005. As such, it provides an opportunity to examine a practical example of CTV programming in the South African context.

GDTV found that the audience for its last four broadcasts was mainly African, although certain programming (documentaries) attracted an Indian and white audience as well (Mayisela 2005).

During the week, the station opened at 7.00 a.m. and closed at midnight; on weekends, it broadcast 24 hours a day, playing music videos or screening talk shows until late at night. As programme manager Lynda Mayisela put it: 'As long as the audience is participating, we don't see the point in closing the show. If somebody comes with a problem, we say let's find a solution to this problem.' Because the station did not have any income, it did not have to pay any fees to the South African Music Rights Organisation (SAMRO). The FRU provided documentaries and African films at no cost to the station.

On Sundays, only Christian religious programmes were broadcast; the station apparently made some attempt to involve people of other religions such as Hindus and Muslims, but these groupings were unwilling to participate (Mayisela 2005).

In terms of news production, some news gathering teams took their own cameras to capture events in the city. The news programmes ran from 5.15 p.m. in four different languages simultaneously.

Viewers apparently enjoyed the opportunity to participate in programming by phone-ins to live talk shows because 'they get really interested hearing their voices on air' (Mayisela 2005). Cellphones provided another means of interaction; the station's telephone number was screened so that viewers could phone in or send an SMS or even a 'please call me' message to indicate that they were watching. Viewers were also invited to send in videos of weddings and funerals, and some brought in home DVDs. Viewer videos consisted mostly of events such as cultural activities, weddings and *Umemulo* (traditional 21st birthday celebrations). Even these limited forms of interaction with the world of television are entertaining for viewers, who are 'excited about being on TV' (Mayisela 2005).

CHAPTER 9

Audience research

CTV audience survey instrument

The purpose of creating an audience survey instrument is to provide CTV with a means to assess its feasibility in the community. A feedback loop is important to the work that a community radio station does. With CTV, as is the case with most radio stations, there exist different forms of interactivity that allow the audience to participate and express their views. This can take the form of call-in shows and outside broadcasts during which audience members have a chance to interact with the presenters. However, when the goal of communication is social change, there is a need for greater accuracy in measuring impact. This is important in two ways. Firstly, if it is not working, what can be done to make it work? Secondly, if it is working, what needs to be done to move to the next stage in the process of social change. Communication for social change is a multi-stage process and the success of communication is measured by its continuity.

The survey instrument we intend to develop will:
- attempt to identify the nature and diversity of CTV's audience;
- investigate perceptions of existing community media by audience sub-sectors;
- assess the feasibility of CTV;
- evaluate the 'community value' of community broadcasting through research into its audience and use by the community;
- identify the unmet media needs of the audience for future community media development; and
- provide, refine and apply a community media audience research methodology appropriate for the sector's diversity, and which can be used at regular intervals in the future once CTV has been established.

The first step will be to develop the survey instrument. In order to do this, we need to look at other instruments that have been used in similar surveys, with a view to incorporating useful elements while modifying and adapting them to suit the needs of CTV. In addition to the use of a questionnaire, focus groups with important sectors of the community will be conducted and, where necessary, in-depth interviews will be undertaken with key individuals in the industry and the community. The overall aims will be to:
- gather information from the potential audience, stakeholders and partners;
- find out what media feedback mechanisms are already in place and how these work; and
- determine how this survey can fill information gaps.

The philosophical basis for this project is to approach the establishment of CTV as an ongoing process. Therefore, the survey will help us to situate CTV's audience in the context of unmet needs and CTV's potential to fulfil these. The theoretical basis for the project is that people begin to and continue to consume media as a function of what they expect to get from it, whether or not it fulfils their needs.

The survey is intended for regular, periodical administration and not for use in a once-off exercise. Over time, this will help to identify the rate of change, which is important for station policy. Developing this survey instrument will serve the greater CTV constituency by providing a model for use by other initiatives and an important tool for training.

The survey must include the following:
- Questions that measure knowledge. We will use 'unaided recall' questions to avoid induced recognition. For example, instead of asking, 'Have you ever heard of CTV?', we would ask respondents to list all channels that they know of or watch, and from this pick up whether or not CTV features.
- Questions that measure attitudes. These questions fall into two categories – the respondent's position (negative or positive) with regard to CTV, and the intensity of the respondent's position.
- Questions that measure behaviour. Aspects concerning past, present and potential future behaviour should be included to assess accurately the behavioural component. For example, it should be established how frequently the respondents consume media, especially TV, whether they are satisfied with what is on offer and whether they would be interested in watching CTV in the future. Behavioural questions will show clearly if needs are being met or not.

Once developed, the questionnaire will be pilot-tested in the form of a mini-survey. This will help to determine questions of reliability (whether or not the questions yield the desired responses consistently) and validity (whether or not the responses that the questions yield reflect reality). This will also help us to incorporate important items that might have been omitted and to remove superfluous ones.

There are three data-collection methods to choose from: personal, telephone and post. Each of these has its strengths and weaknesses. The South African Advertising Research Foundation's data from its Radio Audience Measurement Survey was collected in the same way that Nielsen gathers its television viewership data in the US – by distributing diaries by mail, which are filled in by respondents over a seven-day viewing cycle. They also use the same households repeatedly. While this may be an efficient means of collecting data, it does not serve the needs of community radio as effectively. Telephone may not be viable either, since the level of penetration may not extend to all potential audiences.

Personal data collection involves sending out interviewers to the coverage area, to go door-to-door and interview respondents. This is time-consuming and potentially costly, but yields a wealth of useful data. Another disadvantage is that there is a high risk of interviewer bias; for this reason, interviewer training is imperative.

In keeping with the principles of sustainability and user-friendliness for community media, the design and implementation of this audience survey will make use of volunteers from among the partners and stakeholders. One of the major reasons community media does not frequently carry out audience research surveys is the cost involved. It is generally accepted that the inability of community media to participate in the larger commercial audience surveys adversely affects their ability to provide potential sponsors with market information. Professional research firms charge substantial amounts of money to carry out surveys, the bulk of which goes to the cost of hiring and training interviewers. Training and utilising a station's in-house personnel substantially reduces the costs of the operation. Another very important benefit of this is the capacity-building element. Once trained, the staff own the knowledge and are able to use it and pass it on, not only for their own benefit but also for the sector.

The design of the focus groups and in-depth interviews will be based on the data collected from the survey questionnaire. In this way, they will build on information already obtained and subject it to further interrogation.

This research has to take into account the important fact that 'audience share' is not an absolute priority and that, as community media, servicing an audience ignored by the mainstream is a valuable contribution to the various constituent communities of interest. The purpose of the survey is to acquire better knowledge of audiences and to provide useful information for potential sponsors. Another significant benefit is the opportunity this knowledge provides to tailor programming and thus ensure service to particular communities of interest. This may prove especially beneficial during various licensing processes undertaken by individual stations.

The process of data collection will be based on a random sample drawn from the broadcast footprint over a fixed period of time. Cultural events, especially those that are media-related, can also yield a useful sample of interested respondents. The survey must also take into account the linguistic diversity of the audience, and this will be achieved by translating the main survey instrument and, where necessary, conducting interviews in all languages. The key outcome will be the ultimate usefulness of the research to its primary participants – the audience and the CTV sector as a whole.

CHAPTER 10

Rural CTV

Establishing CTV in rural areas presents particular challenges, which include issues of ownership, production, distribution and reception. Rural areas in South Africa are marked by factors such as poverty and a huge disparity between poor and affluent groupings, which are overlaid by racial divides, lack of electricity, low TV ownership levels and lack of access to production skills and facilities.

It is for this reason that the government and development agencies focus on rural development as a priority. However, the resources allocated do not come close to meeting the goal of uplifting the living standards of rural populations. Communication through the media plays a central role in the development process, providing a means by which vital information can be disseminated to people. In the rural areas, populations who may be beyond the reach of rural extension services run by the government or development agencies can be reached through the media. Radio has long been used as a tool for development.

The modernisation paradigm, which still underpins the planning process in much of the developing world, favours investment in infrastructure for communication. This means ensuring radio and a measure of television coverage in the rural areas. Generally, these services have been provided by the public or government broadcaster, giving the government a means to reach rural populations with development information as well as entertainment and education.

With the liberalisation of communications and the advent of commercial television and radio, the gap between rural and urban has once again widened. There has been a proliferation of commercial, privately owned media, concentrated in urban areas due to the fact that urban markets afford a stronger economic base for commercial and advertising-driven television and radio. Rural populations tend to be poor, with lower spending capacity, and are generally less attractive to advertisers.

In order to participate fully in the political, social and economic development of the country, the rural population should be as well served as urban populations. Without locally relevant information that speaks to a population's specific circumstances, it is impossible to talk meaningfully about democracy (Bagdikian 1997). Although this observation was originally made against the backdrop of media conglomeration in the US, it applies equally to the developing world where the interests of the urban population are prioritised, mainly because the media are usually based in the urban centres. The large gap that needs to be bridged between rural and urban means that the investment required to reverse the trend is correspondingly huge.

Definition of rural

There are difficulties in defining what constitutes a rural area. Does the term include only agricultural regions, for instance, or does it embrace small towns and peri-urban areas? The question of language is also more significant in rural areas where multilingualism is arguably more limited than in urban centres and where people tend to speak indigenous African languages, including Afrikaans, and have very limited ability in English.

In the absence of a commonly accepted definition of the term 'rural', it is extremely difficult to describe or specify the needs of rural populations. There is, for example, a big difference between a township and a rural village. Whereas both a township and a rural village may not have access to running water or electricity, the communications needs of the respective populations will be very different, based on their means of livelihood. While a township population may seek information regarding access to basic services, which could be available close by, rural populations might be seeking information regarding alternative sources of water or energy.

Census 2001 defines an urban area as a structured and organised settlement where land parcels make up formal and permanent structures. Services such as water, electricity and refuse collection are provided, and roads are formally planned and maintained by a council. This definition includes adjacent suburbs, townships, informal settlements, smallholdings and industrial, recreational and institutional establishments (see Stats SA 2001). Thus, a rural area would be any area that does not fall within this classification.

Rural TV coverage

Television coverage in South Africa is fairly widespread, although the existing television broadcast footprint does not cover certain sparsely populated areas such as are found in the Northern Cape. The SABC 1 channel has an expansion target of 90 per cent coverage, and SABC 2 plans to reach 91 per cent of the population, while in 2003 these channels covered 83 per cent and 85.6 per cent respectively (Hope Madikane-Otto 2003).

The discussion on rural TV does not limit itself to areas that may not fall within the national footprint of the public broadcaster; rather, it extends to whether the needs of these rural populations are being met by the services where they exist. This is further compounded by the rationale for coverage. Public and commercial broadcasters roll out coverage infrastructure based on audience figures and associated cost-per-viewer advantages (Emerich 2005). The latter criterion is probably the more problematic when discussing rural CTV. Population densities in rural areas are generally much lower than in urban areas. This means that potential advertisers are reaching fewer people within a broadcast footprint in a rural area than they would in an urban one.

Assuming that the roll-out of the SABC 4 and 5 regional channels follows similar coverage patterns, substantial areas of South Africa will achieve coverage. Although some areas will be too sparsely populated to be served by terrestrial transmitters, the SABC is now offering its channels via satellite as well.

Nevertheless, levels of television ownership are still lower in the rural areas of the country than in urban areas. The social structures of these rural communities allow for communal viewing as opposed to individual household viewing. The only impediment to this is the distances people might have to travel to get to the neighbour's house that has a TV set. In certain areas, central points such as the local commercial or administrative centre have served as places for communal media consumption.

The vagaries of transmission coverage have motivated some rural communities to invest in satellite receiving stations and low-power transmitters to relay SABC TV broadcasts to local populations. These small-town transmitters are owned by the community in the sense that it might raise the capital outlay for the transmitter in order to receive the public broadcaster's programming. There are currently about 500 communities using their own low-power, 1–2W transmitters to cover a radius of up to two kilometres.

The owner of the transmitter is responsible for its maintenance, and Sentech's role is to ensure that they stick to their ICASA-approved frequency. Sentech also helps these mini-broadcasters with their licence applications at no charge.

A problem in applying this redistribution model to CTV is that the low-power transmitters are owned by wealthy communities whose disadvantaged neighbours are largely left out of the equation. Rectification of this situation would require government intervention, although public-private partnerships may also come into play to achieve broadcast reach for poorer communities in these areas.

Satellite distribution

Another problem in rural areas is that the population is thinly spread, which makes it necessary to use powerful land-based transmitters to distribute analogue signals. Setting up such infrastructure can become impractical, given the economic context of public and commercial broadcasting operations.

The obvious means of overcoming coverage limitations is to use satellite broadcasting. The PAS 7 satellite has a footprint that covers the whole of South Africa and spreads into the nearer Southern African Development Community countries as well. To rent the necessary channel space on this satellite would cost R111 000 a month at current rates (Emerich 2005). The downside, of course, is that viewers then have to buy or rent the necessary satellite reception dish and digital decoder; however, various community-oriented broadcasters in South Africa use this mechanism on the DSTV platform.

Communities using DSTV to communicate include the Afrikaans, Portuguese and Indian cultural groups. It must be noted, however, that these are commercial community channels and are not community-owned and managed. Still, developmental communications are delivered on DSTV by Mindset Network, while Trinity Broadcasting Network (TBN) uses the medium to distribute its Christian evangelical programming in the Eastern Cape.

The problem of reception in rural areas could be solved to some extent by a hybrid system that receives a satellite broadcast and then converts the digital data into an analogue low-band transmission that is conveyed through a series of very-low-power repeaters. This system has been used to link rural areas in Britain (Rushton 2004) and relies on broadcasts under the 10 mW level, which falls outside the scope of international frequency regulations. These transmitters use the 2.4 GHz wavelength and have a reach of up to five kilometres with respect to line-of-sight coverage. Networks consisting of such transmitter and relay set-ups could be used to cover rural settlements and could be combined with satellite reception methods to redistribute national content. The distances to be covered in sparsely populated rural settings present a problem here, because these low-frequency transmissions need repeater stations for the signal to cover the distances.

Non-broadcast options

There are other means of reaching rural audiences. African experiences suggest that people in areas that do not have much access to television enjoy the communal experience of watching videos and films (see SACOD Director Tambudzai Madzimuri's observations in Chapter 5). Structures facilitating this could be developed.

Video has been used in Bolivia, Mexico and other parts of Latin America to great effect as a means of development communication (IPDC 2005). In agricultural communities it has served as a means by which information and education can reach the population. The investment needed to set up and provide video services is substantially smaller than the infrastructural needs for setting up television. NGOs with specific reasons to reach these rural populations can also provide sponsorship. An important factor is that the methodology of community video provides for a substantial level of interactivity in that local people can be trained to use video to document their lives and their problems. The issue of scheduling is critical in rural areas, and video provides the flexibility that real-time broadcasting may not. For instance, in agricultural communities, production activities determine when people have time to watch programmes, and a programming schedule that was suitable during the harvesting season may not work in the planting season (IPDC 2005).

GCIS initiatives

In South Africa, the Government Communication and Information System (GCIS) is engaged with a number of projects to use video as a medium for development communications. GCIS is working with the Film Resource Unit (FRU) to distribute African film content through Multi-purpose Community Centres (MPCCs) with the aim of using the films to educate people about issues relevant to governance. Film screenings are held at MPCCs and particular meanings are interpreted and discussed in order to elucidate principles of democracy and development issues (Jacobs 2005). The Latin American experience shows that this system can be enhanced by introducing higher levels of interactivity. For instance, members of the community can give feedback on what kind of programmes they would like to see. Research can determine what information is of most importance to them, which is being done by GCIS through communication officers. This development objective would also be served through viewer groups organised at local levels.

Another GCIS project involves a partnership with the Umsobomvu Youth Fund to run a 35-seater bus that travels the country delivering life skills through an Internet-linked computer and video screenings. GCIS encourages other communication initiatives at MPCCs such as the Community Television Network (CTN), a commercially run project that supplies television set-VCR units to MPCCs. CTN screens monthly videos containing edutainment and commercial material along with information about government programmes. The company is now setting up roadside trading kiosks in township areas. These four-metre high kiosks, called eStokini, provide services that include a news-stand, fast food, staple provisions, a pay telephone and a video screen showing the CTN Stokvel TV channel.

This 'living billboard' concept offers branding and advertising opportunities to commercial clients. It is backed by the Edcon Group, one of South Africa's top retail brands. In association with the South African Council of Churches (SACC), the project will initially roll out from street-edge church properties. CTN Stokvel TV has been a communications channel for the SACC for some time as a tape-based medium distributed to church and stokvel groups to inform people about SACC projects and news.

The commercial element of this approach can be expanded though the provision of other services, such as Internet access, at a small fee. In the US, certain rural communities that do not have local television are served by mobile units, which also provide training to locals in the use of television technology and programming production and development.

This is a very forward-looking strategy based on the principle that in the future even these communities will be in the technological and media mainstream and there will be a need for skilled people. It is safe to assume that the same applies in South Africa and elsewhere. Telephony is an example of the adaptability of technology. In parts of the world where the infrastructure does not allow for landline penetration, cellphones have taken over and provide access. The possibilities of using cellphone technology for television are already being developed.

Utilising MPCCs

While GCIS has embraced the CTN concept, a channel owned and managed by the community would need to find its own distribution mechanism that is distinct from this commercial medium. One idea would be to set up video screens in MPCCs, which could be fed either through satellite transmission or Internet protocol (IP) network distribution. This raises the associated concept of community production, because there is some intention on the part of players such as GCIS, FRU and the Universal Service Agency (USA) to build video production capacity at MPCCs.

The FRU project to develop audio-visual (AV) centres in MPCCs is intended ultimately to include the inception of video production facilities in these centres. This project has the potential to engage with CTV initiatives to produce programming content from rural or small town areas. In turn, this production would be boosted by having a ready outlet in the CTV broadcasts.

The idea of providing video production training to rural populations brings to the fore the problem of low education levels in these areas. Development data show that levels of literacy in rural areas do not compare favourably with urban environments. This is compounded by the migration of educated individuals to urban centres in search of employment, leaving the rural areas with a brain drain that decreases the likelihood of finding individuals who can be trained in the complexities of video technology and production techniques. The ability of AV centres to attract skilled individuals who want to work in rural areas would depend to some degree on the amount of revenue they are able to obtain from production activities.

Large area networks

Because of the economies of scale necessary to run expensive television infrastructure, it is unlikely that a rural CTV broadcaster could survive in just one locality; hence, it would be necessary to develop regional and possibly national networks to give rural CTV a sufficient viewer base. These types of regional distribution already exist in some forms; for instance, the privately owned TBN, Mindset Network's Learn and Health channels and the proposed SABC regional channels. Both Mindset and the SABC require content that will suit audience needs in these outlying areas, so developing production capacity in these regions is crucial.

The nature of these production facilities will be determined by the economic opportunities available to local producers. A national CTV network could provide income, as well as small-scale production opportunities such as video coverage of weddings and funerals in rural areas. The SABC will also want to develop professional producers in these areas, and possibly some means of collaboration between them and the CTV sector could be arranged.

Rural economic development is falling further behind because of the lack of access to high-speed telecommunications services. In terms of the technical requirements of production, it is suggested that low-cost options be investigated. A Wintel or Apple Macintosh PC can be used as an editing platform, with prosumer-level handycams being used for recording purposes.

Where sufficient bandwidth exists for high-speed Internet connectivity, video files can be shared amongst regional or national networks of producers, as well as finished products being transferred to a central broadcast point. This is dependent on the commitment of the government to bring advanced telecommunication services to rural areas. In the US, the government has been able to do this using digital bandwidth. Although the difference is that they have local public stations, this could probably be achieved in South Africa through communications hubs, which the MPCCs are promising to become. For instance, if satellite transmission is used as a national distribution mechanism for rural CTV, then content produced in rural areas could be transferred to a facility such as Multichoice in Johannesburg for uplink to the satellite through broadband connections.

With this kind of set-up in place, production capacity will depend on the skills of the users. The Monash University film and video learnerships are a good step in the direction of equipping people from outlying areas with the basic level of skills required for such operations.

IPDC

The International Programme for the Development of Communication (IPDC) has an ambitious initiative in rural Bolivia, the first priority of which is the strengthening of rural CTV channels and rural AV educational production centres, in order to improve their human resources and programme production capacities. The project seeks to enhance the technological capabilities of these stations, as another element in the improvement of the quality of their programming. It is planned to set out a system of training that will be sensitive to cultural differences in the community and to the various levels of development of the participants; this will promote gender balance in TV production and cover all of the aspects of creating content for TV programming with social development goals (viz. basic concepts of TV production, TV idioms, the technological support and innovation of digital technical resources, and the production of educational messages).

Another such IPDC-sponsored project is TV Serrana in Cuba. The National Association of Farmers sought assistance to meet the information needs of isolated rural populations. Transmissions were done through the existing regional and national channels, but in the more remote areas, the IPDC set up video rooms where the information could be viewed collectively from videotape. The interactive nature of these sessions allowed the farmers to participate and to request the kind of information that they needed most.

Ownership and control

The development of production capacity and distribution channels for CTV is only one part of the equation, the other being community ownership and management. This will require a coordinated effort to involve representative organisations working in the rural areas in CTV development, a similar process to what is happening in the cities.

In the rural areas, an obvious temptation would be to have the existing local government structures take the lead in such ownership and management, because of the skills and resources that reside in government personnel in these regions. However, the question then arises as to whether or not this would cause the same problems as would be the case in an urban setting. It is a widely shared perception that in rural areas the local administration and government structures are closer to the people and are staffed mostly by members of the community, so their level of social investment in the community is arguably greater. Whereas urban community leaders may not necessarily be part of the administrative or local government structure, rural community leaders often are. Nevertheless, community buy-in is dependent upon what tangible benefits are available. This brings the discussion back to the basic premise of the unmet information needs of the community and how these can be satisfied through CTV.

Urban-rural support

Ultimately, the potential for rural television to take root and become sustainable is dependent upon how well CTV develops in South Africa's urban areas. Rural CTV will face the same challenges in addition to macro-level ones such as infrastructure. Urban CTV is in the process of developing and selling its rationale to potential audiences – a process that will ensure buy-in and support. Urban CTV can play a mentorship role for rural CTV in the same way that urban community radio stations have mentored their rural counterparts.

If production facilities remain in urban rather than rural settings, then less infrastructure and lower-technology options, such as the distribution of videotapes rather than CTV, will remain the most viable choice. However, for there to be true ownership and empowerment of rural communities, the focus must be on setting up production in rural areas, allowing the people to tell their own stories and to articulate their needs.

The technical capacity exists for at least a basic set-up, and training is already widely available through the various institutions that exist in urban areas. Once the decision has been made to proceed with this option, the next stage is to look at distribution. The SABC regional channels could facilitate distribution that would provide reasonably wide coverage and reach. There is also the option to use low-power broadcasting or delivery via IP networks to designated centres. The government plans to set up MPCCs all over the country and most of these already exist. Where they do not yet exist, other centres such as schools, libraries and hospitals can be used, especially since these venues are already earmarked for some level of connectivity.

CHAPTER 11

Future technical directions for CTV

In terms of technical aspects, the future of television broadcasting is completely shaped by the dominance of digital technologies and the corresponding obsolescence of their analogue precursors. This has particular implications with respect to the phenomenon of convergence, where disparate communications mediums are collapsing into meta-mediums based on digital storage and transmission technologies.

What this means is that digital technologies are being used for recording, manipulating and storing information, as well as conveying content to users through a variety of channels. Various devices are then used to receive this information, ranging from television sets to computers, personal digital assistants (PDAs) and cellphones. Digitisation is making all of these devices increasingly intelligent in terms of their functionality; in addition, it enables interactivity, so the viewer is no longer a passive receiver of information but can actively participate in a two-way interaction with the content originator.

Digital technologies are also lowering the barriers to entry for video producers, enabling people to produce material at a good level of technical quality at the beginning of the production-transmission chain. This digital information has further benefits: it does not decay during its passage through the production-transmission chain to the same extent as analogue information; it is more readily manipulable and accessible during production; it can be transmitted over multiple channels; and it can be stored by the end-user on multiple devices.

The ubiquity of digital technology in the production chain, from recording to editing, sharing, distributing and transmitting content, indicates that television is no longer a stand-alone medium but rather one that is merging into information and communications technology (ICT) networks. As digital technology progresses and bandwidth availability increases, so television will become available through a variety of Internet protocol (IP)-based distribution channels. Moreover, it will cease to be a passively received medium and will instead contain various levels of interactivity whereby audiences can interact with content.

As proliferating digital technologies drive down barriers to entry, more people will become video producers and their ability to contribute to television programming will be limited by their skills, imagination and ability to use the medium rather than by technology and costs. These factors bode well for CTV because they are making television more accessible for both viewers and producers alike.

Internet TV

Using the Internet as a distribution channel has the advantage of giving viewers the option of seeing archived TV programmes on demand. For instance, a live-show webcast over the Internet from Seattle to a public TV station in Amsterdam uses a combination of asymmetric digital subscriber line (ADSL) and cable modem for transmission to the station. In addition to Seattle programming, the show carries live feeds from contributors in New York, Mexico City, Brussels, Belgium and elsewhere. The segments are edited together at the Salto Studios in Amsterdam (Frishberg 2003).

The Dutch four-hour cable show, *De Hoeksteen* (The Cornerstone) features interviews and round-table discussions using webcam hook-ups and videoconferencing, as well as live studio guests. Audiences participate through a pair of Internet chat rooms and the telephone. Chat-room discussions run as a 'crawl' under the main image (Frishberg 2003).

Despite regular improvements in technology, adoption of Internet TV has been slow, even in the more developed countries. For all the innovations in the past two years, Internet TV remains a choppy image in a small window opened on a monitor.

Even so, Internet TV is beginning to take off in a serious way. Over 700 TV broadcasters, the majority of them commercial stations, everywhere from Afghanistan to Colombia and Australia, are making programming available on 56 KBps connections. Internet portal wwiTV and its North American affiliate, TV4all, list 3 000 live and archived television and radio feeds from every part of the world (Frishberg 2003).

Local neighbourhoods are beginning to use wireless computer networks to create very local TV stations to communicate among themselves. At present, Internet webcasting is used in addition to normal broadcast programming, but not as a main channel for broadcasting.

Several initiatives suggest that the trend toward Internet TV is growing in the public sphere. A group of local stations in Italy has pooled its money to start an Internet service that uses compression, so they can have a 24-hour service to which they all contribute programming.

A webcast TV project in Denmark has grown out of a tenants' rights group in a senior citizens' housing project, originally set up to press their demands for home repairs and better services. The US has about 100 webcasting TV stations, ranging from local commercial channels and a network of Christian Web TV stations to community-access and local-government channels.

In Arizona, Access Phoenix, a community-access station, broadcasts all its shows simultaneously on two cable channels and over the Internet. Anybody with an Internet connection can view the programmes at their regular broadcast time. The shows are also archived and available on demand from the access channel's website.

New York's Manhattan Neighborhood Network runs four channels of public-access television on two cable systems and in streaming formats, live and archived, in broadband and 56 KBps modem versions. On the Hawaiian island of Oahu, community-access provider Olelo has five channels, all streaming on the Internet and over the cable system.

Netcasting

Using IP networks to distribute programming is a path that CTV could follow in order to reach viewers who either do not have TV sets or who wish to obtain televisual information on computers, PDAs or cellphones.

There is an explosion of netcasting taking place worldwide, as broadband capacity is extended by telecommunications providers. In South Africa, providers such as Telkom, Sentech and other third-party providers have extended broadband connectivity speeds through their various fixed-line and wireless products. This has meant that high-speed Internet connectivity is becoming more affordable, although it is still expensive relative to similar products in other countries and consumer uptake is correspondingly slower than in other nations (ICT World 2005b).

Telkom has started providing television broadcasting distribution through its ADSL network. Subscribers to this broadband product can download video streams, and Telkom aims to begin trials shortly on a new broadband service called 'triple play', which includes Internet, music and video-on-demand. One problem with this technology in South Africa is that Telkom is not presently rolling out ADSL services to low-demand areas such as the townships, which means that many people will not be able to access triple-play services (Madlala 2005).

Telkom has content-provision deals with M-Net and MultiChoice to offer DVD-quality broadcasts of video and music-on-demand, downloaded from a content server. According to Steven White, Telkom executive for product development, triple play will be an add-on service, so the standard bandwidth cap for downloading will not apply to video-on-demand. He pointed out that in Europe, the average family downloads 1.5 films per month, meaning that the service would not work as a stand-alone business (in Madlala 2005).

Telkom claims that it is not moving into the realm of content provision, but is merely providing a channel for content distribution. Thus, it would seem that a CTV content provider using a channel such as Telkom's ADSL, would fall outside the definition of a broadcaster in terms of the Convergence Bill. Section 1 of the Bill specifically excludes 'a service or components of a service that make programmes available on demand on a point-to-point basis, including a dial-up service'.

Computer networks for content distribution might be dedicated networks or the Internet, depending on the target audience to be reached. Content distribution in this model would be via terrestrial networks or satellite-based multicasts to PCs and venue-based plasma or television screens, instead of broadcasting television signals over the airwaves (Aldridge 2002b).

A dedicated 'National Empowerment Network' could link educational institutions, disadvantaged communities, the government and the business sector. These sectors would provide both viewer communities and producer groups; in other words, they would be involved as target audiences (receptor sites) and as programming producers (Aldridge 2002b).

The costs of multicasting are significantly lower than television broadcasting, which makes it an attractive option from a cost point of view (Dawkins 2005). On the other hand, there are particular constraints that limit the availability of video-over-data networks, relating to technology and bandwidth availability and cost.

In terms of its ability to reach disadvantaged or marginalised population sectors, the multicasting model relies on video being viewed by groups of people at venues such as MPCCs or taxi ranks rather than by individuals in the privacy of their homes.

The increasing availability of high-speed data networks has considerably broadened the scope for the delivery of video via this medium. Videoconferencing and video streaming are increasingly in use, and cellular and palm-top video is gaining momentum on the latest wave of wireless networking technologies.

Three elements are making multicasting more feasible: cheaper high-bandwidth connections to PCs, changes in content-creation technologies and improvements to video streaming codecs (compression algorithms).

The ability to send high-quality video over data networks will have a significant effect on television broadcasting. US research-firm, Forrester predicts that when Internet video is also viewed on TV sets, a new tier of niche programming – the Internet Tier – will be created. While television already serves mass markets for video, Internet video suppliers will tap niche markets (communities) like ethnic and religious groups, sports and hobby groups or specific age groups.

The feasibility of an empowerment or education-based multicasting system in South Africa is encouraged by several factors:
- the implementation of Multi-purpose Community Centres (MPCCs) and Community Digital Hubs (CDHs) that have broadband Internet connections;
- the establishment of community video centres by the Film Resource Unit (FRU) and the Government Communication Information System (GCIS);
- the need to make information resources available for community upliftment through training, job creation and entrepreneurship;
- the necessity for extensive health education; and
- the scarcity of qualified teaching staff for certain school and tertiary education subjects.

To address these needs, a national network of video-producing centres and receiving stations could be implemented as part of a CTV infrastructure. Receiving stations could be placed at tertiary educational institutions, schools, MPCCs, CDHs, hospitals and clinics. A nationwide 'community' of video producers, some of whom would be based at these self-same institutions, would contribute a large proportion of the content.

Figure 11.1: Video sharing network

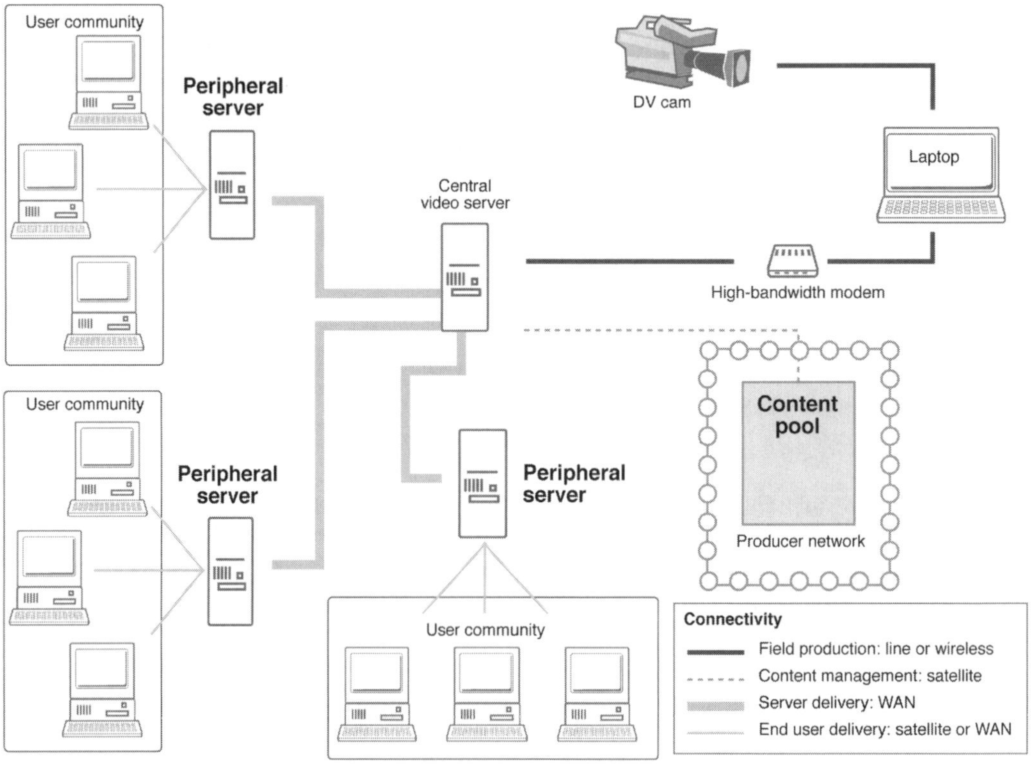

Source: Aldridge (2002b)

The multicast station's reach would include rural areas and could be used to aid empowerment initiatives in these areas. The network can also be extended to other countries, for example those in the SADC region.

Video content delivery over data networks

The delivery of video over data networks offers a cost-effective alternative to the expensive business of television broadcasting. While this method of delivery has been possible for some years, development has been slowed by certain restrictions such as limited bandwidth capacity, which constrains the transmission of information-intensive data such as video. This disability is being overcome today by improvements in video-compression codecs, the development of networking methodologies and the inception of new production technologies.

For example, one South African-developed multicasting system sends data via satellite, a one-way transmission that minimises bandwidth requirements. Error correction occurs through a telephonic IP loop back to the sending station to request the missing packets. This system is cheaper than the VSAT method commonly employed for such transmissions (Roussos 2002).

Figure 11.2: The PanAmSat (PAS) 7 footprint

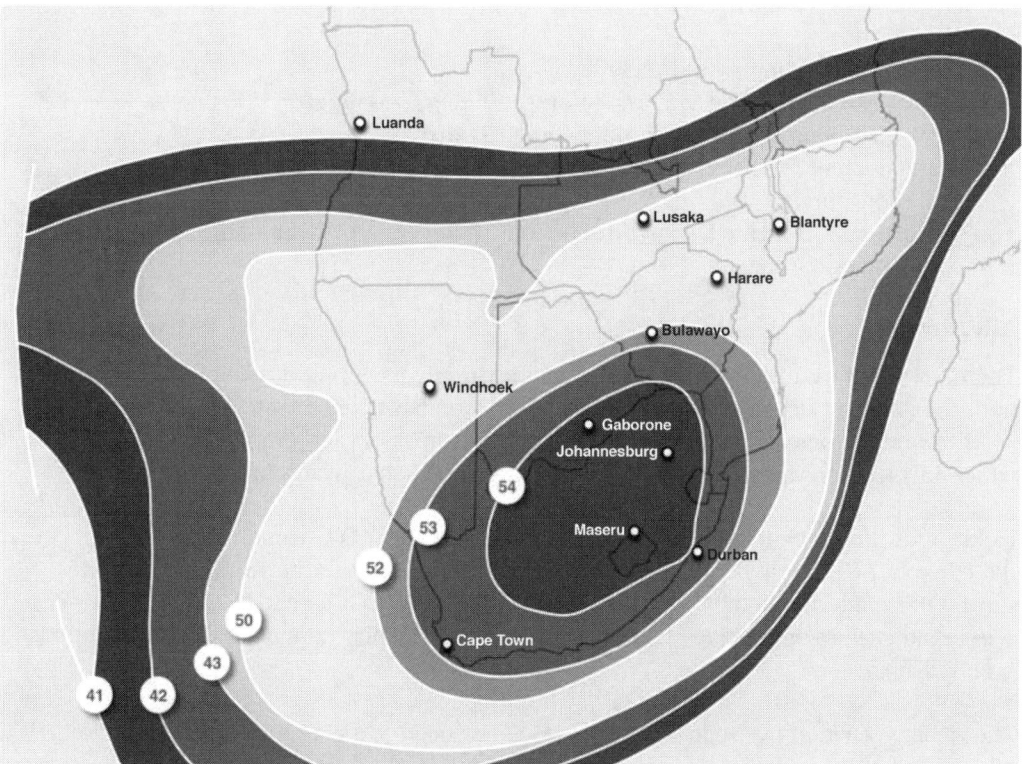

Source: Brock (2002)

Reception is through a satellite dish, the data being uplinked via Sentech transmitters to the PAS-7 satellite. This satellite provides a footprint over the subcontinent – mainly South Africa, Namibia and Mozambique, but extending northwards into Zambia, Tanzania and Angola (see Figure 11.2).

During off-peak times, the data is 'trickled' to receiving stations, where it is stored on a PC that connects to plasma screens or TV sets at the venue. The PC has no keyboard or monitor, and requires no human intervention to operate.

Presently, the major use of this point-to-point multicasting is the creation of 'video posters', showing mainly advertising and in-store promotions, but any content can be delivered in this way and programming can include information, training and entertainment.

Why deliver video through multicasting?

Video is a medium that combines images with narration and music to form an information stream. The medium is ideal for situations where a visual component is required for optimal understanding.

It is envisioned that video multicasting would not compete with television for specific reasons, which include limitations in delivery to mass audiences, and insufficiencies in picture quality and bandwidth availability.

The uses of multicasting would include:
- education (information videos, lectures, training, pedagogical documentaries);
- news (happenings, events, announcements, analysis);
- entertainment (where content is distinct from the normal fare of television, e.g. short films);
- discussions (interviews, panel discussions, interactive programming); and
- local sports coverage.

Advantages

There are significant cost advantages to multicasting versus broadcasting. These relate to both transmission of information over data networks and content-production costs. The latter are being lowered by advances in content-acquisition and editing technologies, which involve improvements in camera technology, PC hardware and software.

Field production technologies today include digital video (DV) cameras that deliver video directly to a PC, from whence the video can be streamed via a network. The stream can be transmitted by telephone or wireless connection to a central distribution server. Wireless transmission can also take place via a GSM cellular connection at ISDN speeds (i.e. 64 KBps).

The quality of video-over-data networks does not need to be as high as that required for television, because:
- the video is not subject to the limitations of transmission over the airwaves, such as interference and signal strength;
- it need not be shown as full-screen, full-motion video; and
- the information value of the content is of greater value than the clarity of the accompanying images.

For these reasons, low-end consumer or prosumer video cameras can be used; they are cheaper than the high-end professional cameras normally used for broadcast purposes and are designed specifically for streaming purposes.

The use of data networks can also facilitate the sharing of video data for producer networks. Videotapes can be automatically scanned and converted to digital data, which is stored in a database. Metadata about the footage can be logged to describe each shot, and the resulting material can be shared by a geographically dispersed producer network.

Multicasting offers a number of advantages. The ability to send particular data to specific IP addresses means that content can be structured according to the nature of the receiving audience. This means that no two audiences need receive the same information, even at particular locales. Content can be scheduled and delivered according to the specific needs of the target audience. Moreover, feedback can be obtained from these receiving audiences via the IP feedback loop, which is ideal for pedagogical or research purposes.

Specific programmes can be sent to particular target groups like learners, sports fans and community organisations, and programmes can be generated by community groups at video access centres, students and trainees at tertiary educational institutions, scholars, local advertising agencies and so on.

Limitations

Multicasting suffers from certain limitations due to the nature of the transmission medium (networks and the Internet). Because video is high-information-density data, optimal viewing – full-screen, full-motion video – is restricted due to limitations of bandwidth, data pathways and compression/decompression technologies.

According to the PAL (phase alternating line) standard of South African and European broadcasting, optimal transmission rates stand at 25 frames per second. Bandwidth and compression/decompression limitations tend to restrict video over IP to lesser frame rates of 12–15 frames per second. Moreover, on-screen viewing is generally at smaller frame sizes (160 X 120, 240 X 180, etc. pixels).

Compression/decompression algorithms (codecs) have improved tremendously in recent times. The latest codecs include the MPEG range (MPEG-1 to MPEG-4), which enable fast compression/decompression. Their limitations are that not all PCs are capable of using them, due to slow processor speeds on the older machines, and that the MPEG standard requires specific hardware (video cards) for editing purposes.

Delivery of video over the Internet is slowed by the limitations of the network as a whole. Data packets find their way across the network via a multitude of servers and are thus subject to network congestion and bottlenecks, and users' modem speeds slow delivery over the 'last mile' between user and Internet service provider.

Solutions

Because of the current limitations of the Internet as a delivery medium, optimal delivery of video data requires the establishment of dedicated media distribution networks. These networks consist of dedicated media servers at the 'edge' or periphery of the network, which then distribute content to the end-user.

There is a difference between content that is delivered to viewers live and that which is delivered to be stored and accessed later. While live streaming requires high bandwidths to deliver television-standard viewing, the storage method enables the viewer to experience DVD-quality video.

The 'trickle' method of data delivery can use satellite as a transmission mechanism, with the IP loop from the end-user being completed by telephone-based feedback to the transmitting station. Using the satellite-delivery methodology avoids tying up users' working bandwidth on landlines. Data can also be 'trickled' to periphery servers (where it is stored for later screening) in off-peak times, so lowering transmission costs. This also obviates the constraint of low frame-rates and slow transmission suffered by live streaming.

Content sharing

Video distribution networks enable content producers to share data and to work collaboratively on video production projects even where they are situated in different locations; thus, producers working on regional, national or international collaborative projects can share video clips and other data to compile a finished product.

New digital asset-management programmes enable video and audio data to be shared by working groups across a network. Video can be automatically input into a database system, and metadata generated about each clip. This enables the continuous development of the asset archive, allowing the users to access project information and media at any time (Datapost 2005). The digital archive is accessible through the LAN or WAN for retrieval of assets and is distributed through LAN, WAN or a satellite network with the capacity to deliver information anywhere in the world.

The system enables content producers in a number of locations to share content via accessing a common pool of stored video and audio data. Producers can collaborate on a single project or use archive material for their own individual purposes.

Cellular communications

The use of cellular communications in South Africa has seen phenomenal growth in the past few years, and cellphone subscribers outnumber fixed-line subscribers, as is the case in Africa as a whole (ITU 2004). Cellular communication is in the process of becoming a medium for the delivery of video content, as handsets and network technologies evolve.

Mobile television is not yet commercially available, but trials are being carried out around the world, and the first TV phones are expected to be available by the end of 2005. Globally, handset makers expect to sell 130 000 TV phones in 2005, rising to 83.5 million by 2010. In five years time, about 125 million consumers internationally will watch television on their mobile phones (Informa Research 2005).

Mobile TV signals will be handled by special chips that sit alongside the chips that process the mobile phone's calls, music and streaming video clips. The difference between TV and streaming video services will be that the TV signals are broadcast to all users at the same time, while mobile operators will deliver streaming video on demand. Mobile TV images are also expected to be of higher quality than mobile video streams (Informa Research 2005).

Cellular network technology has evolved to the point where it can provide mobile users, companies and home users with lower-cost bandwidth and a multitude of high-bandwidth products ranging from video clips to Internet access. Because mobile networks cover nearly every part of South Africa, new applications for cellular technology will significantly increase Internet and email access and penetration (ICT World 2005a).

These networks can provide Internet access at a much lower cost than that of landline connectivity solutions. According to a 2005 survey compiled by Webcheck, South African Internet users spend an average of R209 a month on Telkom costs at home, a figure that excludes the additional fees charged by the Internet service providers. However, existing cellphone networks can provide a permanent connection to the Internet at a far lower cost, which may be as little as R50 per month (ICT World 2005a).

This technology uses a SIM card and a special modem similar to the ones previously used for dial-up Internet access. Using advanced General Packet Radio Services (GPRS), an Internet connection that approximates the speed of a dial-up service can be established almost anywhere in the country.

Unlike a dial-up connection, this is an always-on service. There is no need for time-consuming connections over a landline, and users pay only an access fee similar to that charged for a normal cellphone and for the data that is transferred. The low costs and high reliability of cellular technology have the potential to increase dramatically the number of people who can realistically go online and experience the Internet, email, banking and online commerce at an affordable cost.

Still, landline connectivity is also increasing in speed, using technologies such as the digital subscriber line (DSL). According to one forecast, the number of DSL users globally will grow from 109 million in 2004 to 204 million in 2008, a compound annual growth rate of 17 per cent. The number of global IP TV subscribers will grow from 1.9 million in 2004 to 25.3 million in 2008, a compound annual growth rate of 79 per cent (Global Information Inc. 2005).

These developments mean that there is increasing demand for video content to be delivered via IP networks on a global basis. While CTV is often thought of as being based on local experiences, it must be remembered that communities of interest are international and that CTV can slot into international content networks in terms of content production and acquisition.

However, South Africa is lagging behind international bandwidth uptake. Comparisons with international broadband uptake reveal that South Africa falls behind on a daily basis (ICT World 2005b). South Korea is currently leading the world in broadband uptake, with 24.9 per cent of the population in possession of a broadband connection. The UK and Australia fall in the middle range with 10.5 per cent and 7.7 per cent respectively. In comparison, only 0.002 per cent of South Africans have broadband connections.

While Telkom signed up 17 000 new users after its price reductions in March 2005, there were over 200 000 new broadband subscribers in Australia during the same period. The UK signed up more than 700 000 new subscribers during this time. At the current rate, it will take South Africa nearly 50 years to reach the same penetration percentage as that of Australia (ICT World 2005b).

The culprit in terms of high pricing is South Africa's monopoly telephony provider, Telkom. The company's ADSL prices remain many times more expensive than those of its international counterparts; for instance, a standard 512 KBps ADSL service in South Africa costs more than 50 per cent of the average income of a South African. At the same time, the monopoly made a net profit of R6.8 billion in the 2004–2005 financial year (ICT World 2005b).

Interactive television

New technologies are also enabling viewers at home to participate actively in television programmes. Siemens and Grundy Light Entertainment have developed a system whereby quiz-show contestants will be able to use a Universal Mobile Telecommunications Service (UMTS) cellphone to participate in shows from any location (ICT World 2005c).

Viewers can become part of a live TV show by means of a video link, conducted either via UMTS mobile radio technology or through the fixed-line network, with the help of the Surpass Home Entertainment system from Siemens. In addition, costs for the transmissions can be kept down to the 49 Euro cents normally charged for cellphone calls.

The partnership with the FremantleMedia subsidiary Grundy, which produces the German version of 'American Idol' amongst other shows, is expected to lead to new broadcasting formats on German TV in the near future.

People who do not own a UMTS cellphone can use the Surpass Home Entertainment system and a DSL connection to participate directly in game shows via their own television set. The resolution provided by the broadband DSL connection even makes it possible to transmit a full-screen image of the contestant, although image resolution via the UMTS connection is of lower quality (ICT World 2005c).

Surpass Home Entertainment is designed to allow any television set to be linked to the Internet, thus enabling clear video telephony, as well as transmission of text and multimedia messages on the TV screen. The ability of viewers to influence the outcome of TV shows is intended to lead to greater fun and entertainment when watching television. This concept can also be used with pay-per-view and video-on-demand (ICT World 2005c).

Siemens plans to minimise the bandwidths needed for transmission further by the end of the year, which will provide reception of live TV broadcasts at 1.8 MBps – about the same as the average rate of today's DSL standard (ICT World 2005d). The factors that will make this possible include the new MPEG-4 video data compression, which aims to reduce dramatically the technical requirements for the consumer, while making digital television almost universally available.

Digital broadcasting

Digital terrestrial broadcasting (DTT) will usher in a whole new range of television services for South Africa. The government has announced the formation of a 'migration' task team to look at how the country's analogue television infrastructure can be switched over to digital transmission (Adams 2005).

Digital technology offers a more effective means of transmission than its analogue predecessor, because up to eight channels can be conveyed on one frequency. This opens the way to a greater variety of broadcast channels, which would ease the problems of distributing content in all 11 of South Africa's official languages. Communications Minister Ivy Matsepe-Casaburri has set up a digital broadcasting migration working group and expects the migration to have a far-reaching impact on telecommunications in the country. The minister said the working group would comprise representatives from the industry, ICASA, consumers, business and the government (Adams 2005).

Inputs to, and the report of, the digital broadcasting migration working group will culminate in a national strategy for the migration of broadcasting systems from analogue to digital. Sentech has estimated that the cost for a new digital transmitter network would be in the region of R268 million, and that digital television would enhance services such as e-government, adult education and health services.

CHAPTER 12

Business models

Economic sustainability

In terms of sustainability, there are various factors that constrain the financial operations of CTV. These include its non-profit orientation, ethical considerations, ideological objectives, production values and limited market reach. Despite these factors, CTV has the potential to garner income from various sources. While it is not a typical capitalist enterprise, it nevertheless functions in free-market societies because it offers real communications value to specific sectors of the population.

CTV is an intervention in the realm of capitalist market relations because it aims to put the means of production into the hands of the people. It does this by empowering communities and individuals who otherwise would not have access to the capital required to communicate through television. If community members can access production facilities and skills, they can use these tools to facilitate their collective communication through the converged medium of television, Internet and cellular communications.

The commercial imperative that drives the free-market system is tangential to the priorities of CTV, which favour the development of people-centred communication. Here the financial support of private donors, the government, public fundraising and even religion can balance the lack of interest of the commercial sector in the social project of CTV communications.

While this type of activity may empower emerging video producers and small video businesses, it is not designed to benefit the mainstream audio-visual (AV) industry directly. Instead, the industry gains a greater pool of skilled and experienced personnel and a marginal outlet for its products, while community members gain access to skills, subsequent employment and an outlet for their AV communications.

Economic model

The history of CTV broadcasts in South Africa shows that the majority of broadcast time can be locally produced at minimal cost through live studio productions. Because CTV serves a very different purpose from commercial or public service broadcasting, it differs significantly in its economic model. The purpose of CTV is not to win large-scale audiences to sell on to advertisers; rather, its prime function is to enable communities to communicate among themselves and with the public at large. It follows that financial responsibility should be devolved to communities rather than being the function of the station as an economic engine. This means that the station becomes a medium that communities use for communication purposes, rather than being a mechanism whereby audiences are delivered to advertisers.

What this means in practical terms is that the station has a limited productive function. At the most basic level, a CTV station would consist of a transmitter, communications links and a playout station. In this scenario, community producers submit content to the channel, which then broadcasts it according to a mutually agreed schedule. It would be useful to add a live AV studio to this baseline set-up in order to produce live broadcasts, which can then form the mainstay of broadcast output in the early stages of establishment. This model has been successfully demonstrated by Greater Durban TV (GDTV) in the course of its transmissions to date. Where the station has its own dedicated teams of production crews (the Cue TV model), it can produce a limited amount of outside programming every day. The ideal set-up is where participating communities undertake their own production activities; in other words, where production takes place outside of the station and is financed by the communities themselves.

In professional broadcasting circles much is made of the notion of high-quality programming that brings in viewers, a prerequisite for the economic sustainability of media enterprises. The idea of quality is defined in economic terms; it is assumed that quality is linked to the amount of money spent on content creation and that a lowering of quality standards will result in fewer viewers for the TV station. The term 'quality' then pertains to: the cost of equipment and consumables; the cost of hiring qualified, experienced personnel; and peripheral costs such as travel. It is true that investment in these attributes of professional television results in high-quality images, narratives and related technical standards, and that commercial and public service channels tend to be successful in translating these values into large-scale audiences.

However, the above formula is not the basis for CTV, which requires very different principles to evaluate its sustainability. The foundation of CTV, as it has been formulated for the South African broadcasting landscape, lies in the notion of public access to the airwaves. The dynamics of making this sustainable do not lie in the commercial terrain, but rather in the value that communication holds for various stakeholders and communities throughout our society.

Developing a social communications network

The key to economic sustainability in this situation is to convert the value of this social communications network into income for the station. It has been observed that commercial operations are generally inimical to the democratic functioning of CTV, which allows minority or disadvantaged groupings to voice their concerns through CTV (Ross in Aldridge 1996). The fact that some scope is given for commercially oriented operations for CTV in the South African context is a response to two impediments, these being lack of legislated investment in the medium and the need to contribute to wider economic empowerment in society. In order to address these issues and to create a sustainable CTV sector in South Africa, CTV must address itself to issues of both economic success and democratic engagement.

The optimum response for CTV would be to find a holistic base that encompasses a wide diversity of interests throughout society. These interests are based in local communities but also have national and international components. The nature and scope of local CTV means that different interest groups must harmonise their intentions and productive capacities across barriers of race, class, income and other disparities. In this way, the CTV sector will be able to receive its income through a variety of channels and this will militate against dominance by any one sector. This would be a significant departure from the intention to serve only marginalised population sectors, to a position where some form of cross-subsidisation occurs whereby the wealthier sectors subsidise the less affluent. For example, the station may broadcast some programming that aims at higher Living Standards Measures (LSMs) in order to draw advertising that targets these sectors; or constituent communities of interest may have wealthy sectors within them that can support production activities for their lower-income compatriots.

The definition of quality in the CTV context pertains primarily to the interest value of its content to the particular community targeted; it does not refer to image quality, production values or mass-market appeal that characterise commercial broadcasting productions. It is for this reason that CTV can afford to have very different production values to professional operations; in addition, CTV gains equity from volunteerism and 'in-kind' contributions from various actors in the community environment. Volunteers within community sectors will be able to produce broadcast programming using consumer- or prosumer-level equipment such as digital video (DV) cameras and PCs. This will also enable the development of micro-enterprises or video collectives that can produce low-budget content for CTV and other community-wide distribution. Many video professionals are aghast at this 'de-professionalisation' of the medium, but it has proved successful internationally in empowering citizens to communicate, and must be given every opportunity to succeed in South Africa.

Production costs

A continuum of production costs in per-minute measures has been outlined by the Association of Christian Broadcasters (Rosenthal 2005), reflecting a range that covers the costs of producing professional programming for commercial, public service and independent broadcasters, and includes a low-budget professional option. This final category is priced at R1 400 a minute and, because it can be applied to a small or micro video-business level, should be considered as a measure of the bottom or entry level of the professional video industry. This would also represent the top end of the CTV sector, where NGOs, community volunteers, AV students and broadcasting learners develop their skills to a level at which they can become effective CTV programme producers who are then able to enter into other commercial production activities outside of the CTV sector.

The notion of 'quality programming' will be reinterpreted by the endeavours of this CTV community into formats that will appeal to particular audiences or niche markets within the broadcast area. In this regard, a minimum 'per-minute' cost can be established to ensure reasonable income for independent productions, to be calculated in terms of the minimum amount needed to sustain a small-scale production business.

To illustrate the above calculation we could say that an amount of R250 per minute would ensure that a micro-enterprise could generate a monthly income of R26 000 through producing one half-hour programme every week, assuming that the programme consists of 26 minutes of content and four minutes of sponsorship/advertising messages. If the production company has capital expenses of R100 000 for prosumer production equipment and a high-powered PC for post-production, it would be able to recover its capital outlay within a two-year period, as well as paying staff salaries, rent and vehicle expenses.

The responsibility for programme production should be placed in the hands of communities, which are also responsible for raising funds and broadcast fees for their productions. The station would monitor and provide guidelines for fundraising, while concerning itself principally with the costs of running a small playout, transmission and marketing operation (as Triangle TV does in New Zealand). The basic set-up can be broadened to include components for access productions such as a live broadcasting studio, AV equipment and edit PCs to add a limited production and experiential training environment to the channel, as well as enabling marginalised communities to produce programming at little cost.

Volunteers and independent producers

Volunteerism is a useful mechanism as it enables viewers to employ the channel's resources to produce content. However, the relationship between these volunteers and the channel should be clearly established to determine whether or not they fall into the category of 'independent producers' for the purposes of the ICASA content quota. Nevertheless, volunteerism is not without its problems. In the South African context, volunteers from marginalised communities often require some basic forms of support, such as daily subsistence and travel costs, or non-cash means to meet these needs. Volunteers can also be an unreliable and shifting population that causes headaches for production targets and logistics.

While ICASA may wish to promote the development of an independent video sector through CTV, this does not necessarily translate into an extensive involvement of the professional industry in providing CTV content. This content can be produced by other 'independent producers', like NGOs or community groups, which might make extensive use of volunteer or student labour in their production processes. This level of enterprise might not result in the type of 'quality' content produced by professionals, but it will serve the interests of community communication and meet ICASA's independent production requirements. This does not exclude the acquisition of content produced by independent professional organisations, but it is expected that this would largely be paid for by CTV supporters such as large NGOs, parastatals and companies rather than by the channel itself.

The core of the station is its transmission capacity, so this must be guaranteed. A regular source of income is required to sustain this central capacity, and each station will have to find its own balance between commercial and community funding sources to support this. Community funders will be found in various sports and religious organisations, civil society NGOs and educational institutions. Commercial funders would include corporates, parastatals and local businesses. These bodies could also carry the production costs in addition to contributing to broadcast costs.

An essential component of CTV will be interactivity between the broadcaster and the community. Because this is best effected by telephone and Internet links, telephony providers would have a definite financial interest in CTV that they could sustain through supporting the channels.

Advertising and demographics

Content, audience and revenue

CTV is very different to commercial and public service television in its mode of operations, funding modality and relations with audiences and advertisers. Programming is generally provided by those who want to communicate with particular communities of interest and is often created and scheduled for broadcast according to the wants and needs of participating producers and communities, rather than as an attempt to maximise audience reach for commercial interests.

The commercial operations of the existing players in the South African television arena are in marked contrast to the CTV model because they favour the interests of advertisers who wish to maximise audience reach in particular target sectors, predominantly the upper LSMs. The primary objective of CTV is to enable audiences to have access to the airwaves through participation in programming as well as in the management and ownership of the channel. Together with the fact that the majority of South Africa's population are in the lower to middle LSMs, this means that CTV channels will have a very different programming style and content to their commercial and public service cousins.

These factors notwithstanding, CTV in South Africa is supposed to derive income from advertising as well as from grants, sponsorships and donations, which presents a challenge to a medium that is not by nature very friendly to the notion of commercial exploitation. CTV channels will have to weigh the dynamics of commercial operations very carefully against the principles of access in establishing their programming, marketing and funding strategies. At the same time, the notion that CTV will find sustainability through advertising revenue alone is mistaken because the medium does not naturally fit into a commercial framework.

In fact, research by Naidoo (2005b) indicates that CTV will not have the appeal to attract sustainable advertising revenue, based on the assumption that advertisers will be reluctant to invest in a new, untried medium and that CTV audience demographics will not be appealing to major advertisers. Naidoo lists four factors that will limit adspend on CTV: competition from commercial media; inability to deliver audience size and profile; inability to differentiate itself from its commercial and public service rivals; and interference in programme content by revenue contributors such as the government.

However, CTV will have to source some income from commercial endeavours and so must have an understanding of how it might exploit commercial opportunities. In the context of commercial media operations, it is essential for a media organisation to understand its audiences in order both to plan content and to attract advertising revenue. It is a fact that in the media and advertising industries, audience profile drives advertisers' decisions as to where they place their media investment.

If a CTV station targets advertising as part of its revenue model then it can expect to compete against mainstream media for its share of the pie. It is to be expected that CTV stations will lack the resources and the audience numbers of the national broadcasters to compete on an equal footing. For CTV to be competitive, it is essential that it is able to differentiate itself in terms of its audience profile in order to attract advertisers through being a channel to reach their target markets.

Understanding audience profiles also plays a critical role in TV programming, because programming content is the most significant driver of audiences. Thus, the relationship between audience, advertising and content shapes the strategies of many commercial broadcasters, and CTV stations have to understand this fact if they are to position themselves to attract advertising revenue in a very competitive market.

This analysis dissects the national South African television audience to provide an indication of demographic profiles in KwaZulu-Natal (KZN), Gauteng and the Western Cape. It offers insight as to the demographic trends in each province that can be used by the CTV stations in deciding where to focus their resources to be most effective in the television environment (Naidoo 2005a).

South Africa has an estimated population of 45 million (Stats SA 2005). Of the three provinces, KZN is the most populous, followed by Gauteng. The total population is expected to grow by about 1.5 per cent per annum over the next five years. There are just over ten million households and that figure is expected to grow to 13 million by 2010 (ICASA 2003c).

It is a norm globally and in South Africa to target the bulk of media advertising at the higher LSMs with their greater disposable income, but with these markets increasingly being saturated by TV penetration, more attention is being focused on the 'bottom of the pyramid' – the market that is less affluent but which collectively has enormous purchasing power. Innovative advertising is finding its way into the less affluent urban areas, and the advertisers targeting this gap are looking for partnerships with media. This must provide opportunities for community-based media like CTV.

Pay TV channels with their high-end LSM viewers continue to attract the lion's share of TV advertising revenue. Still, CTV should take heart from the extent to which eTV has changed the broadcasting landscape in South Africa, proving that free-to-air TV has the potential to alter audience trends and to attract adspend.

CTV stations should take cognisance of ICASA's expectation that they attract a level of commercial funding via advertising. In this sense, their business models will have to consider the challenges of delivering compelling content that leads to defined audiences in order to attract sustainable advertising revenue streams.

Where the funding for any type of programme production, or capital start-up costs for that matter, will come from is another matter. Naidoo (2005b) argues that revenue (i.e. income resulting from operations) will constitute only 20 per cent of income, while funding (income from other sources) will constitute some 80 per cent of income. At the same time, he projects that 80 per cent of funding will be derived from the government or government-supported agencies, and 20 per cent from donor funding; while 80 per cent of revenue will be derived from sponsorships and only 20 per cent from advertising. In this instance:

> ...the most viable business model SA CTV can expect to rely on for sustainability is approximately 64% of government or government related income, 16% on income from the non-profit or donor sector, 16% from sponsorship and only 4% from advertising. (Naidoo 2005b: 50)

The prospect of such overwhelming reliance on government support for CTV is a gloomy one, for inevitably this will result in CTV channels becoming mere mouthpieces for the government and lacking the ability to engage in substantive criticism in the political arena. At present, such a situation is explicitly precluded by ICASA regulations (see the regulatory overview in Chapter 2).

The requirement that CTV engage in commercial activities could force stations to compromise on their community development potential, although we must bear in mind that it is vital to pursue the entertainment format even in pedagogical or social upliftment programmes in order to maintain audience attention.

Nevertheless, it will be essential for CTV stations to understand and measure their audiences. One of the problems that community broadcast media face is that the South African Advertising Research Foundation (SAARF) does not measure audience responses to this media sector, which is then forced to perform its own measurements with scarce resources to perform this task.

The analysis below categorises audiences by the demographics of race, language, age and LSM level. It must be noted that race is a problematic factor in South Africa that has served to divide people according to particular ideological perspectives. In the media context, advertisers have largely abandoned race as a defining factor of target markets. Race, like language and age, does influence culture and in this way has an effect on consumers' purchasing decisions. However, advertisers place far more weight on LSM levels in making their media placement decisions; consequently, it would be a serious mistake for CTV channels to base their programming decisions and marketing strategy on the racial profiles of their audiences. In fact, cultural divisions within race groups arguably play as great a role in demarcating difference as does the race factor alone.

TV audience (TVA) analysis

Points to consider:
- TV reaches 68 per cent of the total population. The highest penetration is in the Gauteng and KZN regions, with 20 per cent of TV viewers in these provinces. The Western Cape lags behind with only 10 per cent. Between them, these three regions account for 50 per cent of the total TV audience.
- Of the approximately 30 per cent of the population that TV does not reach, 90 per cent are in the lower LSM categories. However, in the last five years the number of lower LSMs with access to television has grown by 200 per cent.
- TV reaches over 40 per cent of households (HHs) in South Africa. The highest penetration of households is in Gauteng, followed by KZN.

Figure 12.1: Total TV viewing

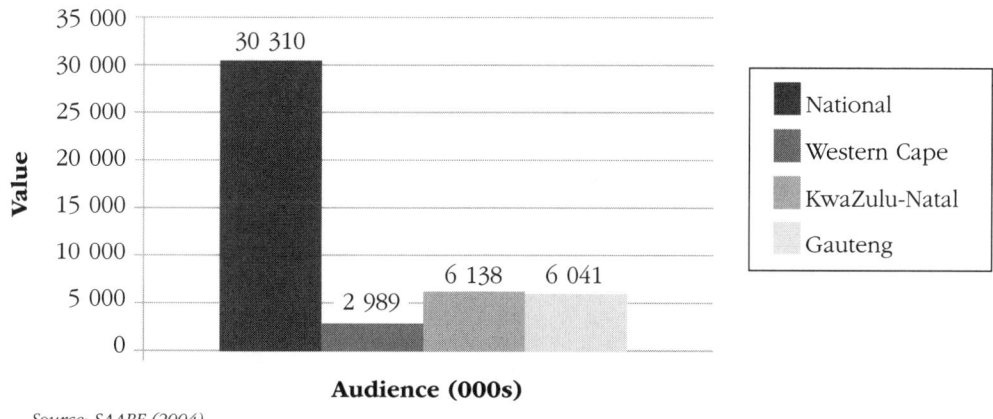

Source: SAARF (2004)

Figure 12.2: Total TV households (TVHHs)

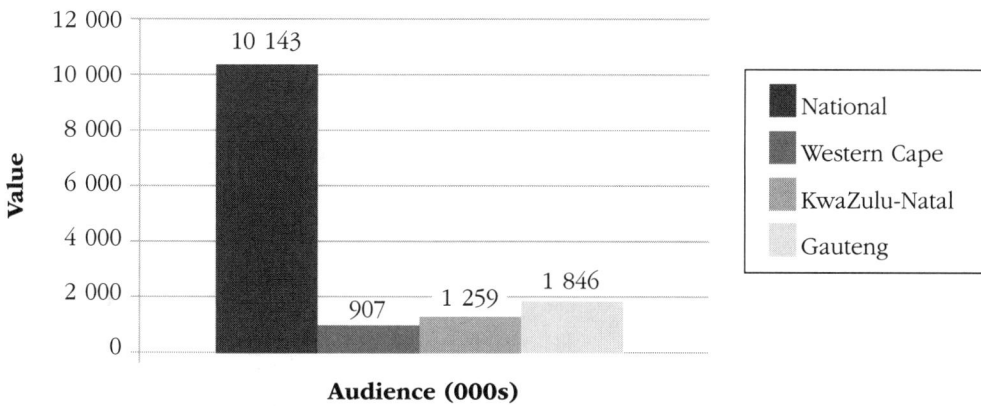

Source: SAARF (2004)

Implications for CTV:
- There is a business case for launching CTV stations in these areas with high TVA and TVHH penetration, using a 'churning' strategy to attract viewers rather than targeting 'new' viewers (i.e. attracting viewers away from the other broadcast stations).
- ICASA forecasts that TVHH penetration will increase between 70 per cent and 75 per cent by 2010. Even if the lower-end scenario is considered, the forecast indicates a continued burgeoning of TV in the country.
- Growth is expected mainly in the less affluent, previously disadvantaged TVHHs, which is a primary target market of CTV in South Africa.

TVA per channel analysis

Figure 12.3: Audience share, all adults (South Africa)

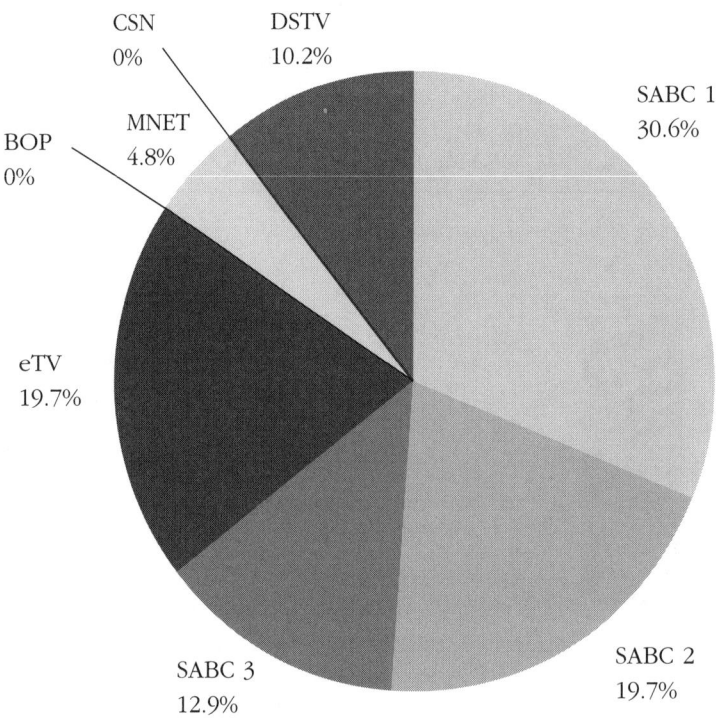

Source: SAARF (2004)

Points to consider:
- Most channels have increased their audience year on year.
- The most popular channel by far in South Africa is SABC 1, followed by SABC 2.
- Both of these channels air content in indigenous languages, particularly in their news bulletins.
- The rapid growth of eTV can be seen with its almost 20 per cent of national TV audience.
- Pay TV channels have increased their market share rapidly in recent years and now reach over 10 per cent of viewers.

Figure 12.4: Audience share, all adults (Western Cape)

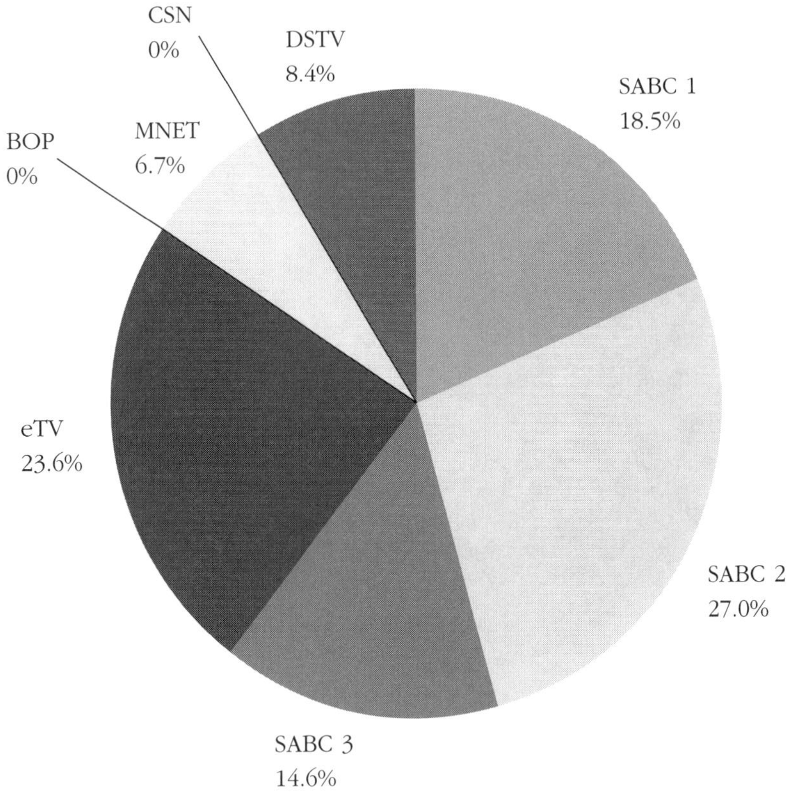

Source: SAARF (2004)

Figure 12.5: Audience share, all adults (Gauteng)

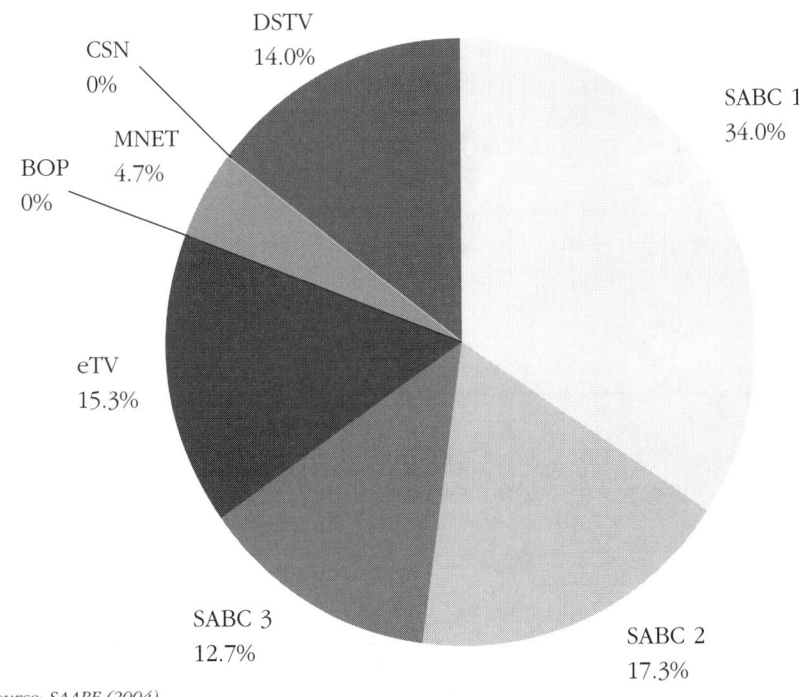

Source: SAARF (2004)

Figure 12.6: Audience share, all adults (KwaZulu-Natal)

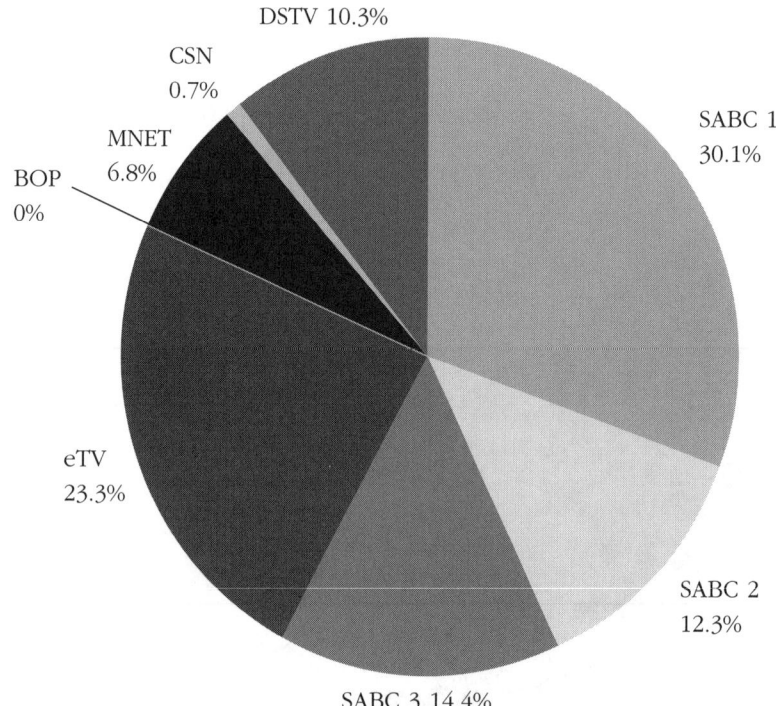

Source: SAARF (2004)

Implications for CTV:
- National audience trends are generally reflected on a similar basis at provincial level, except in the Western Cape where SABC 2 is the most watched channel, primarily because of its Afrikaans programmes.
- In the last five years, SABC 1 has increased its audience in the lower LSMs by over 100 per cent, indicating the growing reach of TV in this segment. Advertisers, too, are increasingly targeting this segment.
- The ability of eTV to attract TVA from the SABC stations in a relatively short space of time indicates that there is a potential market for free-to-air TV services that can provide compelling content.
- The SABC's three TV channels dominate TVA, and therefore present the largest target in terms of drawing viewers away by using a differentiating content strategy.

Analysis by race

Points to consider:
- African viewers contribute over 75 per cent of TVA, yet form the lowest proportion of pay-TV subscribers.
- White viewers constitute 14 per cent of the audience, coloured viewers 9 per cent and Indian viewers just less than 2 per cent.
- KZN has the highest total of African viewers, with the Western Cape having the least. Gauteng has the most white viewers.
- The Western Cape has the highest number of coloured viewers, as this group forms the majority of the province's population, one of only two provinces in the country where the majority is not African.
- KZN has the largest Indian audience, though they are nevertheless a minority population group in the province.

BUSINESS MODELS

Figure 12.7: African audience share

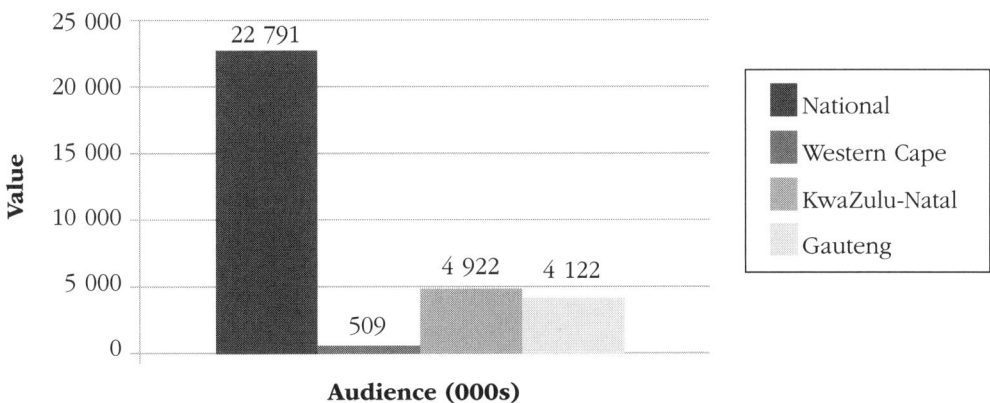

Source: SAARF (2004)

Figure 12.8: White audience share

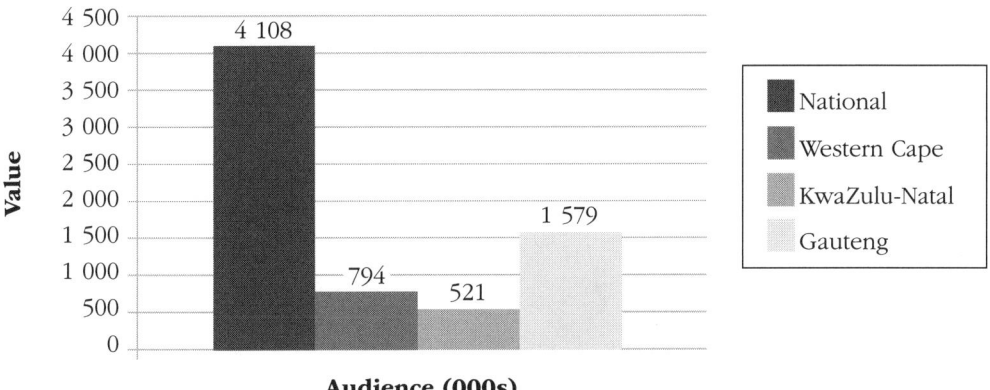

Source: SAARF (2004)

Figure 12.9: Coloured audience share

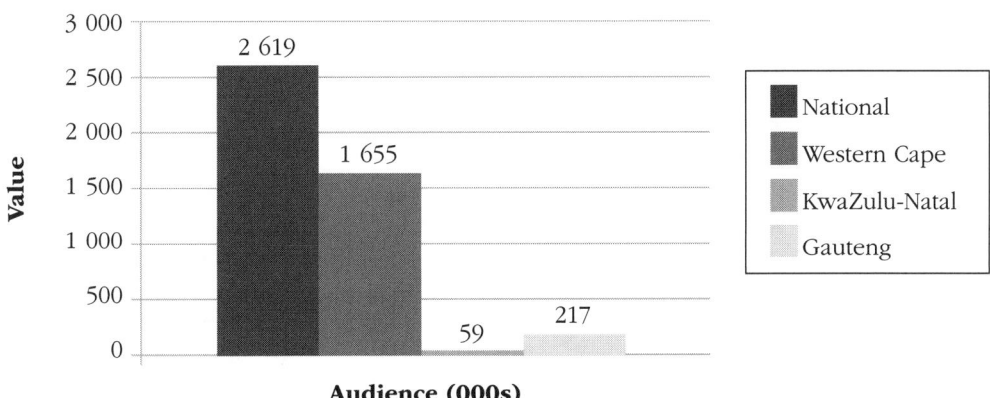

Source: SAARF (2004)

Figure 12.10: Indian audience share

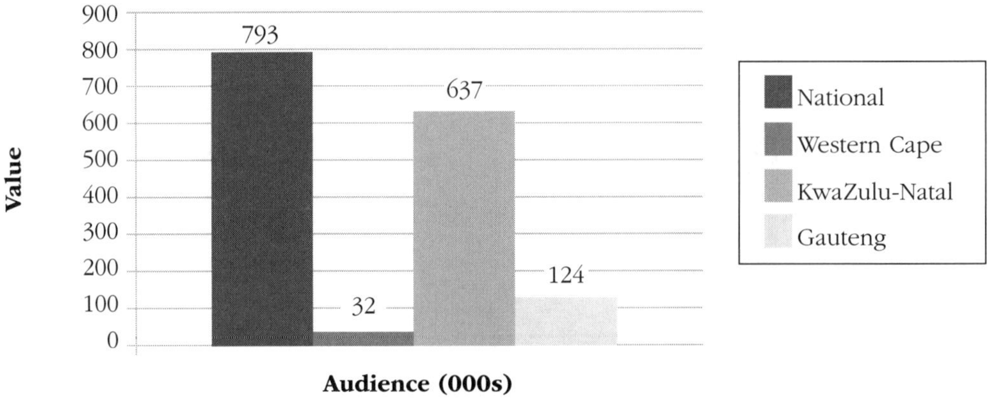

[Bar chart showing Audience (000s): National 793, Western Cape 32, KwaZulu-Natal 637, Gauteng 124]

Source: SAARF (2004)

Implications for CTV:
- The implications of the race breakdown in terms of 'community' representation will not be lost on CTV stations.
- There are still significant numbers of African people who do not have access to TV.
- This segment resides mostly outside of Gauteng, the Western Cape and KZN.
- The more affluent white, coloured and Indian viewers are concentrated in these three provinces.

Analysis by language

Points to consider:
- Afrikaans as a first language is more popular than English, particularly in the Western Cape.
- IsiZulu is the most popular language, predominantly in KZN and Gauteng.
- South Sotho is the most common language in Gauteng.
- IsiXhosa is not a majority first language of audiences in any of the three provinces, even though it is the second most widely spoken language (after isiZulu) in the country.

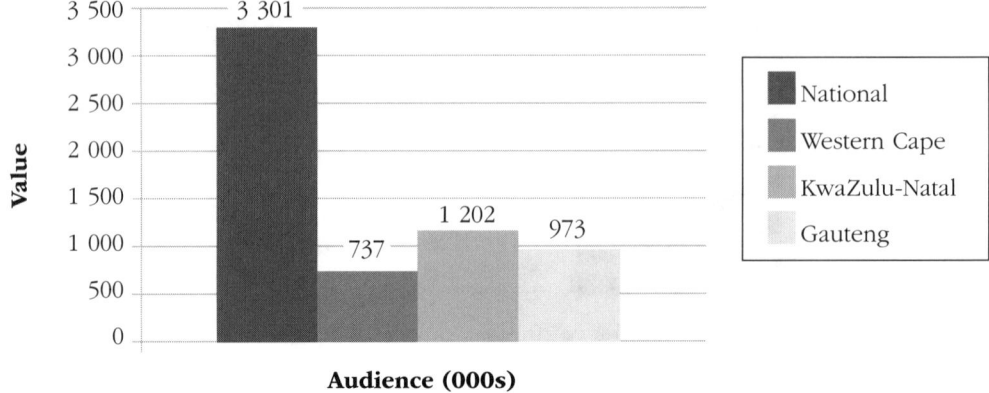

Figure 12.11: English audience (home language)

Source: SAARF (2004)

Figure 12.12: Afrikaans audience (home language)

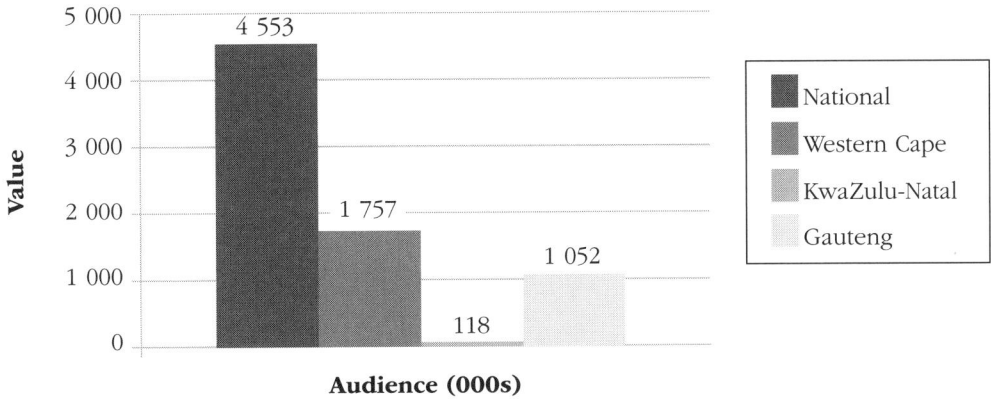

Source: SAARF (2004)

Figure 12.13: IsiXhosa audience (home language)

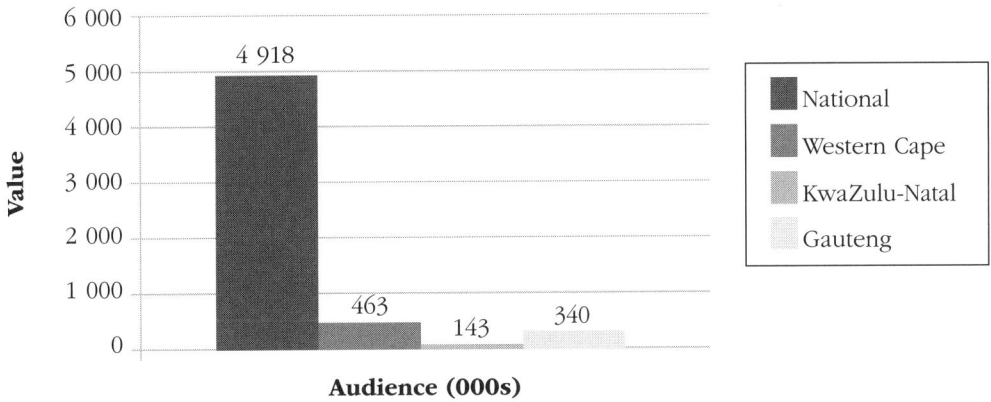

Source: SAARF (2004)

Figure 12.14: South Sotho audience (home language)

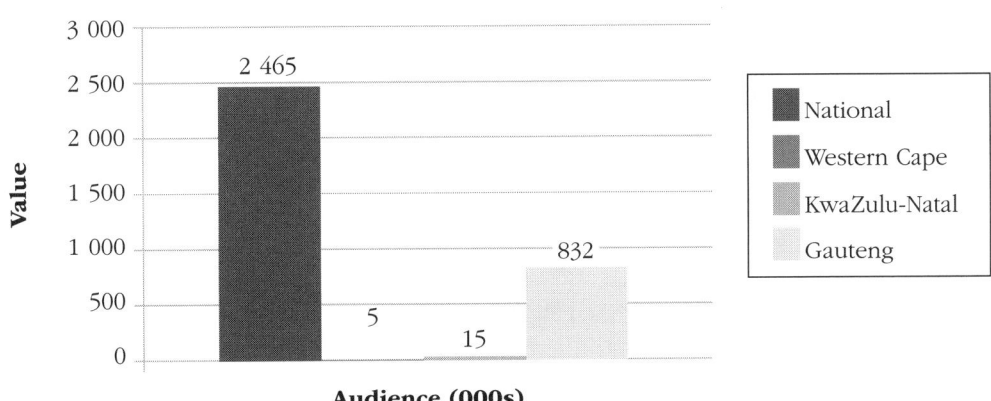

Source: SAARF (2004)

Figure 12.15: IsiZulu audience (home language)

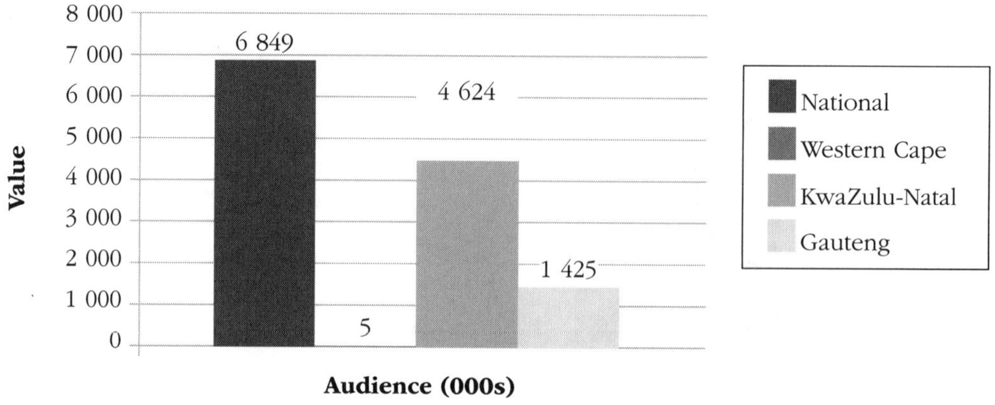

[Bar chart showing IsiZulu audience values: National 6 849; Western Cape 5; KwaZulu-Natal 4 624; Gauteng 1 425. Y-axis: Value; X-axis: Audience (000s)]

Source: SAARF (2004)

Implications for CTV:
- The first choice of language by TVA and TVHH is an important factor when considering the 55 per cent local content programming quotas set by ICASA for CTV stations.
- Television advertising in South Africa predominantly uses English as a first language.

Analysis by age group

Points to consider:
- TVAs across the aggregate age groups of 16–24, 25–34 and 35–49 years are almost equal at around eight million each, nationally.
- KZN has the most viewers in the 16–24 and 25–34 age groups, while Gauteng has the most viewers in the 35–49 age group.
- The highest TVA in KZN is the 16–24 age group, while the Western Cape and Gauteng have their highest TVA in the 35–49 age group.

Figure 12.16: Audience by age group, 16–24 years

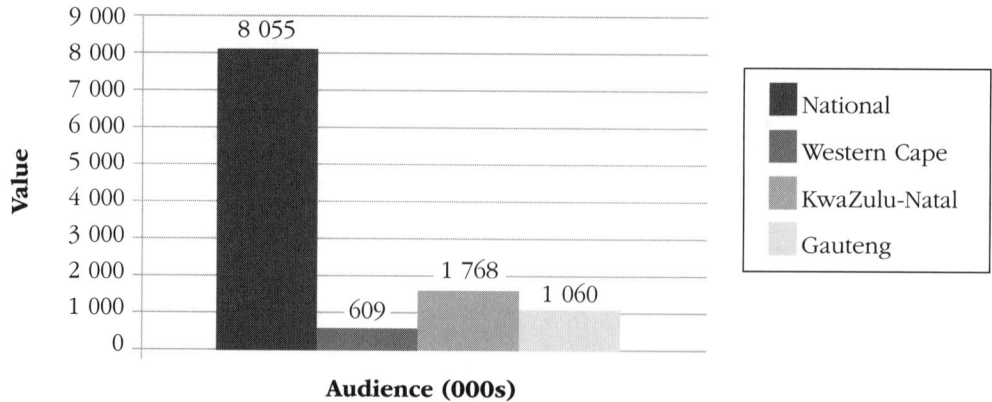

[Bar chart showing audience 16–24 years: National 8 055; Western Cape 609; KwaZulu-Natal 1 768; Gauteng 1 060]

Source: SAARF (2004)

Figure 12.17: Audience by age group, 25–34 years

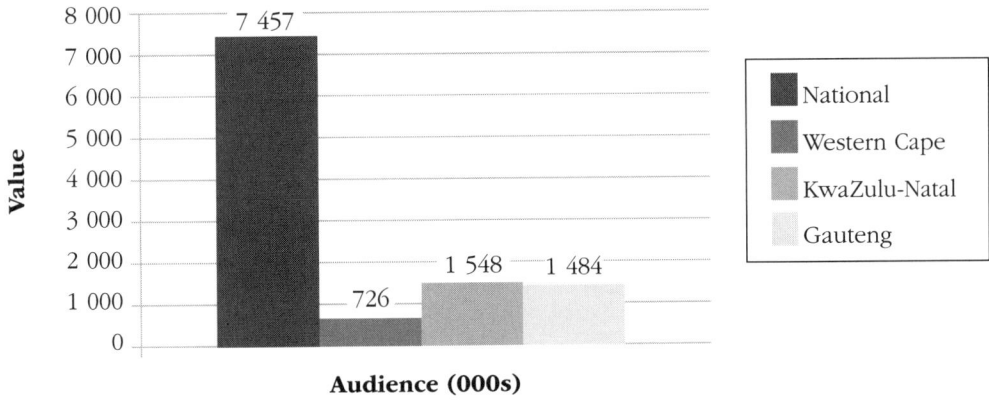

Source: SAARF (2004)

Figure 12.18: Audience by age group, 35–49 years

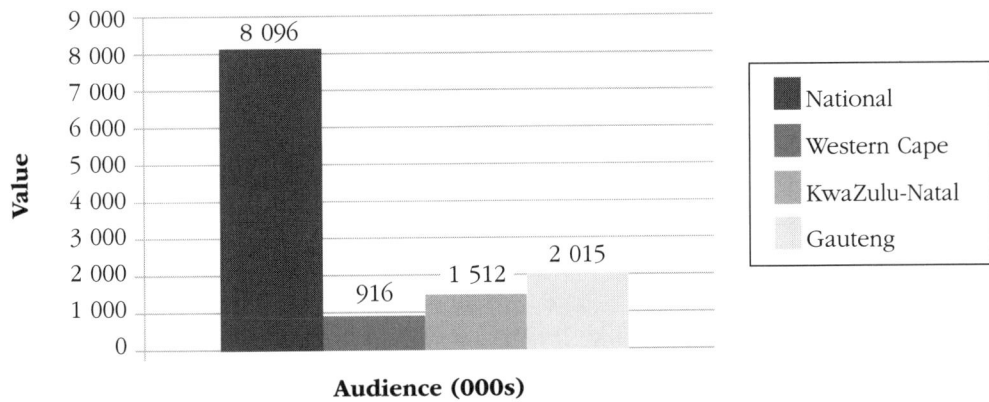

Source: SAARF (2004)

Implications for CTV:
- Programming content will have to appeal to a spectrum of age groups in order to lure viewers away from the established broadcasters.
- The under-16 age group is the fastest-growing segment of this demographic.

Analysis of TVA and TVHH by LSMs

LSMs have proven to be the most important demographic measure influencing placement of media-spend by advertisers. The bulk of advertising revenue in South Africa is targeted at the higher LSMs.

Aggregated LSM groupings and TVA percentages are as follows: lower LSMs (1–4) constitute 51 per cent of TVA; middle LSMs (5–7) constitute 33 per cent of TVA; and upper LSMs (8–10) constitute 16 per cent of TVA.

Points to consider:
- Year on year, there has been a slight shift from the lower to the middle LSMs in TVA.
- TVA and TVHH follow similar patterns in terms of proportions.
- Over 70 per cent of South Africa's upper LSMs live in Gauteng, the Western Cape and KZN.

- The lower LSMs form the largest proportion of audiences, except in the Western Cape where the middle LSMs are in the majority.
- Over 50 per cent of TVA and TVHH are in the lower LSMs.
- The majority of upper LSM viewers and households are in Gauteng.
- KZN audiences are dominated by lower LSM viewers and households.
- KZN has the fewest viewers in the upper LSMs.
- The Western Cape has the highest proportion of upper LSMs in its TVA and TVHH.

Figure 12.19: Universal LSM 3, TVA

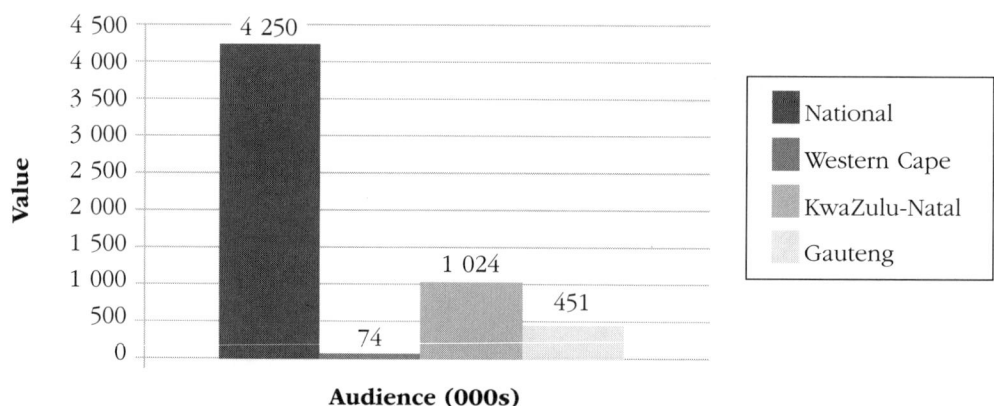

Source: SAARF (2004)

Figure 12.20: Universal LSM 3, TVHH

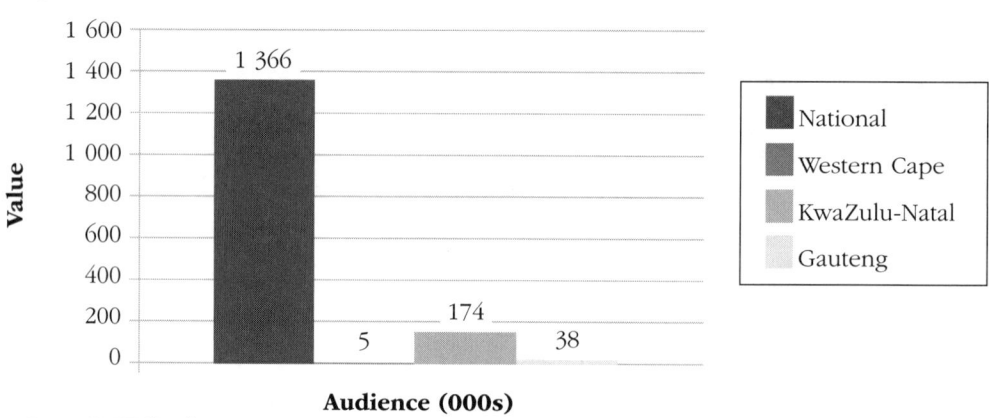

Source: SAARF (2004)

Figure 12.21: Universal LSM 6, TVA

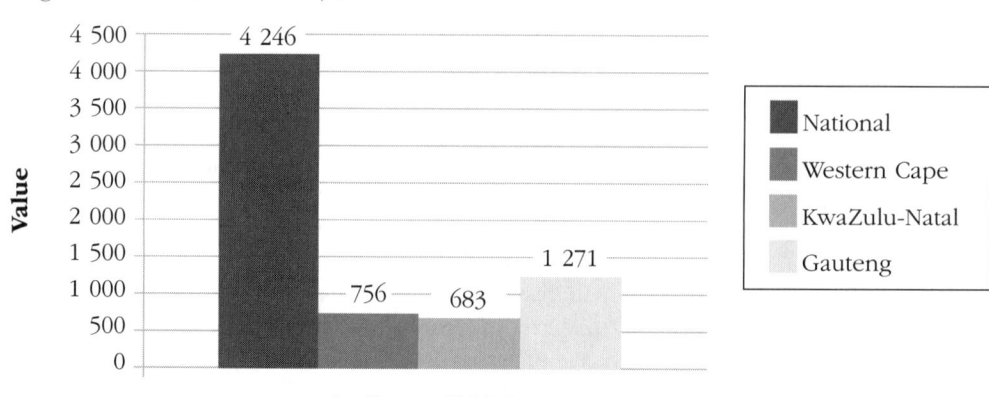

Source: SAARF (2004)

Figure 12.22: Universal LSM 6, TVHH

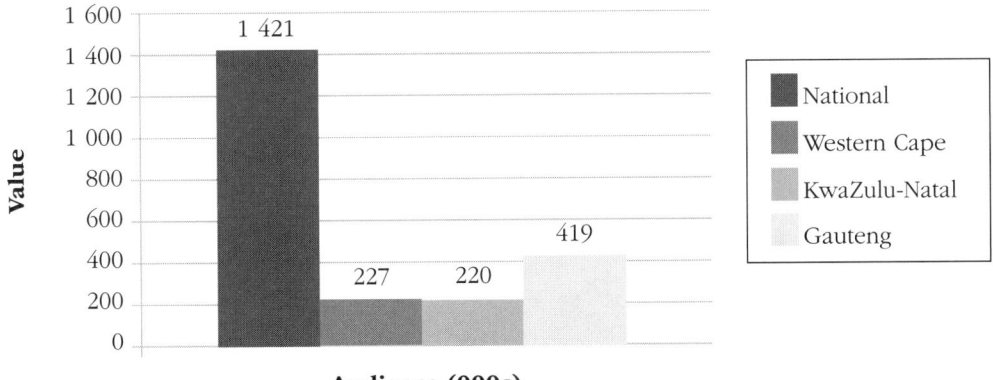

Source: SAARF (2004)

Figure 12.23: Universal LSM 8, TVA

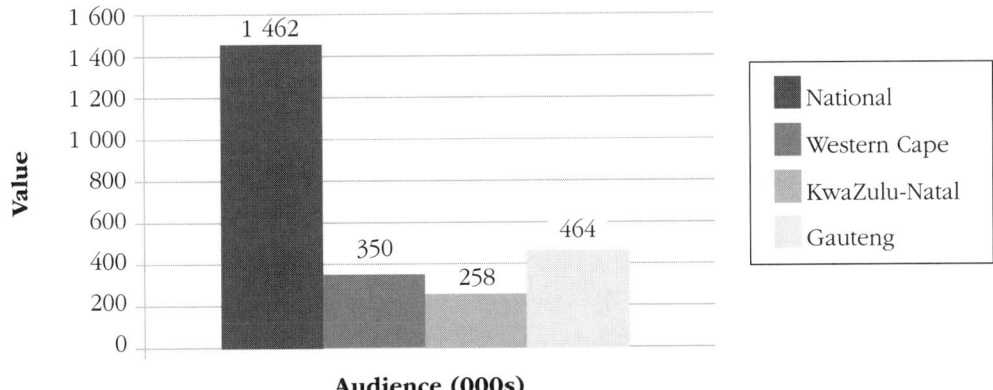

Source: SAARF (2004)

Figure 12.24: Universal LSM 8, TVHH

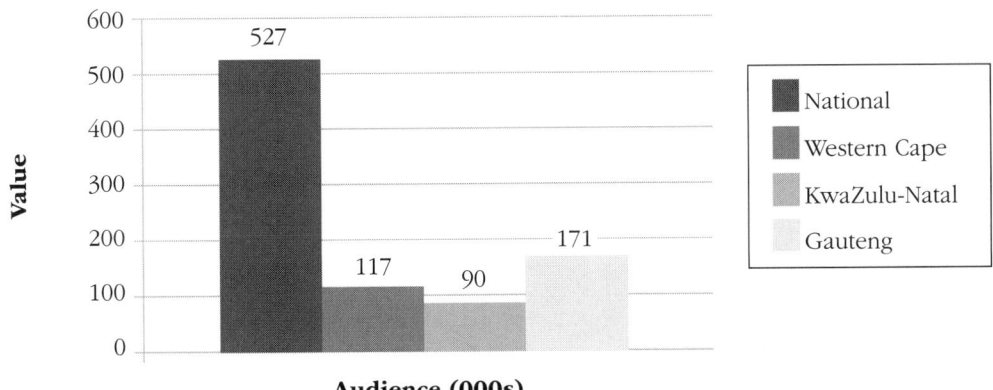

Source: SAARF (2004)

Figure 12.25: Universal LSM 10, TVA

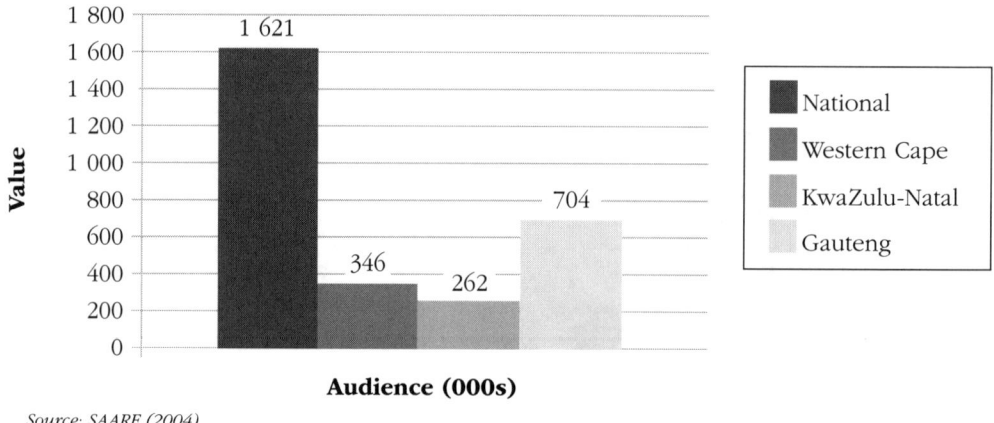

Source: SAARF (2004)

Figure 12.26: Universal LSM 10, TVHH

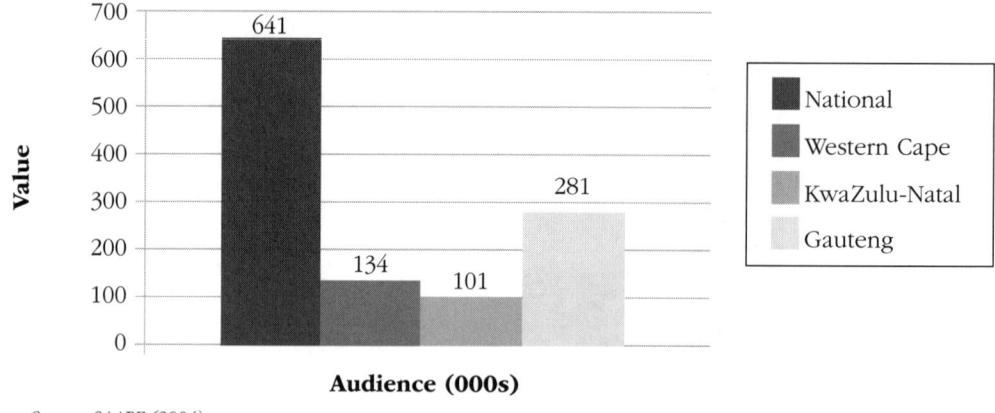

Source: SAARF (2004)

Implications for CTV:
- Overall household population growth corresponds to a steady increase in TVHH, which shows that TV consumption is an important part of the South African lifestyle.
- The competition for the higher LSM market is aggressive, and pay TV commands the bulk of upper LSM viewers.
- The growth market for TVA lies in the lower LSMs (with the exception of the Western Cape) because significant numbers still do not have access to TV.
- Even though the lower LSMs are limited by their lack of disposable income, their purchasing power far exceeds that of the middle and upper LSMs.

Recommendations
- CTV should compete for TVA in the lower LSM categories, both to reach previously disadvantaged communities as a social development goal and to avoid competition with commercial media for adspend.
- CTV needs to articulate its programming differentiation clearly in order to appeal to the broad-based, free-to-air market where audiences desires change, and to attract revenue from advertisers looking for new media channels.

- The sustainability of CTV stations will depend to some extent on the relationship between content, audience and advertising. It is advisable to have experienced professionals managing this relationship.
- Other CTV revenue sources such as grants and sponsorships will also require audience reach, although more leeway will be allowable in these instances.

CHAPTER 13

Conclusion

It is clear from the enthusiasm shown and the commitment expressed by stakeholders during the course of this research that the need for CTV in South Africa is considered an urgent and important priority. Indeed, it is something many people have been fighting for over considerably longer than a decade.

The conviction about CTV's value derives in part from the constitutional provisions and human rights that are bolstered as a consequence of the introduction of a community tier of television broadcasting. These rights include the right to communicate, the right to equality and dignity and to linguistic and cultural expression, as well as the right of access to the media and access to information. The imperative for the rapid development of CTV also derives from the very real benefits that other countries have experienced from CTV in terms of development and empowerment, most particularly where this concerns vulnerable communities.

South Africa has taken some substantial steps toward the diversification of the country's media, most notably in the realm of community radio. Few would disagree, however, that a great deal more needs to be done before ordinary South Africans can claim to have easy access to media that speak their language, understand their particular concerns and express their specific local, national and global aspirations.

This report demonstrates that the technology, the people, the will, the models and the experience exist to make sustainable CTV in South Africa a reality.

A variety of international models have been assessed during the course of this report, and relevant aspects have been highlighted. An overview of the regulatory environment has been presented, beginning with the constitutional framework, and various pieces of legislation and policy that will impact on the development of CTV have been examined. A range of case studies has been evaluated depicting the CTV experience as it has evolved in South Africa to date. Potential partnerships have been explored, and technical matters concerning signal distribution, frequencies and transmission options have been considered. This report has also dealt with matters of production, programming, audience research, business models and the special challenges faced by CTV in rural areas.

The authors of this report suggest that a 'consortium model' should be adopted, along the lines of CTV in Australia. This model draws on government funding for specific projects only, and relies mainly on partnerships and the involvement of stakeholders. We recommend, too, that an element of commercial advertising be allowed in the sector but urge that democracy, accountability, accessibility and the right to communicate are held up as founding principles for the sector.

The authors support the establishment of media access centres for communities, the creation of a development fund for broadcasting and a high level of independence for producers. The government should be encouraged to enter into partnerships with CTV licensees that encompass issues of programming, policy support and possibly funding. Various other recommendations are made concerning technical, management and structural issues, all of which are aimed at bolstering the sustainability of the sector.

The democratic, access-oriented nature of the nascent CTV sector has been reflected by the determinedly participative methodology engaged in by the research team. At every turn, the experience, knowledge and aspirations of stakeholder groups have been sought out and tested.

The result, we believe, is a report that encapsulates the development, hopes and environment of a vital sector. In formalising the progress that has been made, and by capturing the debates, needs and obstacles confronting the sector, it is hoped that this report will be a significant contribution to CTV in South Africa and, therefore, to the consolidation of our young democracy and the principles it holds dear. By providing genuine community access to broadcasting, television is literally being re-visioned. In so doing, it is also providing a brighter, better picture for all.

CHAPTER 14

Case Study: CTV Cape Town business model

As the Cape Town CTV initiative continues to lay down structures towards a firm beginning, the issue of financial sustainability and business modelling continues to be a key concern. This is within the context of debates about the viability of the sector, not only in South Africa but all over the world. As has been variously mentioned in the present report and other literature on the subject, CTV has thrived in other countries thanks to systems of support and subsidisation either by government or by the commercial media sector, underpinned by legislation. Two issues emerge from this scenario: CTV is deemed important enough to ensure measures that guarantee its continued existence, and it faces massive challenges of self-sustainability. This scenario is further burdened by the size of the media market in which the Cape Town initiative plans to operate, adding constraints to its short-, mid- and long-term viability.

CTV in Cape Town will serve as an important means by which the various communities, both geographic and interest-based, can gain access to the media. It is envisaged to fill the role of providing entertainment, information and education in its programming, while affording the local population access to training and skills development. All of this must take into account local specificities in a way that the available mainstream media do not.

In this sense, the initiative must partner with the community as a whole and with representative bodies to provide useful information, accurate representation and meaningful access by making infrastructure and skills training available. In this way, the community becomes an active participant as opposed to a passive consumer of information and communication.

The discussion thus moves from considering whether or not CTV is a necessary and integral part of the media landscape in Cape Town to elaborating means by which it can be brought to fruition and maintained viably.

The options for viability are limited and require innovative thinking. Modelling such an initiative on business principles must be framed within the limitations of the audience as a viable market, the socio-economic conditions prevailing and the guiding principles and values to which the initiative commits itself. Therefore, it must be useful to its audience and attractive to advertising to ensure viewership as well as revenue. This is a twin challenge, considering that commercial radio is attractive to advertising because it targets a large spending population and depends on advertising income for sustainability. CTV is primarily responsible to its audience, whether or not they are attractive to advertisers.

The initiative must rely on diverse and innovative sources of revenue in order to survive. Much of the literature on CTV has focused on the PEG and C-PEG formats that have been discussed elsewhere in the report. This is a combination of public access educational and government broadcasting and, in the case of C-PEG, a commercial element to supplement it. PEG and C-PEG apply to programming formats as well, but in the context of business modelling these must be seen individually and in combination as sources of revenue. There must also be emphasis on reducing costs to a minimum.

Aldridge (1997) points out that, in itself, the PEG model fills a niche that is not well covered by the public or commercial broadcasters. However, this is also where the challenge lies, in that it is not covered because it does not make money for these broadcasters. Whereas entertainment sells, it is not as beneficial to the community in terms of fulfilling educational and information needs or in its ability to engage in democratic government. The inclusion of a commercial element (C-PEG) will necessitate providing entertainment that can draw audiences as well as advertising and sponsorship revenue. The whole process must be predicated upon a full understanding of the audience through research, and consultation with all stakeholders, with a view to identifying needs and potentialities, on the basis of which the programming is designed.

Income streams

Education

Literature on CTV and on the experiences of community radio point to the growing need for media to carry educational programming. Issues of access have made the media the only way in which the educational needs of certain groups can be met. Many educational institutions have been using the media for some time, and those in Cape Town are no exception. Furthermore, in the last few years, there has been a rise in the number of institutions offering courses by correspondence (Damelin, Intec and Unisa, for example).

One of the problems faced by the students is access to materials, which may be costly. Community radio is working on an initiative whereby course materials will be discussed and elaborated upon at allotted times for the students. It is envisaged that increased access will boost enrolment at the institutions, while the stations will benefit from dedicated audiences and bankable programming. Although this will take time to be realised, there have been steps in the right direction. Bush Radio, for instance, has found it viable to air broadcasts of set-books for matric students around examination time, thus attracting advertising from businesses targeting this group.

Interest groups also have a range of targeted programming for their members. In Cape Town, this is of particular importance, given that there is a strong interest group and sector orientation in organisational membership. An example of this is Worker's World Media Productions (WWMP), which counts the labour movement as its constituency. CTV will provide WWMP with an additional means to reach its members with educational programming.

Aldridge (1997) talks about the potential that exists for corporate clients to provide cost-effective staff training through CTV. There are many companies in Cape Town that can be approached in this regard. The advantage that CTV has over the mainstream media here is that it provides greater flexibility in terms of scheduling, and offers better rates than commercial media. Also it can be localised; for example, Standard Bank in Cape Town can provide training for its staff over a period of time that is specifically convenient for them. This can also tie into the notion of corporate social investment.

Mindset Network has become a major player in providing educational programming. Mindset has been broadcasting its materials on DSTV channels as well as to institutions, and has a large amount of material, produced in-house and commissioned, which it is willing to make available to CTV. For example, their Health Channel is broadcast to health centres and clinics, targeting both patients and health-care workers. Their educational service is broadcast to a number of schools countrywide. Broadcasting on CTV will be mutually beneficial, by providing CT CTV with high quality, useful programming while delivering greater audiences to Mindset. Mindset also offers a chance for local producers to showcase their work, providing valuable exposure to local talent, the only caveat being that productions must meet the network's quality criteria and fit into the fixed areas in which Mindset specialises.

Schools in the Cape Town area would be an ideal outlet for educational programming developed by the station. They would also be a source of content through coverage of all manner of events, which would be sure to draw audiences of interested parents and community members. This is the quintessence of local television. Sponsorship and advertising would derive from local businesses interested in increasing visibility at a local level. For example, a local music goods outlet could sponsor coverage and broadcasting of school concerts, while a sporting goods outlet might do the same for local sporting events. School governing boards could also be co-opted into contributing if school meetings were to be covered by the station. The advantage of this format of programming is that it has a longer shelf life and can be rebroadcast in the interests of continuity.

Government programming

Since 1994, community radio has viewed government funding, whether local, provincial or national, with scepticism. There is always the fear that it will come with strings attached and that recipient stations will wind up being government mouthpieces, unable to question and criticise where due. This has made for very difficult choices for a sector that could well do with the support. A similar argument could well apply to revenue from advertising, where there is an even greater risk of programming control. The argument advanced by some in the sector is that if community media serve the people, who pay taxes, then the government does have an obligation to support the sector. In the absence of legislation formalising government support for the sector, as is the case in other countries, it is left to stations to negotiate a symbiotic relationship whereby they can serve as a communication link between the government and the people, with the former paying for the service and even providing funding for specific projects. In the long term, it is necessary to engage policy structures through the National Community Radio Forum (NCRF) and other bodies by lobbying for legislative support for the sector. Audiences must be involved in this exercise, by CTV providing a quality service that proves useful to them.

The Department of Communications has provided equipment to community radio stations to increase their technical capacity. This has worked quite well for the recipient stations, enabling them not only to carry live feeds for government events but also to use for their own regular work and to provide training for staff. The greatest risk of government interference is when the entire relationship between the government and the station is based on one particular department. What has worked successfully in the past is when the relationships and funding are spread across many departments in the form of specific issues and projects. For example, in Cape Town, CTV could provide an emergency services helpline for the Department of Public Safety, a service that would constantly keep citizens well informed. CTV could also borrow a leaf from the US, where highway information on road closures, accidents and other related issues are constantly provided on local radio and public access TV.

Providing these kinds of services allows the government to have a one-stop information link to the public, while allowing CTV to secure itself as a source of vital information to its viewers.

The Government Communication and Information System (GCIS) is a key partner for CTV in terms of government involvement. GCIS has a large amount of ready-made programming, in addition to having a long list of events for which live coverage is required. Community radio has worked in partnership with GCIS successfully, and television would add a new dimension to the flow of communication between the government and citizens. A partnership with GCIS would cater for communication with national and provincial government.

'C' is for commercial

The experience of community radio since its inception has demonstrated that commercial advertising is difficult to secure unless the content and quality of programming is of a high standard. The requisite standards are difficult to attain unless there is the means with which to acquire good-quality equipment and skilled production staff. In addition, most advertising revolves around entertainment formats that attract the largest audience. The sector has learnt that providing useful information may be a valuable service, but it is one that is not necessarily popular enough to draw audiences and advertising.

The perfect balance, which remains fairly elusive, is a scenario whereby CTV will have large enough audiences, including the higher range of Living Standards Measures (LSMs), to attract advertising and revenues while fulfilling its mandate to provide important information and education to the communities that it represents. In addition to this, community access and provision of training must remain central to its functioning. This then begs the question: How does a station ensure high-quality programming while providing access and/or training as well? Aldridge (1997) has suggested that subsidisation and a fair spread of income sources is the key to answering this. By avoiding over-reliance on any of the three income streams, the station could fulfil all its functions and steadily grow its market share. This can only be achieved with a strong station policy that clearly lays out the parameters for partnerships with the government, education/training institutions, advertisers and the community.

One approach to commercial advertising would be to segment the potential partners into large national corporates, local corporates and small, medium and micro enterprises (SMMEs). The large national corporates tend to seek audiences large or small, and focus on reaching as many consumers in as many markets as possible. Selling airtime to this group is more about timely communication when yearly budgets are drawn up. CTV can attract local corporates and SMMEs by offering lower rates than they would get from commercial stations. The local nature of CTV is also a unique selling point for this group. Lower rates for advertising can be achieved by offering in-house production of adverts, skills permitting. Over and above this, the trend towards increased corporate social investment means that local corporates can be encouraged to support local initiatives to build the community in which they operate. Again, targeting becomes important; advertising and sponsorship can be pegged to specific programmes that fall within the potential advertiser's area of business.

Multimedia classified advertising continues to grow in South Africa, as evidenced by its increasing visibility at airports and in other public spaces. CTV can flight these during off-air periods to fill up space. Internet connectivity would allow the station to feature advertisers' sites, affording them even more exposure.

Partnerships with other community media, both radio and print, will increase the appeal of CTV as a carrier of advertising. Offering multimedia packages will increase reach. This is one of the focus areas for the newly constituted NCRF hub structure, in which CTV should seek to play an active part. In terms of revenue generation, the structure aims to bring community stations together to formulate a concerted marketing strategy that would offer potential advertisers and sponsors packages that include all the member stations.

Programming

In the interests of balance and fulfilling its mandate, the station would need to plan its programming carefully, dividing it into peak and off-peak; the former carrying programming that is most likely to draw revenue, such as entertainment, news and other information, while the latter carries community notices and announcements as well as educational programming.

The likelihood is that in the initial set-up phase, it will be difficult to produce substantial in-house programming, unless there is funding for capital costs. A possible source of revenue is to sell chunks of airtime to producers, whether individuals or organisations, to flight their own programming. If such a system works well, it could be maintained in the long run, so that the station can focus on training and providing a broadcast service. This, however, needs to be governed by clear partnership guidelines that prevent powerful interest groups from controlling the station.

News is an integral part of programming and probably the most expensive to produce. Whereas it is desirable for this to be done in-house, it would require a high level of skill, good-quality equipment and a dedicated team. It may be possible to partner with local news producers such as community radio stations to achieve this. Community radio stations in Cape Town like Bush Radio have well-established news departments with whom partnerships in news gathering and production can be formed.

At the heart of any business plan is a high level of innovative thinking. Generating revenue is about limiting costs, and this requires the business of making television to be as inexpensive as possible without compromising on quality. This poses a challenge for programming. Audiences must be included and encouraged to feel a sense of ownership in the station. Live television provides this, whether it is coverage of a local event, in-studio interviews with community members, or even a live-cam in a part of the city, sponsored by a local business. These are some ideas that need to be explored.

The non-governmental organisation (NGO) sector is an integral part of any local community. NGOs and community-based organisations (CBOs) have as much presence in local communities as the government does, providing services to the population. NGOs increasingly make use of the media to inform communities of the services that they provide. The problem in the past has been that they have not been able to access media effectively. Community radio provides media training for NGO staff, equipping them to make more use of the media in their work; as a result, some NGOs are able to produce programming for community media.

Transmission costs for CTV will probably form the bulk of expenditure. At present, the Cape Town initiative is exploring the different options available from Sentech, depending on the coverage area required. Obviously, the greater the number of transmitters needed, the more the service will cost. However, it will only be possible to make this determination once a clear needs assessment has been done, focusing on how dispersed the target population is and who is most likely to use CTV. This can be done through an audience research survey, as elaborated in Chapter 12 of this report. An interim solution is to procure a time slot on an SABC channel during which programmes can be aired. Based on discussions with the SABC, this remains a possibility. This would afford the

CT CTV initiative time to develop capacity while creating a name and a presence in the community, without the financial pressure of running a fully fledged station. The station could then have a media-access facility where training, marketing and some production work is done, while making use of studio facilities elsewhere. Greater Durban TV (GDTV) has shown that event-based broadcasting can be a great way to initiate and maintain recognition in the community. So far, GDTV has relied on special-event broadcasts to develop and entrench itself in the community with reasonable success.

Keys to success

The key to sustainability is a comprehensive business plan that seeks to achieve a reliable revenue-generation stream coupled with cost-containment. This begins with a feasibility study, which includes an assessment of the audience in terms of needs, potential viewership and marketing potential. The media environment can provide competition and the risk of duplication of effort, especially with regard to community radio. A well-thought-out approach offers great potential for the creation of cross-media partnerships and synergies to the ultimate benefit of the community and the CT CTV initiative.

Partnerships within the initiative can reduce costs through maximising the competencies that already exist. Strong partnerships lead to concerted planning, fund-raising and management of the initiative. Cape Town has a strong partnership base that comprises organisations with complimentary competencies that can yield great results if well managed.

Human resources capacity is central to the success of the initiative. This is why training and access must be assured. It is important to learn from community radio that with a good training system in place there is also a high attrition rate, with staff being absorbed into mainstream media and other more lucrative sectors; however, this can be a source of strength and can attract funding for training.

In the case of CT CTV, the planning process needs to be multi-tiered and flexible to allow for the initiative to get off the ground with the resources it has at its disposal, which include organisational competence, strong partnerships and human resources. Based on this, the decision remains whether to start as a broadcast service provider exclusively, to engage in programme production as well, or even to produce programming to be carried by another broadcast service provider such as the SABC.

Audience analysis

According to statistics from the 1996 Census, 70 per cent of economically active persons in the City of Cape Town earn less than R2 500 per month, including a large portion who earn no income whatsoever. This economic sector represents some 80 per cent of African households, while 90 per cent of coloured households receive an income of under R4 500 a month. These figures show that the majority of the urban population is relatively poor. In terms of the economics of commercial media production, these people are not an attractive target market for advertisers (Bosch 2003); hence, community media like community radio stations struggle to obtain advertising revenue.

Table 14.1 shows a sample of the All Media Products Survey (AMPS) ratings for South Africa's four free-to-air TV channels in the Western Cape, Cape Town and surrounding areas. The figures reveal that Cape Town audience figures across all four channels hover around the 1.5 million mark, with 'fringe' audiences in the outlying areas varying from about 190 000 to 250 000. These figures indicate that a CTV broadcast reaching the entire

Cape Town area has a potential audience of between 1.5 to 2 million people, spread across all income groups. This is a substantial audience for news and current affairs programmes, which could be turned into significant income generators for the channel.

Table 14.1: AMPS audience ratings (000s), April 2004

	eTV	SABC 1	SABC 2	SABC 3
Total	19 076	23 288	18 858	14 145
Western Cape	2 494	2 418	2 527	2 146
Cape Town	1 689	1 645	1 578	1 469
Cape Town fringe	244	218	252	193

Source: SAARF 2004

Table 14.2 shows the city's population broken down by income level. The categories have been arbitrarily ascribed to give a rough idea of income divides: the 'Low' category falls between zero income and a monthly personal income of up to R2 500; the 'Middle' category reflects a monthly personal income of R2 501 to R16 000; and the 'High' category begins at R16 001 with a peak pegged at over R30 000 a month.

Table 14.2: Cape Town income demographics

Personal annual income (Rands)	Personal monthly income (Rands)	Population	High income	Middle income	Low income
None		208 218			208 218
1 000–2 400	100–200	24 935			24 935
2 401–6 000	201–500	68 462			68 462
6 001–12 000	501–1 000	141 348			141 348
12 001–18 000	1 001–1 500	182 542			182 542
18 001–30 000	1 501–2 500	158 263			158 263
30 001–42 000	2 501–3 500	92 894		92 894	
42 001–54 000	3 501–4 500	61 451		61 451	
54 001–72 000	4 501–6 000	54 116		54 116	
72 001–96 000	6 001–8 000	30 533		30 533	
96 001–132 000	8 001–11 000	21 374		21 374	
132 001–192 000	11 001–16 000	13 164		13 164	
192 001–360 000	16 001–30 000	7 878	7 878		
+360 000	+30 000	2 705	2 705		
Not stated		90 585			
Total		1 158 468	10 583	273 532	783 768

Source: Dorrington (2000)

Figure 14.1: Cape Town income demographics

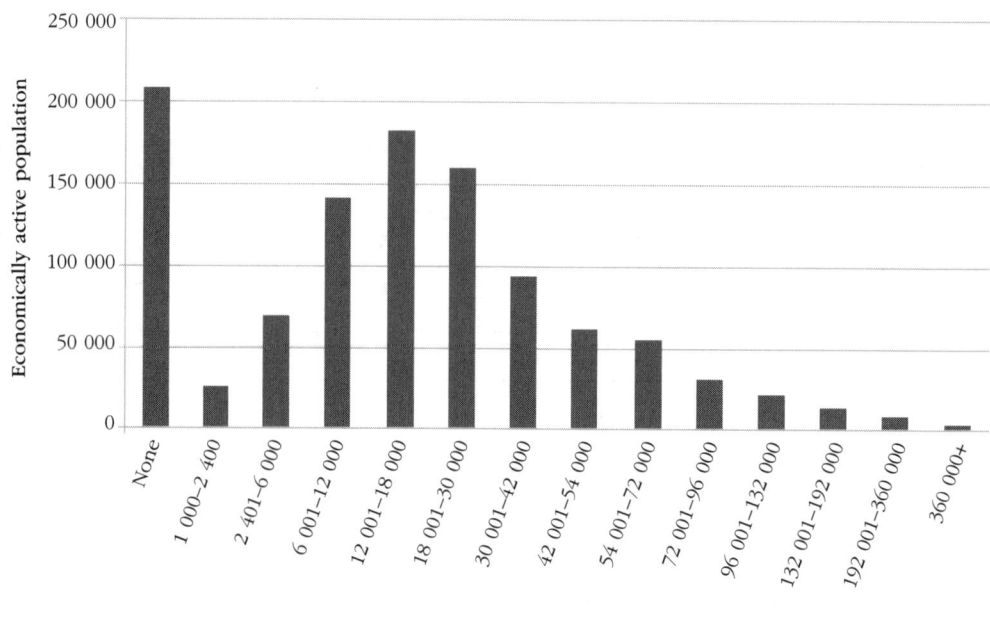

Source: Dorrington (2000)

These statistics are graphically represented in Figure 14.1 above. Here we see the extent of South Africa's economic insufficiencies, where the majority of the population has a relatively low income, with a large proportion of unemployed persons.

This shows that the 'urban poor', which in this model represent those earning a personal income of less than R2 500 per month, right down to zero income per month, constitute some 70 per cent of the urban population. The bulk of the population falls into the R2 401–R72 000 bracket, which represents relatively low income levels of under R6 000 a month.

These figures demonstrate that in reaching the bulk of the population, a CTV station covering the Cape Town area will serve mainly lower-income audiences. While there is a very high number of unemployed people who have extremely little or no income, CTV broadcasters should avoid the urge to reach very low income groups, because these people are least likely to have access to television sets, although many might be members of income-earning households. It must also be borne in mind that communities of interest tend to cross income levels, so it would be a mistake to consider audience targets only in economic terms. Moreover, the LSMs are not directly related to income levels, which may then be misleading in terms of defining commercially useful market segments.

The above figures should be correlated with the TV audience analysis in Chapter 12. We must bear in mind, too, that CTV does not operate along the same lines as the public service and commercial channels, which delineate specific audience profiles that programming is targeted to reach; instead, CTV relies on programming produced by and for particular communities of interest that cross boundaries such as income level, class and race.

Available infrastructure

It is envisaged that in its initial phase, a CTV station in Cape Town would rely to a large extent on existing infrastructure. In the long term, it is desirable to establish a video access centre that will enable Capetonians to gain basic video production training outside of existing institutions, as well as access to the tools of video production. Various member organisations in the CT CTVC will have production capacity by virtue of possessing the necessary equipment and staff, students and volunteers with at least a basic level of production training. At the time of writing, only the Arts and Media Access Centre (AMAC) and the Community Video Education Trust (CVET) have video production capacity.

There are several tertiary educational institutions in Cape Town that could provide infrastructural items such as video equipment, studios, student volunteers and programming. They are the University of the Western Cape (UWC), the University of Cape Town (UCT), City Varsity and the South African School of Motion Picture Medium and Live Performance (AFDA). All have expressed an interest in and a willingness to work with the CT CTV initiative, although the extent of their involvement has yet to be negotiated.

While South African universities have been involved in CTV activities in the past (Rhodes University and the University of KwaZulu-Natal), their ability to engage with the wider community in terms of allowing people outside of the student community to have access to their facilities is limited. Since students are the paying clients of these institutions, they have a legitimate claim to the use of the institution's audio-visual (AV) facilities, and their involvement in CTV activities can even form part of their studies. While institutional AV departments may make their facilities available to outside clients on occasion, their primary responsibility is to the institution itself and its student and staff constituency; thus, allowing community members to access these facilities is likely to be problematic.

A formal agreement may be entered into between the institution and the CTV initiative, whereby payment is guaranteed for the hire of equipment and responsibility is taken for the safety and return of equipment and the use of studio facilities. However, the most likely scenario is one where the students themselves undertake production activities as part of the CTV initiative, making use of the institutional facilities to this end. Community volunteers would most probably be accommodated by NGOs such as CVET and AMAC that have a specific community development mandate.

Two institutions were surveyed as part of the local infrastructure scoping report, these being UCT and UWC. Other institutions have a range of sophisticated production equipment, but were not surveyed as they are private institutions that are unlikely to lend their facilities to a CTV initiative for the purposes of hosting a broadcast or other production activities outside of their existing student curriculum.

University of Cape Town

The University of Cape Town has a fully fledged AV Centre that is used primarily by students of the Film and Media Studies Department and the Department of Drama. It has a range of prosumer-level digital video (DV) cameras and accessories, including tripods, microphones and mobile lighting kits. It also has a variety of analogue and digital editing suites, the latter equipped with professional digital editing software on both Apple Mac and Wintel PC platforms.

The Centre has a 9 m x 12 m studio space equipped with cold lighting, backdrops, an autocue and studio control with a vision mixer, audio console and DV recording machines. Related facilities include a sound studio and an iMac G5 audio editing workspace. The facility does not have a server-based network, nor does it have broadcast ability or external network links.

These production facilities are in constant use by full-time UCT students and are not usually available for use by outside parties. However, the Centre has indicated that it would like to participate in a CTV broadcast in terms of providing facilities and personnel, depending on the schedule for such broadcast(s) and the time of year such participation would be required.

See Appendix A for further details.

University of the Western Cape

The University of the Western Cape also has an AV department, but it has been concerned solely with recording events for the institution and has had only limited engagement with the student community. The only interaction with students that has occurred has been with the Bush TV initiative on campus, although it plans to extend this involvement during 2006. The department is also in the process of upgrading its facilities through building a small studio and acquiring new equipment.

At the time of writing, the department has only one PD170 digital camera with tripod, microphone and lighting kit. It has one Wintel PC edit system. The head of the department, UWC's Digital Media Coordinator André Daniels is currently a member of the CT CTVC steering committee and is interested in involving the department in CTV production activities. This is likely to be principally through the activities of students involved in the Bush TV initiative on campus, which has gone through a period of inactivity but is likely to be revived with the support of the department as well as CVET.

See Appendix B for further details.

City Varsity

This private tertiary institution teaches a range of subjects, including film and video production. According to Director Martin Botha, City Varsity produces about 250 student productions per year. This tally includes ten 12-minute 35 mm films, music videos by 12 directors, public service announcements (PSAs) and various other small-scale productions. At the second-year level, the institution has an average of 30 students who are divided into crews of ten persons each. The school is in its tenth year of operations and has about 2 000 productions in its archives.

City Varsity has 16 mm film cameras and has agreements with camera-hire companies to use their 35 mm cameras. It has its own range of DV cameras and various editing facilities ranging from Avid to Media 100s. Its animation department uses software such as Combustion and Maya.

AFDA

The South African School of Motion Picture Medium and Live Performance (AFDA) claims to be the biggest training provider in the country for the film and video industries. According to Director Garth Holmes, the institution could get involved with CTV in terms of training and content provision. The institution produces about 300 films a year between its Johannesburg and Cape Town campuses.

First-year students produce two one-minute films in the year, resulting in a total of around 60 productions, all of which have been sold to the SABC. Second-year students produce five-minute films, and this group is split into about 50 crews that make five films each per year. Third-year students make ten-minute films, and about 30 of these experimental films are produced annually. All of the third-year films are sold to the SABC. Fourth-year students produce genre films, and here students focus on specific profiles; some students make commercials, while others make music videos as a category of short film. Dramatic narrative development is an important component of all of these short films, documentaries and series. Fourth-year films are sold to the SABC and M-Net. AFDA also has a Master of Fine Arts programme and is busy negotiating a movie-of-the-month deal to create two feature films per two-year cycle.

The organisation has all the equipment needed to make high-quality films and videos, but concentrates mainly on film as a medium. AFDA has a particular interest in local television and is looking at segmented platforms in terms of developing the product and the market simultaneously. The intended outcome is to produce popular cinema or 'cinema for the masses', as Holmes puts it. 'The aim is to produce local cinema that has local characters, heroes, villains, aspirational problem-solving and fulfilment for audiences, so that people will go to see it,' he says.

Fourth-year students are encouraged to shoot their productions somewhere different to where they are studying. They give lectures to school students in that region in exchange for financial assistance from the provincial government. AFDA also provides a course for assistants, where second-year students are trained to crew for the fourth-year productions.

Holmes says the biggest problem with internships and courses is ensuring sustainability. 'You need intellectual capital to create the intellectual property,' he says. 'Our biggest problem is to train a nucleus of intellectual capital in the key positions – writing, directing, scripting and performance.'

AFDA is prepared to get involved in CTV activities through providing content and student volunteers.

SABC

The SABC has committed itself to supporting CTV in terms of the agreement entered into in 1996 between the Open Window Network, representing the CTV sector, and the Corporation. The SABC has given extensive support to GDTV as a result of the agreement and this support is likely to continue in the near term.

The former regional head of the SABC in the Western Cape, Lawrence Mitchell, referred to a previous occasion when the SABC supported a 'break-away' community broadcast for Cape Town, the Cape Community Broadcast Channel (CCBC), in 1998. This channel broadcast for 15 days on a special event licence, providing three hours of content in the evening and one hour in the morning. Mitchell, who has since moved on to head up the Cape Film Commission (CFC), expressed the view that the CFC would have an interest in supporting such an initiative.

Broadcasting under the wing of the SABC has its pros and cons. On the one hand, it would enjoy the benefit of SABC facilities and equipment; on the other, it could be constrained by the SABC's licence provisions, editorial policy, programming guidelines and technical standards. The nuts and bolts of the arrangement would have to be negotiated with the SABC at both regional and national level – regional for facilities, and national to gain a window on one of the SABC channel's frequencies. In the longer term, the relationship between CTV channels and the SABC will have to take into account the Corporation's regional, indigenous language stations, which will have a profound effect on the terrain in which CTV operates in terms of competition for revenue sources and overlap in local coverage.

In terms of logistics, Mitchell points out that it is difficult to produce compelling television that people want to watch, and that the CCBC project showed that community producers struggle to produce sufficient programming to fill the time available. Current affairs and discussion programmes are best in this regard, but they have to compete against other media such as newspapers and the Internet.

Mitchell believes that this kind of project requires people 'who have worked on television and on live television who understand what it is about'. He also cautions that those who wish to address ideological issues such as gender, community access or left-wing politics can diminish the kind of mass viewership on which the SABC predicates its advertising-driven public service style of broadcasting. In this situation, it is essential to understand audience patterns to produce relevant content, and this is why the SABC has a large audience research department that enables it to refine its content and editorial policies in order to appeal to mass markets.

These observations reinforce the old adage that 'content is king'. As Mitchell comments, 'To me, the carrier and the frequency is immaterial. It is the content that counts and to use other channels to promote it and drive those audiences. If nobody is aware of it, then there is no point.'

SABC Cape Town facilities

According to Airtime Cape Town head Dave Terblanche, the SABC's regional office has various facilities that could be used for a CTV broadcast. These include a three-camera studio in Sea Point. There are three areas that can be used for broadcast: one is a newsreader-type situation for a single presenter and the second is a round desk that can seat three to four people. The background is a set of Table Mountain that can be changed if necessary. The third area is a 'lounge arrangement' with a couch and a green-screen background.

Adjacent to the studio are a waiting room and a make-up room. The building has a canteen on the fifth floor. The studio has equipment to take phone-in inputs and make them audible in the studio. The radio studio's auditorium, which seats 150 people, can be used for panel discussions. Camera outputs from this venue feed directly back to the studio, but an outside broadcast set-up would be necessary in terms of recording equipment.

The studio has two DVCAM VTRs because the SABC's news operations in the Western Cape run on DVCAM standard. The VTRs are Sony DSR1000 hard drives that can take six hours of material and can take feeds from any format. They can also record at the same time as they play out and can be used to input material such as adverts, logos and 'stings' into the broadcast. The studio is equipped with a caption generator, autocue, lighting grid, sound mixer and remote inputs to connect with outside broadcast facilities. There is also a device that turns computer graphics into video by running a VGA PC monitor in parallel and mixing it into the broadcast video stream.

There are edit suites in the building, but they belong to news and are fully utilised; however, Terblanche says that there is space in the building where non-linear edit suites could be set up. For local broadcasting, there is a fibre-optic cable, which links the studio to Sentech's Milnerton office, and can be rented from the SABC. Sentech routes the data to whatever transmitter is being used for broadcast. There are also communication links with Sentech that can be used during broadcasts.

Transmission

We do not consider low-power transmission options here because the economics of broadcast media require maximum audience reach to be successful, especially in the terrain of television production. It could be possible for a CTV broadcaster to buy one or more low-power transmitters to reach small local regions, for example the inner city, provided that funding could be found for an ongoing project of this nature. However, frequency scarcity would then preclude any other or any larger-scale CTV broadcaster from operating in the wider city environs.

The number of transmitters and the relative power (Wattage) required to reach a citywide area varies according to topography. In Cape Town, the SABC uses at least nine transmitters to cover the total area. These are located at Tygerberg, Constantiaberg, Table Mountain, Fish Hoek, Clifton, Aurora, Amanda Glen, Hout Bay and Grabouw. This number has significant financial implications because each transmitter has its own costs; for example, the 20 kW Constantiaberg transmitter costs R148 000 a month, while the 1 kW Tygerberg transmitter costs R33 000 a month.

Lesser-powered transmitters can still be used effectively; for instance, GDTV used a single 100 W transmitter that reached a radius of at least 50 km, although reception was patchy and particular areas within that radius received a weak signal or even no signal at all. For a Cape Town CTV station, using just one transmitter at the Tygerberg site would provide the most cost-effective way of reaching the majority of Cape Town's population, particularly those in the lower-income groups who live predominantly in the so-called 'Cape Flats' areas (see Figure 14.2). This would leave out the western coastline beyond Table Mountain and the Twelve Apostles as well as most of the southern peninsula, with the exception of the eastern seaboard around Simonstown.

RE-VISIONING TELEVISION

Figure 14.2: Coverage for CT CTV

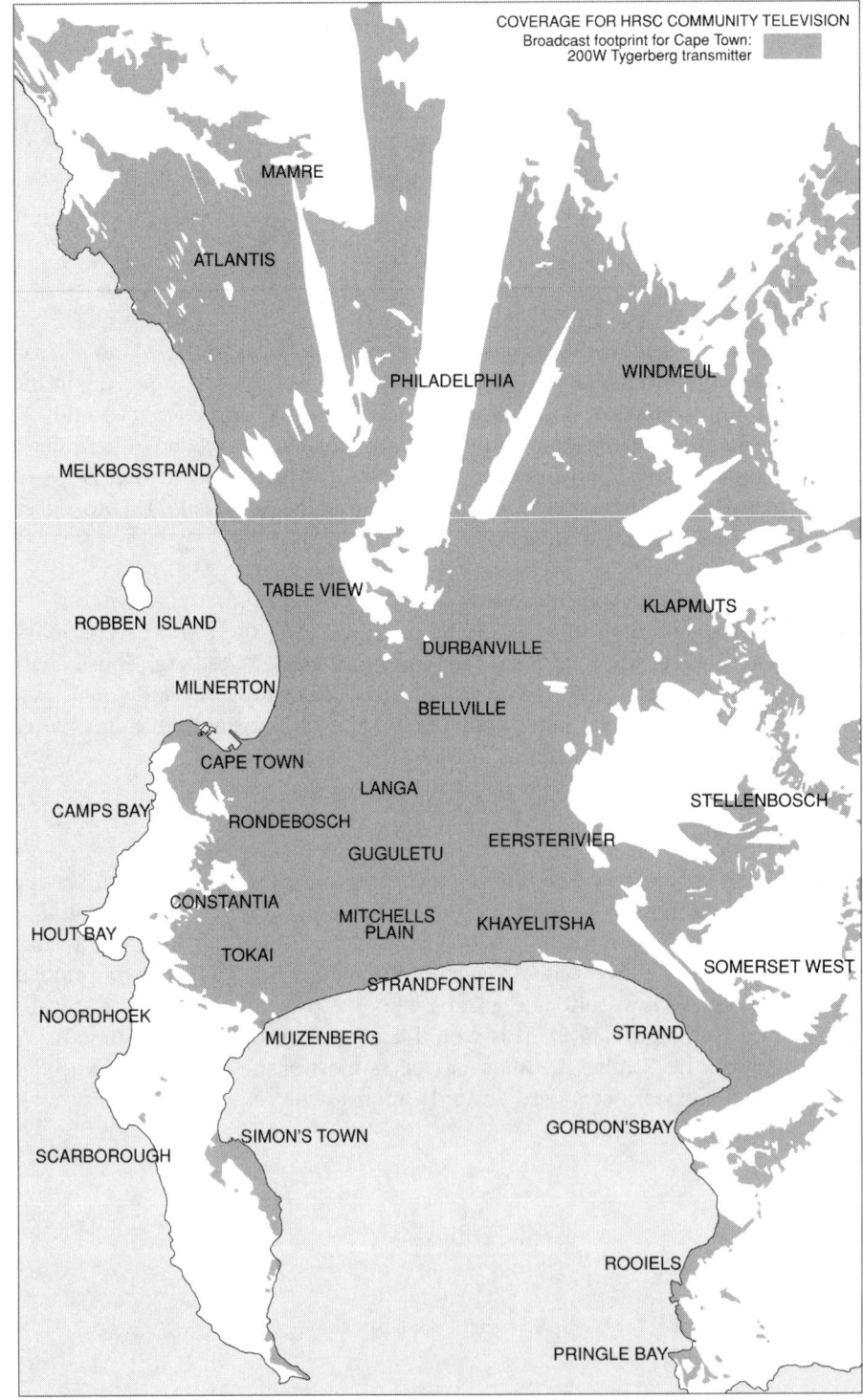

Source: Sentech 2005
Note: The shaded area represents coverage of the greater Cape Town area using a 200 W transmitter located at the Tygerberg site (just south of the deep middle indent into the coverage area).

Conclusion

Various potential income streams and support areas have been identified in terms of the C-PEG model, although the real support of players within these environments must still be established.

Cape Town has a variety of tertiary education, NGO and independent production facilities that can be utilised for a CTV broadcast. Relative to other South African cities, it has a strong tertiary education component that produces a high volume of students and graduates with video and film production skills. These facilities and a base of young video producers, together with the city's vigorous film and video industry, place it in a strong position with regard to attracting volunteers and generating content for CTV. Nevertheless, we must bear in mind that tertiary educational institutions have their own priorities, which centre on educating students rather than acting as a long-term base for production activities.

The city has seen previous CTV broadcasts, including one on an SABC 'break-away' channel. The SABC is willing to support similar initiatives in the future and this could represent a means of establishing a presence for CTV in Cape Town at minimal cost to the CTV broadcaster. Using SABC facilities and transmitters would ensure audience reach across the entire Cape Town municipal region.

In the longer term, CTV will not be able to linger under the wing of the SABC, and will have to fly on its own in terms of broadcast facilities and transmitters. On the one hand, this will increase the station's costs in terms of investment in facilities, personnel, production and transmission. On the other hand, the channel will be able to increase its broadcast duration, which will leave more space to bring in advertising and sponsorship income. However, a lesser footprint resulting from fewer transmitters will have a negative impact on revenue potential and viewership, unless revenues can be found to support multiple transmitters.

Different transmission mediums – including webcasting, IP-based network transmissions and cellular communications – can also be leveraged to widen the channel's reach and increase its revenue potential. It is often argued that the relative scarcity of Internet connectivity amongst the lower-income population militates against the use of these mediums to reach CTV's priority audience. Nevertheless, there is already a wide array of television stations worldwide making use of these mediums to convey both video and print information to global audiences. These varied technologies make the world a small place, and communities of interest are often global in nature. This means that even a local CTV station can communicate with global audiences through the Internet, distribute multimedia content to other sites over IP networks and interact with cellular users through video and text.

The penetration of these digital technologies into lower-income groups is increasing. The City of Cape Town has initiated a 'Smart Cape' strategy that has placed Internet-enabled computers into libraries across the city, which are available for use free of charge. Schools are increasingly utilising computer labs to teach scholars how to use information and communications technology and cyber cafés abound in urban areas. The national government has its Multi-purpose Community Centre, Telecentre and community digital hub projects, and as broadband technologies proliferate, bandwidth becomes cheaper.

Cellular uptake has been surprisingly high in South Africa and there are more cellphone owners than landline owners in the country. The new high-speed wireless technologies such as 3G and HSDPA offer users the ability to access the Internet, download video and conduct video telephony in addition to the variety of other functions currently bundled into cellphones. While this technology is currently available mainly to higher-income earners, the next few years are sure to see prices drop and accessibility increase. Moreover, cellphones with the ability to receive television broadcasts are now coming onto the market and, again, these will become more accessible to lower-income groups as time goes by.

It will be essential for CTV broadcasters to leverage the interactivity that these digital mediums allow. GDTV, for example, has used cellphones to good effect in the live studio setting, and this kind of interaction with audiences should be maximised by CTV broadcasters to enhance viewer participation and feedback.

To sum up, the City of Cape Town is well placed to host further CTV broadcasts. The Cape Town CTV Collective has begun mobilising community sectors to discuss and participate in CTV activities. The Collective has established a set of principles to guide its actions and is planning pilot broadcasts for 2006. Its strategy involves mobilising extensive community involvement in the channel, and it is this people-centred approach that holds the most promise for its ongoing sustainability.

APPENDIX A

Local CTV scoping report: technical parameters – University of Cape Town

Production facilities

Video cameras – make, model, tape format

4 x Sony TRV15 (DV)
1 x Sony TRV16 (DV)
2 x Sony TRV19 (DV)
2 x Sony HC2DE (DV)
1 x Panasonic EZ35 (3CCD DV)
2 x Sony PD100 (3CCD DVCAM)
5 x Sony PD150 (3CCD DVCAM)
3 x Sony PD170 (3CCD DVCAM)

Lights/lighting kits

4 x 800w (Redheads) (in kit)
Lowell kit (3 lights)

Camera tripods and heads – make, model

4 x Still cam-type
13 x Manfrotto 128
1 x Manfrotto 520

Microphones – make, model, type

11 x Azden Radio lapel mics
4 x Dynamic Handheld mics
7 x Azden Handheld mics
10 x Sennheiser EW12 (Radio lapel mic kits)
1 x Beyer Semi-rifle mic
6 x Semi Rifle Kits (Sennheisser ME6)

Video editing facilities – analogue

SVHS, VHS analogue suite – cuts only

Video editing facilities – digital

4 x Powermac G5 Dual 18 GHz, 1.25 Gig RAM, 160 + 250 Gig HDDs, Mac OS X 10.3.9, DVD-R/RW, Final Cut Pro and DVD Studio Pro
1 x emac G4 (1.25 GHz, 512 MB RAM, 80 Gig, DVD-R/RW, OS 10.3) with Final Cut Pro and DVD Studio Pro
1x Avid DV Express Pro (using HP Intel 3.2 GHz machine)

Studio facilities – total area, lighting, cameras, autocue, backdrops/props, communications

9 m x 12 m floor space
Cold studio fluorescent lights (x 5)
Grey or black backdrop
Can accommodate component camera system
Homemade autocue

Studio control – monitors, mixing desks, personnel/seats

Panasonic MX70 Vision mixer, 24-channel audio console and necessary monitors
DVCAM and DV record machine

Work flow – servers (type, capacity, speed) and network

N/A

Broadcast ability – microwave links, media servers, external bandwidth

N/A

Production

What is your annual production budget?
N/A

How many productions do you produce a) weekly b) monthly c) yearly?
N/A

What types of production do you undertake (e.g. training, corporate, educational, documentary, drama)?
N/A

What is the duration of an average production (can be differentiated according to types, e.g. documentary, insert)?
N/A

How long does it take you to produce?
N/A

How many people are involved in each production?
N/A

How much tape stock do you use? (can be per production or weekly/monthly/annually).
N/A

Do you reuse tape stock – if so, how many times are tapes reused?
N/A

What additional costs are associated with each production (e.g. telephone, transport, personnel)?
N/A

Personnel

How many personnel do you have? List job titles.
N/A (Educational institution)

What is their operational level? List qualifications and experience.
N/A (Educational institution)

How many are engaged in direct training activities? List training areas.
N/A (Educational institution)

How many are engaged in support functions? List areas.
Two persons running studio and edit facilities.

General

What related production facilities do you have (e.g. sound studios, animation or graphics facilities, music library)?
Sound studio and iMac G5 pro tools-based audio editing workspace

Are your production facilities available for use by others?
No

If yes, would you hire them out or sponsor them for CTV purposes (give costs)?
N/A

What is their availability (i.e. when do they stand idle and for how long)?
In constant use by full-time students enrolled at the University of Cape Town

Would your staff be available for training or mentorship of CTV personnel? Give details.
N/A

Would your facility participate in a CTV broadcast in terms of a) facilities b) personnel c) production costs?
We would like to participate in terms of facilities and personnel, depending on the schedule for such broadcast(s) and the time of year such participation would be required.

Could your facility host a CTV broadcast?
Possibly

Have you engaged in broadcast activities in the past? Are you considering this option for the future? If yes, give details.
No

Have you ever engaged in netcasting? Are you considering this option for the future? If yes, give details.
No

APPENDIX B

Local CTV scoping report: technical parameters – University of the Western Cape

Production facilities

Video cameras – make, model, tape format

PD170, shooting Mini DV or DVCAM

Lights/lighting kits

3-light kit (redheads)

Camera tripods and heads – make, model

ActionPro tripod

Microphones – make, model, type

Sony UWP series wireless microphones

Video editing facilities – analogue

Still in the process of setting these up

Video editing facilities – digital

2 PCs
200 Gig space
512 RAM/1 Gig RAM
Adobe Premiere

Studio facilities – total area, lighting, cameras, autocue, backdrops/props, communications

Still in the process of setting up

Studio control – monitors, mixing desks, personnel/seats

As above

Work flow – servers (type, capacity, speed) and network

N/A

Broadcast ability – microwave links, media servers, external bandwidth

N/A

Production

What is your annual production budget?
None

How many productions do you produce a) weekly b) monthly c) yearly?
This is dependent on the number and size of projects put forward but could be between five and ten

What types of production do you undertake (e.g. training, corporate, educational, documentary, drama)?
Training, educational, documentary

What is the duration of an average production (can be differentiated according to types, e.g. documentary, insert)?
Mainly inserts of about ten minutes

How long does it take you to produce?
Not answered

How many people are involved in each production?
2–4 people

How much tape stock do you use (can be per production or weekly/monthly/annually)?
We request as it is required

Do you reuse tape stock – if so, how many times are tapes reused?
Hardly, only when not available

What additional costs are associated with each production (e.g. telephone, transport, personnel)?
Might be equipment or gear that we do not have ourselves, as well as transport

Personnel

How many personnel do you have? List job titles.
Two positions: Digital Media Coordinator; Digital Media Assistant

What is their operational level? List qualifications and experience.
Not answered

How many are engaged in direct training activities? List training areas.
Not answered

How many are engaged in support functions? List areas.
Not answered

General

What related production facilities do you have (e.g. sound studios, animation or graphics facilities, music library)?
Not answered

Are your production facilities available for use by others?
Not currently (only used for in-house productions)

If yes, would you hire them out or sponsor them for CTV purposes (give costs)?
Not at this stage

What is their availability (i.e. when do they stand idle and for how long)?
Not answered

Would your staff be available for training or mentorship of CTV personnel? Give details.
Time permitting we will; with such a small staff it is difficult to tell

Would your facility participate in a CTV broadcast in terms of a) facilities b) personnel c) production costs?

Could your facility host a CTV broadcast?
Not currently

Have you engaged in broadcast activities in the past? Are you considering this option for the future? If yes, give details.
Yes, as UWC represents a large part of the Cape Town community

Have you ever engaged in netcasting? Are you considering this option for the future? If yes, give details.
No, but hoping to in the near future

GLOSSARY

Asynchronous Digital Subscriber Line (ADSL). A method of high-speed data transfer over a digital telephone connection. The term 'asynchronous' refers to the disparity in transfer rates between 'upstream' and 'downstream' data flows, in other words the rates at which the user's PC sends requests for data to the server and at which it downloads relevant data from the server. ADSL data rates range from 1.5 to 9 MBps when receiving data (the downstream rate) and from 16 to 640 KBps when sending data (upstream rate).

Advanced Television Systems Committee (ATSC). A committee formed to establish technical standards for US advanced television systems. Also, the name given to the 8-VSB transmission standard itself.

All Media Products Survey (AMPS). A measurement used by SAARF to establish patterns of media consumption according to various demographic and consumer criteria.

Arts and Media Access Centre (AMAC). Cape Town NGO concerned with providing training and facilities in fine arts, performing arts and media production to previously disadvantaged individuals.

Association of Christian Broadcasters (ACB). A national body representing the interests of evangelical Christian community radio stations and professional television broadcasters.

Blonde. A hot light used in video work. These range in power from 1 000–2 000W, but are usually pitched at the higher rating. They are used as key floodlights for lighting large areas.

Byte. A group of data bits that are processed together. A byte consists of eight bits. There are kilobytes, megabytes, gigabytes, terabytes, etc:
1 byte = 8 bits
1 kilobyte = 1 000 bytes
1 megabyte = 1 000 000 bytes
1 gigabyte = 1 000 000 000 bytes
1 terabyte = 1 000 000 000 000 bytes

Charge-coupled device (CCD). A light-sensitive chip or image sensor used in scanners and digital cameras that converts light into proportional (analogue) electrical current. The analogue/digital converter converts analogue signals into pixel values.

Chrominance. Refers to the colour coding of the video signal, relative to a specified reference colour. It sets the parameters for the depiction of colours split into the red-green-blue (RGB) video signal.

Community digital hub (CDH). A type of facility planned by the Universal Service Agency that will enable people in disadvantaged communities to use computers and to access the Internet.

Complementary metal oxide semiconductor (CMOS). An emerging light sensor technology offered as an alternative to CCD. CMOS offers more dense light sensors per square centimetre than CCD and has a broader dynamic light range than CCD; thus, it will yield more shadow detail and more highlight detail with less colour distortion from uncontrolled light sources. As the technology matures, CMOS will eventually be less expensive to produce than CCD.

Community Video Education Trust (CVET). A Cape Town-based NGO concerned with development through video. The organisation provides video production training to organisations and individuals with a development orientation as well as visual literacy courses in marginalised communities.

DVCAM. A digital format that uses 8-bit digital component recording with a 5:1 compression ratio and a sampling rate of 4:2:0. The unique compression algorithm provides excellent picture quality and superb multi-generation performance. The DVCAM format has a wider track pitch of 15 µm (compared with 10 µm for the DV format), which gives higher reliability for professional editing.

Genlock. A method of synchronising video cameras so that their respective images synchronise at the vertical, horizontal, and chroma-phase levels. This enables cross-camera cuts, mixes and cross-fades without noticeable roll, jump or chroma shift in the picture.

Global System for Mobile Communications (GSM). A digital communications standard for cellular telephone networks. It is a second generation (2G) system that is now being superseded by third generation (3G) standards.

Government Communications and Information System (GCIS). A government department tasked with facilitating communications between government departments and citizens.

High-speed downlink packet access (HSDPA). A high-bandwidth cellular technology that when used with 3G networks delivers speeds of around 384 KBps upstream and 1 800 KBps downstream. These speeds are set to increase to 9 MBps in the near term and up to 50 MBps in the long term.

Human Sciences Research Council (HSRC). A state-sponsored research organisation concerned with establishing the nature of social trends, developmental needs, appropriate means of intervention, and so on.

Institute for Democracy in South Africa (IDASA). Formerly, the Institute of Democratic Alternatives for South Africa. An NGO concerned with promoting democracy in South Africa.

Living Standards Measure (LSM). A marketing segmentation tool developed by the South African Advertising Research Foundation (SAARF). The LSM levels range from one to ten, with one representing the poorest people and ten representing the most wealthy.

Luminance. A measure of brightness. In video terminology, it refers to an algorithm that measures the intensity of the combined RGB (red, green and blue) components of a video image on a screen.

Moving Picture Experts Group (MPEG). The standard for compression and storage of motion video, for example, videos available though the World Wide Web.

MPEG IMX. A format based on Digital Betacam and developed by Sony. It uses the MPEG compression system, but at a higher bit rate than Betacam SX.

Multi-purpose Community Centre (MPCC). Facilities established by GCIS in disadvantaged communities to enable people to access various government services. Other services can also be housed in these centres, for example NGOs, small businesses for job-creation purposes and computer training schools.

National Electronic Media Institute of South Africa (NEMISA). A tertiary training institution established by the national Department of Communications, with the intention of providing training in various electronic media for emerging African professionals.

NTSC. A signal distribution coding that originated in the United States. The acronym derives from the National Television Systems Committee, the US organisation that first defined the standard. It is now used in various countries around the world.

Phase alternating line (PAL). The colour video and broadcasting standard used mainly in western Europe and South America. PAL screen resolution is 625 lines, and its refresh rate is 50 Hz.

RCA. An analogue electrical connection used in audio and video cabling. The name derives from the Radio Corporation of America, which first introduced the device. It consists of a 'male' component with a plug and ring that fits into a corresponding 'female' component.

Redhead. General-purpose lights widely used in video work. This category of lighting equipment typically operates at 800W, but can range from 650–1 000W. Redheads can be used as a key floodlight for large areas, but are also useful as fill and backlights.

Sector Education and Training Authorities (SETAs). Government bodies set up in each industry sector to establish and fund means to train people in the skills needed in that sector, as well as to recognise existing skills sets in terms of formal and informal qualifications standards.

Society of Motion Picture and Television Engineers (SMPTE). The organisation that established the SMPTE standard time code for video playback.

Universal Mobile Telecommunications Service (UMTS). A 3G standard, supporting a theoretical data throughput of up to 2 MBps.

XLR. A cable connector for electronic appliances, particularly in the audio and video spheres. It has a rugged construction that includes a latch mechanism and rubber padding. 'Female' and 'male' components connect with multiple pins that slide into corresponding slots.

REFERENCES

Adams S (2005) SA moving towards digitised broadcasting, *The Star* 20 May.

AGN (1995) *Information brochure*. Johannesburg: Africa Growth Network.

Aldridge M (1996) *Consciousness, culture and creativity: Harmonising the techno-cultural interface*. MA thesis, Centre for Cultural and Media Studies, University of Natal, Durban.

Aldridge M (1997) *Community television broadcasting in South Africa: Theoretical overview and business plan*. Open Window Network. <http://www.mediastream.co.za/community-tv/html/ctv_business_plan.htm. August 2005.

Aldridge M (2002a) Own your own TV station, in *Brainstorm*. Johannesburg: ITWeb Publications.

Aldridge M (2002b) National empowerment multicasting network. Cape Town: Media Stream.

Aldridge M (2004a) A solid foundation for CSI, in *Professional Management Review*. Johannesburg: PMR Publications.

Aldridge M (2004b) Independent World Television, in *Screen Africa*. Johannesburg: Sun Circle Publishers.

Armstrong C (2004) *Community TV and video in South Africa: From special event to main event? A scoping document, 1990–2005*. Johannesburg: Wits Link Centre.

Auret M (2005) Author interview with Sithengi Film Market CEO Michael Auret.

Banzi K (2005a) *Cue TV case study*. Cape Town: Human Sciences Research Council.

Banzi K (2005b) *Bush TV case study*. Cape Town: Human Sciences Research Council.

Bagdikian B (1997) *The media monopoly*. Boston: Beacon Press.

Berlin Declaration (1997) Fourth Convention of the German Open Channels, Berlin 13–16 November.

Bosch T (2003) *Radio, community and identity in South Africa: A rhizomatic study of Bush Radio in Cape Town*. Doctoral dissertation, Ohio University College of Communication.

Bray A (2003) *Video over IP*. <www.lightreading.com/document.asp?doc_id=40811> June 2005.

Briz31 (2005) <www.briz31.tv/news.asp> August.

Brock R (2002) *Successful implementation of satellite IP multicast in media & retail environments and hybrid networks*. Johannesburg: CPC.

C31 Melbourne (2005) <http://www.channel31.org.au/> 16 August.

CBAA (2003) *Community Television Code of Practice: Code 1 – Governance, Community and Access Principles*. Community Broadcasting Association of Australia. <www.cbaa.org.au/content.php/345.html> November 2005.

Chait M & Tilley N (2005) Author interview with Dr Melanie Chait and Nikki Tilley of the Monash University Film and TV Unit.

CT CTVC (2005) *Cape Consortium minutes, 7 July*. Cape Town Community Television Collective.

Currie D (2004) RTS Fleming Memorial Lecture 2004: Television and the digital future. *Citynews*, City University London, 11 October.

Datapost (2005) *The datapost solution*. Johannesburg: Datapost.

Dawkins R (2005) Author interview with Richard Dawkins, Executive: Customer Acquisition and Retention, Orbicom.

Deep Dish TV (2005) <www.deepdishtv.org>

De Vos D (2005) Author Interview with media lawyer Dirk de Vos on his contribution to regional television broadcasting for the DoC.

Doherty C (2004) Interactive advertising, *AV Specialist* 81: 26–29.

Dooms P (2002) The licensing of community radio: Responses from stations. FXI research paper. <www.fxi.org>

Dorrington RE (2000) *Projection of the population of the Cape Metropolitan Area 1996–2031*. Cape Town City Council.

DPLG (2005) *Information pamphlet*. Pretoria: Department of Provincial and Local Government.

Droz J (2003) *Mac vs. PC: A comprehensive survey of over four hundred reports, studies and articles*. <http://mac.unimaas.nl/docs/MACvsPCCombined.pdf> June 2003.

Dublin Community Television (2005) <www.dctv.ie/> 11 August.

El-Khoury C (2005) South African CTV links. Email correspondence from C31 Director Christine El-Khoury.

Emerich R (2005) Author interview with Sentech Portfolio Manager: Signal Distribution, Rian Emerich.

Frishberg M (2003) *Roll-your-own net TV takes off*. USA: Wired News.

Fulton C (2000) *Why I prefer the open source solution for video editing*. O'Reilly Network, <www.oreillynet.com/pub/a/network/2000/08/11/magazine/author_view.html>

Fulton C (2000) *Broadcast 2000 brings DV editing to Linux*. O'Reilly Network, <www.oreillynet.com/pub/a/network/2000/08/11/magazine/broadcast2000.html>

GCIS (2005a) Author interview with David Jacobs, Lydia Maredi and Charlotte Mmatli of the Directorate Local Liaison and Communication, Government Communication and Information System, Pretoria.

GCIS (2005b) *Building a South Africa that truly belongs to all: Programme of action 2005*. Pretoria: Government Communication and Information System.

Global Information Inc. (2005) *IP TV global forecast – 2005 to 2008 semiannual IP TV global forecast update*. <http://www.gii.co.jp/english/mr27396_ip_tv.html>

Hadland A & Thorne K (2004) *The people's voice: The development and current state of the South African small media sector*. Cape Town: HSRC Press.

Haysom L (2005a) GDTV report: 'Summer sizzler' broadcast 29 December 2004 to 27 January 2005. Unpublished document.

Haysom L (2005b) Author interview with Lou Haysom, GDTV supporter, Durban.

Hill A & Weinshenker D (2005) Presentation on the Centre for Digital Storytelling, <www.storycenter.org> City Varsity, Cape Town.

Hill T (2004) *New revenue alert from SMS*. Telecommunications Magazine website <http://horizontest.bvdep.com/telecom/default.asp?journalid=2&func=articles&page=0402i14&year=2004&month=2> September 2005.

Hope Madikane-Otto Research & Consulting (2003) *Content analysis on television broadcasting from September 2002 to February 2003*. Pretoria: Department of Communications.

IBA (1995) *Triple Inquiry Report*. Johannesburg: Independent Broadcasting Authority.

ICASA (2003a) *Revised Code of Conduct for Broadcasters*. Johannesburg: Independent Communications Authority of South Africa.

ICASA (2003b) *Local Television Discussion Paper*. ICASA, Johannesburg.

ICASA (2003c) *Regional Television Broadcasting Services*. Position Paper, 26. November, Johannesburg. (http://www.icasa.org.za/Repository/esources/Broadcasting/Policy/Local%20TV%20Discussion%20Paper.pdf, July 2005)

ICASA (2004) *Community television broadcasting services: Position paper*. Johannesburg: Independent Communications Authority of South Africa.

ICASA (2006) *SA Television Content Regulations, 2006*. Johannesburg: Independent Communications Authority of South Africa.

ICT World (2005a) *Everything going broadband*. Issue 146 <www.ictworld.co.za>

ICT World (2005b) *Local ADSL uptake 'pathetically' slow*. Issue 140, Category: Local News, 9 June.

ICT World (2005c) *Siemens develops way for TV participation from home*. Issue 146, Category: Global News, 20 July.

ICT World (2005d) *Siemens offers interactive TV across the Internet*. Issue 150, Category: Global News, 18 August.

Informa Research (2005) quoted in *Cellphone TV set to reach masses*. Amsterdam: Reuters News Service.

IPDC (2005) <www.unesco.org/webworld/ipdc> 13 August.

ITU (2004) *African telecommunication indicators 2004*. Report prepared for Africa Telecom 2004, Cairo, May.

ITWeb (2005) *Cellphone TV set to reach masses*. Amsterdam: Reuters News Service.

Jacobs D (2005) Author interview with GCIS Directorate officer David Jacobs.

Kantor L (2005) Author interview with SABC Head of Regulatory Affairs Lara Kantor.

Leitch (2004) *Integrated content environment overview*. Canada: Leitch Technology Corporation.

Letsebe H (2005) Author interview with Harry Letsebe of the MDDA.

Link TV (2005) <http://www.linktv.org> August.

Lishivha P (2005a) Re: Community television research. Email response to questions posed by researcher Mike Aldridge.

Lishivha P (2005b) Re: Questions for ICASA. Email response to questions posed by researcher Mike Aldridge.

Louw P (1991) *Communication and counter hegemony in contemporary South Africa: Considerations on a leftist media theory and praxis*. PhD, University of Natal, Durban.

Lundby K (1995) *Community media in Norway and Zimbabwe*. Seminar at the Centre for Cultural & Media Studies, University of KwaZulu-Natal, October.

Lungu P (2005) Author interview with GDTV Chairperson Patrick Lungu. Durban.

Madlala L (2005) *Digital divide hits township hard.* <www.tectonic.co.za/view.php?id=610> 22 September.

Madzimuri T (2005) Author interview with SACOD Director Tambudzai Madzimuri.

Marshall S (2005) *The trouble with open source.* ITNOWextra – September 2005, <http://www.bcs.org/BCS/Products/publishing/itnow/OnlineArchive/sep05/itnowextra/memberview.htm>

Martinis D (2005) Author interview with Dimitri Martinis of the National Film and Video Foundation.

Mayan TV (2005) <http://ayantv.webcrayon.com/> 11 August.

Mayisela L (2005) Author interview with Lynda Mayisela, GDTV Programming Committee.

McAskill N (2005) Author interview with CVET Coordinator Natalie McAskill, regarding CVET production capacity.

Mdladlana M (2000) The African Renaissance will be driven by investments: The role of government. Presentation by the Minister of Labour to the AHI 2000 Congress.

Mindset Network (2005) <www.mindset.co.za> August.

Mindset Network (2005) Conversation between author and unknown video editor at Mindset Network.

Mjwara (2005) Author interview with J Mjwara, Deputy Director, Department of Communication.

Moalosi D & Thorne K (2003) Submission to ICASA on the Inquiry into Local Television. NCRF discussion paper.

Molema (2005) Author interview with NEMISA Acting Head Stanley Molema.

Mthembu D (2005) Author interview with FRU Project Manager Desmond Mthembu.

Naidoo A (2005a) *Analysis of South Africa's demographics in the context of community TV.* Cape Town: Human Sciences Research Council.

Naidoo A (2005b) *Is community TV sustainable in South Africa? Identifying its challenges and building a viable business model for CTV in SA.* MBA research report, Graduate School of Business, University of Cape Town.

Nandi CTV Fiji (2005) <www.communitymedia.se/cat/fiji/index.htm> 11 August.

Olson B (2000) *The History of Public Access Television.* Available at <http://www.geocities.com/iconostar/history-public-access-TV.html <http://www.geocities.com/iconostar/history-public-access-TV.html> > June 2006.

Open Channels for Europe (2005) <http://www.openchannel.se/europe/index.htm> August.

Peppas M (2005) Author interview with Dr Mikhail Peppas, GDTV Station Manager. Durban.

RMB (2000) <www.rmb.co.za> November.

Roodt J & Conradie P (2003) *Creating a learning culture in rural schools via educational satellite TV broadcasts.* Presentation at Globalisation, Regionalisation and the Information Society – A European and South(ern) African encounter, Bruges, Belgium.

Rosenthal P (2005) *Comment on October 2005 draft of 'Re-versioning television' document on community TV.* Submission to HSRC CTV research project. Cape Town: Association of Christian Broadcasters.

Ross JM (1996) Email correspondence between community TV producer Jesikah Maria Ross and Mike Aldridge concerning the GDTV broadcast, in Aldridge M *Local sounds, local visions: The struggle for community television in South Africa*. Unpublished paper.

Roussos A (2002) *Multicast communications technology overview*. Johannesburg: Sentech.

RTV South Korea (2005) <http://www.rtv.or.kr/eng/info/english.jsp> 16 August.

Rushton D (2004) *Draft report: International TV think piece*. London: GAMOS.

SAARF (South African Research Foundation) (2004) All Media Products Survey. (Available at http//:www.saarf.co.za)

SAMRO (2005) *South African Music Rights Organisation website* <www.samro.co.za> August.

Schramm W (1964) *Mass media and national development: The role of information in the developing countries*. Stanford, CA: Stanford University Press.

Sentech (2005) Map of coverage for HSRC Community Television: Tygerberg C1.9. Pretoria: Sentech

Shamberg M (1971) *Guerilla Television*. New York: Henry Holt

Smith R (2005) Author interview with MISA-SA Director Rene Smith.

Sony Electronics Inc. (2005) *Live content producer AWS-G500 product brochure*. <www.sony.com/AnycastStation> August.

Soweto TV (2004) *Soweto TV business plan*. Johannesburg.

Stats SA (2001) *Census 2001*. Pretoria: Statistics South Africa.

Stats SA (2005) *Mid-year population estimates 2005*. Pretoria: Statistics South Africa.

Stead A (2005) To HD or not to HD – that is the question, *Screen Africa* 17: 24.

Terblanche D (2005) Author interview with Dave Terblanche, SABC Manager Airtime Cape Town.

Thafeng T (2005) Conversation between Soweto TV CEO Tshepo Thafeng and the author concerning his organisation's negotiations with NEMISA for use of its facilities for a temporary event broadcast.

Thorne K (2005) Discussion document: On the principles and practice of a proposed community television (CTV) service in the greater Cape Town metropolitan area. Cape Town CTV Collective.

Triangle Television (2005) <www.tritv.co.nz> August.

Van Zyl J (2002) *Civil society and broadcasting in South Africa: Protecting the right to communicate*. Communicatio 20(2). <www.unisa.ac.za/default.asp?Cmd=ViewContent&ContentID=7156>

Van Zyl J (2006) id21 online discussion on community radio for development, January. A project of the Institute of Development Studies, University of Sussex, England.

Wainer C (2005) Author interview with Colin Wainer, MD of Broadcast Visions consultants.

Wits LINK Centre (2005) *Submission to the Parliamentary Portfolio Committee on Communications on the 2005 Convergence Bill (Notice 27294 of 2005)*. University of the Witwatersrand.